Earth System Govern...

Earth System Governance

Frank Biermann and Oran R. Young, series editors

Oran R. Young, *Institutional Dynamics: Emergent Patterns in International Environmental Governance*

Frank Biermann and Philipp Pattberg, eds., *Global Environmental Governance Reconsidered*

Olav Schram Stokke, *Disaggregating International Regimes: A New Approach to Evaluation and Comparison*

Aarti Gupta and Michael Mason, eds., *Transparency in Global Environmental Governance*

Sikina Jinnah, *Post-Treaty Politics: Secretariat Influence in Global Environmental Governance*

Frank Biermann, *Earth System Governance: World Politics in the Anthropocene*

Related books from Institutional Dimensions of Global Environmental Change: A Core Research Project of the International Human Dimensions Programme on Global Environmental Change

Oran R. Young, Leslie A. King, and Heike Schroeder, eds., *Institutions and Environmental Change: Principal Findings, Applications, and Research Frontiers*

Frank Biermann and Bernd Siebenhüner, eds., *Managers of Global Change: The Influence of International Environmental Bureaucracies*

Sebastian Oberthür and Olav Schram Stokke, eds., *Managing Institutional Complexity: Regime Interplay and Global Environmental Change*

Earth System Governance

World Politics in the Anthropocene

Frank Biermann

The MIT Press
Cambridge, Massachusetts
London, England

MIT Press books may be purchased at special quantity discounts for business or sales promotional use. For information, please email special_sales@mitpress.mit.edu.

This book was set in Sabon LT Std 10/13 by Toppan Best-set Premedia Limited, Hong Kong. Printed and bound in the United States of America.

Library of Congress Cataloging-in-Publication Data

Biermann, Frank, 1967–
  Earth system governance : world politics in the anthropocene / Frank Biermann.
    pages ; cm — (Earth system governance)
  Includes bibliographical references and index.
  ISBN 978-0-262-02822-6 (hardcover : alk. paper) — ISBN 978-0-262-52669-2 (pbk. : alk. paper)
1. Global environmental change—International cooperation. 2. Global environmental change—Government policy. 3. Climatic changes—International cooperation. 4. Climatic changes—Government policy. 5. Environmental policy—International cooperation. 6. Nature—Effect of human beings on. I. Title.
  GE149.B54 2014
  333.7—dc23
                                2014013242

10 9 8 7 6 5 4 3 2 1

Contents

Series Foreword   vii
Preface   ix
A Word on the Poems   xiii
List of Abbreviations   xvii

1   Introduction   1

2   Conceptualization   15

3   Agency   47

4   Architecture   81

5   Accountability and Legitimacy   121

6   Allocation   145

7   Adaptiveness   175

8   Conclusion   203

References   215
Index   261

Series Foreword

Humans now influence all biological and physical systems of the planet. Almost no species, land area, or part of the oceans has remained unaffected by the expansion of the human species. Recent scientific findings suggest that the entire earth system now operates outside the normal state exhibited over at least the past 500,000 years. Yet at the same time, it is apparent that the institutions, organizations, and mechanisms by which humans govern their relationship with the natural environment and global biogeochemical systems are utterly insufficient—and poorly understood. More fundamental and applied research is needed.

Such research is no easy undertaking. It must span the entire globe because only integrated global solutions can ensure a sustainable coevolution of biophysical and socioeconomic systems. But it must also draw on local experiences and insights. Research on earth system governance must be about places in all their diversity, yet seek to integrate place-based research within a global understanding of the myriad human interactions with the earth system. Eventually, the task is to develop integrated systems of governance, from the local to the global level, that ensure the sustainable development of the coupled socioecological system that the Earth has become.

The series Earth System Governance is designed to address this research challenge. Books in this series will pursue this challenge from a variety of disciplinary perspectives, at different levels of governance, and with a range of methods. Yet all will further one common aim: analyzing current systems of earth system governance with a view to increased understanding and possible improvements and reform. Books in this series will be of interest to the academic community but will also inform practitioners and at times contribute to policy debates.

This series is related to the long-term international research program "Earth System Governance Project."

Frank Biermann, *VU University Amsterdam* and *Lund University*
Oran R. Young, *Bren School, University of California, Santa Barbara*
Earth System Governance Series Editors

Preface

This book seeks to develop a new perspective on the governance of human-nature coevolution at the planetary scale. It is the result of a research trajectory over several years that has evolved from dissatisfaction with current concepts of environmental policy to a felt need for new paradigms that bring our thinking and acting in line with new realities of planetary transformation. I began exploring one such paradigm in 2000, that of "earth system governance," with this term first appearing in a policy-oriented paper in 2002 (Biermann 2002c), followed by two conceptual publications that identified key governance principles and research challenges in this domain (Biermann 2005a and 2007).

The notion of earth system governance now underpins a long-term global research network, the "Earth System Governance Project," launched in 2009 under the auspices of the International Human Dimensions Programme on Global Environmental Change (IHDP). This network has evolved into a vibrant global community of researchers who share an interest in the analysis of earth system governance and in exploring how to reform the ways in which human societies (fail to) steer their coevolution with nature at the planetary scale. More than 2,500 colleagues subscribe to the Earth System Governance newsletter, and about 200 researchers belong to the group of lead faculty and research fellows affiliated with the Project. This large network incorporates a diversity of conceptualizations, research approaches, methods, and political opinions on earth system governance. In this book, I develop my own insights on the complex issues of earth system governance, which are at the same time deeply influenced by the lively debates within this research community.

In exploring the concept, principles, and challenges of earth system governance, I have had the pleasure of working with many outstanding colleagues in a variety of research and policy contexts. Some of these colleagues deserve special acknowledgment as coauthors of articles or book chapters upon which I draw in parts of this book. I wish to mention in particular Harro van Asselt, Philipp Pattberg, and Fariborz Zelli, who published with me earlier on the concept of architecture and the problem of fragmentation; Sander Chan, Ayşem Mert, and (again) Philipp Pattberg, with whom I coauthored a number of studies that resulted from our joint project on transnational public-private partnerships; Klaus Dingwerth, with whom I wrote on the role of the state; Ingrid Boas, who published with me on the topic of climate migrants; and Aarti Gupta, with whom I edited a special journal issue on the accountability and legitimacy of earth system governance.

In addition to those with whom I have coauthored papers on subthemes of earth system governance, I am indebted to numerous colleagues who have helped me to explore this concept in more detail. These include, in particular, my fellow members of the scientific planning committee of the Earth System Governance Project, with whom I could share the excitement of developing its science and implementation plan. These include Michele M. Betsill, Ken Conca, Bharat Desai, Leila da Costa Ferreira, Joyeeta Gupta, Norichika Kanie, Louis Lebel, Diana Liverman, Heike Schroeder, Bernd Siebenhüner, and Simon Tay. Many thanks also to the members of the Project's scientific steering committee who joined this group after its launch: Karin Bäckstrand, Susana Camargo Vieira, and Pius Z. Yanda.

Three people were especially important in setting up the Earth System Governance Project: Oran R. Young was closely involved and very supportive of this project from the very start, first as chair of the former IHDP core project on Institutional Dimensions of Global Environmental Change, and later as chair of the Scientific Committee of the IHDP. Since 2011, he has been a lead faculty member of the project and one of the guiding lights in our community. The Earth System Governance Project would not have been possible without the relentless efforts of Ruben Zondervan, who has smoothly and effectively managed this initiative from its first planning phase and today serves as the project's executive director at our international project office at Lund University, Sweden. This international project office would in turn not have been possible without the strong support of Lennart Olsson of the Lund University Centre for Sustainability Studies, who not only secured generous funding for our project office from Lund University but also provided invaluable intellectual input in getting the project off the ground. Since 2011, I have been a visiting professor of earth system governance at Lund University. This book would certainly have taken much longer without the benefits of this part-time position in Sweden.

In addition to those mentioned, my research on earth system governance has benefited greatly from interaction with colleagues—too many to be listed here by name—in numerous research programs associated with this research agenda. My thinking on international bureaucracies has been influenced by my colleagues from the research project Managers of Global Change (MANUS). Questions of architecture, agency, and adaptiveness have been intensively discussed within a working group with the somewhat cryptic acronym "P.3.a" in the European Union integrated project ADAM, which stood for Adaptation and Mitigation Strategies: Supporting European Climate Policy. Accountability and legitimacy of earth system governance was the central theme in a series of workshops that culminated in a special issue of the journal *Ecological Economics*, and I have drawn on fruitful discussions with the many colleagues who contributed to that issue. Many of these questions have been discussed, in one way or another, with colleagues from the Global Governance Project, a network of European research institutions that was active from 2001 to 2012. Last but surely not least, I am grateful to the thirty colleagues of the Department of Environmental Policy Analysis at the Institute for Environmental Studies of the VU University Amsterdam. This group has influenced my thinking about environmental and earth system governance in multiple ways. The Institute for Environmental Studies has provided a welcoming and supportive environment to conduct this study program over the years.

Given that this research builds on a ten-year trajectory, it is not possible to list all funding institutions that have financed parts of this work. I am particularly indebted to three institutions that have, through various programs, funded most of my research in recent years, namely the European Union with its various programs and institutions (primarily under the sixth and seventh research framework programs), the Netherlands Organization for Scientific Research, and the Volkswagen Foundation in Germany, which financed my earlier work.

This book itself has benefited substantially from numerous comments, suggestions, and advice from many colleagues. I am particularly grateful to the extensive valuable and constructive comments by four anonymous reviewers for the MIT Press. Clay Morgan of the Press was, as always, very supportive and helpful in guiding the manuscript through the submission and review phase, until his retirement in February 2014 after many years of being a central, much-respected supporter of environmental research in the world of academic publishing. After Clay's retirement, Beth Clevenger oversaw the final production stages with enthusiasm and energy. Special thanks also to copyeditor Matthew Abbate, whose sharp eye and linguistic dexterity have helped ensure a much smoother read. The index has been compiled with great precision by Lillan Henseler. Very special thanks to Tineke Reus, who has gone the extra mile in checking and standardizing the many references listed in this book, and provided vital general support.

My deepest-felt thanks, however, go to my wonderful wife, Aarti—my most valued critic, strongest support, and closest friend throughout all these years. We both may be too old to experience earth system disruptions ourselves. Earth system governance is about the type of planet we leave to our children. This book is hence for our daughter, Sophia Nalini, and her generation.

A Word on the Poems

Globalization is changing our lives in multiple ways. One facet is the global harmonization of cultures, belief systems, and languages. English, in particular, has become the global medium of scholarly and political discourse. This is important from the perspective that this book offers— the perspective of earth system governance. Our joint efforts in navigating the coevolution of humans and nature at planetary scale, our common quest to protect "earth system boundaries," will not be successful if we cannot generate and maintain common discourses and communities of values and mutual understanding, aided by a common language.

On the other hand, cultural and linguistic globalization costs us dearly. It chips away at the diversity that constitutes the beauty of our world. This is not a minor concern. There is, however, one powerful medium that celebrates the diversity of national and local languages while speaking a universal tongue. It is poetry.

I have thus illustrated this book with poetry from my own culture, which is European and, more precisely, German. I have chosen poems that I find beautiful, but which are also, in a variety of ways, topical. They all add a special message, a particular connotation, and a unique vision, on the challenges of earth system governance. In all cases, however, the link is implicit. The poems are from times when greenhouse gases, planetary tipping points, or holes in the stratospheric ozone layer were unknown. One might surmise that these challenges of our times were also unknowable. Yet what is surprising when reading the poems of long ago is that they all share a message. A warning. A certain degree of unease.

The best-known of these poems, and still the most surprising perhaps, is Jakob van Hoddis's vision of the end of the world, "Weltende." The poem became a symbol of European expressionism. It was written in 1911, only a few years before the beginning of the onslaught of the Great

War. Jakob van Hoddis—born Hans Davidsohn—met a terrible end, first in a mental asylum and many years later murdered in a Nazi concentration camp. He surely had no knowledge of what we today see as the threat of earth system transformation. Yet reading some of his lines— "From bourgeois' pointed heads their bowlers flew, the whole atmosphere's like full of cry ... and on the coast, one reads, the water's high. The storm is here, the seven seas do wildly hop onto the land to bust thick dams. The folk have cold, so many noses need a mop ..."—one gets an eerie feeling.

Bertolt Brecht's poem "Concerning Spring" ("Über das Frühjahr") was written somewhat later, in 1928. Again, environmental pollution was not a political issue then, at least not on the scale that we perceive it to be today. Yet again the visionary text could not be timelier. What else can one say about the climate problem than that before "we swooped on oil, iron and ammonia," we used to have a "time of irresistible violent leafing of trees"? What better describes the current lack of attention and concern than Brecht's "Spring is noticed, if at all / By people sitting in railway trains." As in Hoddis's poem, published seventeen years earlier, one might feel an uneasiness over modernization and industrialization and a growing fear of their consequences: "High above, it is true / There seem to be storms: / All they touch now is / Our aerials."

The uneasiness endures even with much older texts. One example is the short extract from Goethe's *Faust (II)*, a dialogue between Faust, the hero, and the devil to whom he has given his soul, Mephistopheles. Faust is frantically building dikes, improving his waterworks. Yet Mephistopheles is categorical—there is no way out of the predicament, and dikes and defenses will be to no avail. Within the larger context of the Faustian saga, one might feel immediately reminded of the current discourse on geoengineering. Will we engage in a new Faustian bargain?

Another poem by Goethe is very topical for the question of agency— his take on the ancient myth of Prometheus, the Greek Titan who once brought fire to the mortals and was severely punished by Zeus. The myth of Prometheus can stand in for the beginnings of human civilization and the dawn of a fossil-based economy. Prometheus set in motion the wheel of anthropogenic earth system transformation, the consequences of which we face today. The Prometheus myth signals the turning point that ended the Holocene and launched the Anthropocene. In his fearless deed that disobeyed the will of the gods, Prometheus can be seen as the key agent who brought us both fire and freedom. It is up to our generation to reconcile the two.

A more optimistic poem is from Kurt Schwitters, the most famous poet from my hometown, Hannover. Schwitters was a Dadaist, and so isolated that even other Dadaists did not include him in their circles. What can Dada contribute to the theory of earth system governance? This question sounds Dadaistic in itself, and Dadaists might be amused. I chose here one poem, "Earliness Rounds Rain Blue," that at least mentions the word *grün* ("green") seven times in eight lines. May it be seen as Dada's response to what lies ahead.

Another poem is from the earlier years of Brecht, the "Morning Address to a Tree Named Green" ("Morgendliche Rede an den Baum Griehn"—Brecht uses the English word "green" here as proper name for the tree). The poem is open to many interpretations, and whoever has lived in a backyard in the old parts of Berlin knows the type of tree that is spoken to here. I include this poem as a symbol of hope, and the tree named Green as a metaphor for the human race. Growing, surviving, coping, managing: it has never been easy. Yet there is hope that humanity will, in the end, also cope with one of the greatest challenges it has ever wrought—the transformation of the entire planetary system.

Humanity and hope: what better can describe the work of Friedrich von Schiller, in its various facets around reason and rebellion, justice and freedom? I include here a short piece of an unfinished play by Schiller, *Demetrius,* with its strong claims for justice and fairness, as the opening for the chapter on allocation and justice in earth system governance.

The very last poem is again from Bert Brecht, from his *Children Songs* published in 1934: "The Tailor of Ulm (Ulm 1592)." This poem, about the tailor who believed he could fly and the bishop who responded that people never would fly, is based on a true story from the early nineteenth century (Brecht changed the timing to 1592, to link it to the journey of Christopher Columbus from 1492). This poem opens the discussion in the concluding chapter of this book, inviting readers to make their own assessment of the parable of the tailor and the bishop as it relates to the fundamental leaps of imagination and courage that effective earth system governance might require.

Most poems have today entered the public domain. The poem by Kurt Schwitters has been taken, with kind permission by the publisher, from Kurt Schwitters, *Die literarischen Werke*, edited by Friedhelm Lach, vol. 1 (Köln: Dumont Buchverlag, 1979), and has been translated by me. As for the poems by Bertolt Brecht, "Concerning Spring" was originally published in German in 1928 as "Über das Frühjahr" and has been translated by Christopher Middleton (copyright 1960, 1976 by Bertolt-Brecht-Erben/Suhrkamp Verlag). "Morning Address to a Tree Named Green" was originally published in German as "Morgendliche Rede an den Baum Griehn" and has been translated by Lesley Lendrum (copyright 1960, 1976 by Bertolt-Brecht-Erben/Suhrkamp Verlag). "Tailor of Ulm" was originally published in German in 1934 as "Der Schneider von Ulm" and has been translated by Michael Hamburger (copyright 1939, 1961 by Bertolt-Brecht-Erben/Suhrkamp Verlag). All Brecht poems are from *Bertolt Brecht Poems, 1913–1956* by Bertolt Brecht, edited by John Willet and Ralph Manheim (used by permission of Liveright Publishing Corporation). The translation of the poem by Friedrich Schiller is based on an incomplete online version at http://pdfbooks.co.za, corrected by me. The translation of Goethe's *Prometheus* is from *The Works of J. W. von Goethe*, edited by Nathan H. Dole (London: Francis A. Niccolls and Co.), and the translation of the fragment from *Faust* is from http://poetryintranslation.com/, by A. S. Kline. The translation of the poem by Jakob van Hoddis is from widely used Internet sources.

List of Abbreviations

CDM	Clean Development Mechanism
CSD	UN Commission on Sustainable Development
ECOSOC	UN Economic and Social Council
EU	European Union
FAO	Food and Agriculture Organization of the United Nations
GATT	General Agreement on Tariffs and Trade
GEF	Global Environment Facility
GDP	gross domestic product
ICAO	International Civil Aviation Organization
ICJ	International Court of Justice
ICSU	International Council for Science
IDGEC	Institutional Dimensions of Global Environmental Change, a former core project of the IHDP
IHDP	International Human Dimensions Programme on Global Environmental Change
IISD	International Institute for Sustainable Development
ILO	International Labor Organization
IMF	International Monetary Fund
IMO	International Maritime Organization
IPCC	Intergovernmental Panel on Climate Change
IOM	International Organization for Migration
OECD	Organisation for Economic Co-operation and Development
REDD	reduced emissions from deforestation and forest degradation (in climate governance)
SDIN	Sustainable Development Issues Network
TRIPS	Agreement on Trade-Related Aspects of Intellectual Property Rights (under the World Trade Organization)

UN	United Nations
UNDP	United Nations Development Programme
UNEP	United Nations Environment Programme
UNGA	United Nations General Assembly
UNESCO	United Nations Educational, Scientific and Cultural Organization
WHO	World Health Organization
WMO	World Meteorological Organization
WTO	World Trade Organization

Weltende

Dem Bürger fliegt vom spitzen Kopf der
   Hut,

In allen Lüften hallt es wie Geschrei.

Dachdecker stürzen ab und gehn entzwei

Und an den Küsten—liest man—steigt die
   Flut.

Der Sturm ist da, die wilden Meere hupfen

An Land, um dicke Dämme zu zerdrücken.

Die meisten Menschen haben einen
   Schnupfen.

Die Eisenbahnen fallen von den Brücken.

Jakob van Hoddis (born Hans Davidsohn), 1911

End of the World

From bourgeois' pointed heads their
   bowlers flew,

the whole atmosphere's like full of cry.

Tile layers fall from roofs and break in
   two,

and on the coast, one reads, the water's
   high.

The storm is here, the seven seas do wildly
   hop

onto the land to bust thick dams.

The folk have cold, so many noses need
   a mop.

From viaducts fall down the trams.

1

Introduction

Humans have altered their environment since prehistoric times. Today we have begun to transform our planet. Humankind has become a planetary force that influences global biogeochemical systems. Humans are no longer spectators who need to adapt to the natural environment; we have become a powerful agent of earth system evolution. The Amsterdam Declaration "Challenges of a Changing Earth," adopted in 2001 by a coalition of international research programs, concluded that human impacts on the earth's land surface, the oceans, the atmosphere, biological diversity, the water cycle, and biogeochemical cycles "are clearly identifiable beyond natural variability" and are "equal to some of the great forces of nature in their extent and impact" (Amsterdam Declaration 2001; see also Steffen, Sanderson, et al. 2004; UNEP 2012b). The later 2012 State of the Planet Declaration (2012, 2) confirmed, "[h]umanity's impact on the Earth system has become comparable to planetary-scale geological processes such as ice ages. ... That the Earth has experienced large-scale, abrupt changes in the past indicates that it could experience similar changes in the future." This complex transformation of planetary systems by humankind is becoming one of the key political challenges of the twenty-first century. Political responses that fail to recognize this changed context are bound to fail. A new paradigm in both research and policymaking is needed.

In this book, I explore a new perspective on environmental politics: "earth system" governance. Environmental politics, from its very beginning, has focused on the surroundings of human settlements. Environmentalism is essentially centered on people. It is about the protection of what is around us, as humans, as is visible in the root of the word *environment* in English (based on old French "encircling, surrounding"), or the *Umwelt* ("surrounding world") in German and the *ambiente* in Romance languages. Target parameters of environmental policy were often defined in relation to impacts on humans, such as air or water quality standards. Today, however, this traditional concept of environmental policy is too limited. Humans are not only reshaping their local environment. They are changing the entire planet.

The most prominent example is global climate change. When Charles D. Keeling began to measure atmospheric carbon dioxide on Mauna Loa, Hawaii, in the 1950s, he found concentrations of around 310 parts per million. When he died in 2005, the value was around 380. In May 2013, it passed the symbolic value of 400 parts per million, which is about 40 percent higher than before the start of the industrial revolution (Peters et al. 2012). Ice core records show that over the last 420,000 years, the atmospheric carbon dioxide concentration remained roughly between 200 and 300 parts per million (Petit et al. 1999)—before humans began to burn about 40 percent of all known oil reserves, shooting up carbon dioxide concentrations in the atmosphere at unprecedented speed and to unprecedented levels. Also the concentration of methane—another powerful greenhouse gas—has more than doubled, from about 0.7 ppmv to 1.75 ppmv.

Today, global mean warming is already 0.85 degrees Celsius above preindustrial levels. The Intergovernmental Panel on Climate Change (IPCC) expects that without additional mitigation efforts beyond those in place, global temperatures will rise to 3.7 to 4.8 degrees Celsius above preindustrial levels within this century (IPCC 2013 and 2014b; see also World Bank 2012). The result could be the highest temperatures in the entire Quaternary Period of the last 2.6 million years. According to calculations by the World Bank, if current commitments are not implemented, a warming of 4 degrees Celsius could occur as early as the 2060s (World Bank 2012). With 50 additional parts per million of carbon dioxide in the atmosphere, coral reefs might stop growing and later start to dissolve. Sea levels are currently rising at 3.2 centimeters per decade (World Bank 2012), and are expected to rise within this century by up to 98 centimeters (IPCC 2013). More dramatic sea level rise is conceivable. In past periods of planetary history, comparably high atmospheric concentrations of carbon dioxide often occurred with sea levels that were several meters higher.

In the last few thousand years, the human species has also colonized the rest of the biosphere. Humans consume or exploit about 42 percent of the terrestrial net primary production of the planet today (Vitousek et al. 1997). The global forest cover has shrunk by about 40 percent from the time when our ancestors turned from hunters and gatherers to settled farmers (Andreae, Talaue-McManus, and Matson 2004, 250). The biological diversity of our planet is dramatically declining, directly through human action and indirectly through global warming and other changes in the earth system. Over the past centuries, humans have increased the species extinction rate a thousand times. Between ten and thirty percent of mammal, bird, and amphibian species are threatened with extinction. In earth history, there have been five mass extinctions of species, the most recent 65 million years ago. The current mass extinction is the sixth, and the first induced by one species alone.

Human-made chemicals have flooded all parts of the globe. Persistent organic pollutants have spread throughout the ecosystems up to unsettled polar regions. Stratospheric ozone depletion through emission of chlorofluorocarbons since the 1920s has increased ultraviolet radiation. The high losses of stratospheric ozone discovered in the 1990s might have been the most dramatic interference of humans with the earth system so far. The time interval between discovery of the new chemicals and the discovery of their planetary impacts was about fifty years. In other words, it took us two generations before we figured out what we were doing.

The sheer number of humans has increased as well. A thousand years ago, there were probably about 300 million people on the planet, and 790 million at the beginning of the industrial revolution. In the last 200 years, this number has risen to over seven billion people. Intensive agriculture to feed the large number of people led to a fivefold increase of nitrogen fertilizer production in a thirty-year period from 1960 to 1990, and it continues to rise (Andreae, Talaue-McManus, and Matson 2004, 247). The amount of biologically available nitrogen from human activities has increased ninefold in the last hundred years. Eighty percent more nitrogen now reaches the oceans than in 1860. The flow of phosphorus to the seas is today three times higher than historical background rates. Marine resources are depleted. Humans now use one tenth of the renewable freshwater available in lakes, rivers, or glaciers worldwide.

That said, the environmental impact of the seven billion humans is hardly equal. The richest 20 percent claim 76.6 percent of the world's private consumption, and are most responsible for some core impacts on planetary systems. The poorest 20 percent account for just 1.5 percent of global consumption. Globally, one billion people still have insufficient access to water, and 2.6 billion lack basic sanitation (see chapter 6, on "Allocation"). Regardless of these huge social inequalities, the fact that the human species has increased its numbers twenty times in merely one thousand years is a major factor in the current earth system transformation.

The Anthropocene

In short, the earth system has moved outside the range of natural variability that it has exhibited over the last half a million years. As stated in the Amsterdam Declaration of 2001, "[t]he nature of changes now occurring simultaneously in the Earth System, their magnitudes and rates of change are unprecedented" (Amsterdam Declaration 2001; see also UNEP 2012b).

To classify this new state of the earth system that societies and their governance systems have to respond to, some scientists argue that we have entered a new epoch in planetary history. The interglacial epoch of the last 12,000 years is described in geology as the Holocene, within the Quaternary Period denoting the last 2.6 million years. In the Quaternary, humans developed as a species. In the Holocene, human civilization emerged. Today, scientists claim that by reshaping the planet, humans have forced a new epoch in geological time, defined by our species: the "Anthropocene." This term was invented by the ecologist Eugene F. Stoermer in the 1980s, and later advanced in a joint publication with Nobel laureate Paul Crutzen (Crutzen and Stoermer 2000; Crutzen 2002). It is used to describe today's global environment as influenced, and dominated, by human action (overviews in Zalasiewicz et al. 2011; Steffen et al. 2011). In 2008, members of the Stratigraphy Commission of the Geological Society of London concurred that

[w]e have entered a distinctive phase of Earth's evolution that satisfies geologists' criteria for its recognition as a distinctive stratigraphic unit, to which the name Anthropocene has already been informally given. ... Sufficient evidence has emerged of stratigraphically significant change ... for recognition of the Anthropocene—currently a vivid yet informal metaphor of global environmental change—as a new geological epoch to be considered for formalization by international discussion. (Zalasiewicz et al. 2008, 6 and 7)

Four years later, the State of the Planet Declaration, adopted at a major conference organized by the main global change research programs, argued that

consensus is growing that we have driven the planet into a new epoch, the Anthropocene, in which many Earth-system processes and the living fabric of ecosystems are now dominated by human activities. (State of the Planet Declaration 2012, 2)

This ongoing human perturbation of the Earth system is a major planetary experiment; in fact, it is the largest experiment humans have conducted. As with all experiments, the exact outcomes and changes in system parameters are not known ahead of time. Maybe there is no reason for immediate concern. Earth system transformation is a long-term process and may not be experienced in a dramatic way by our present generation, except for some ongoing effects such as the melting of the snowfields on Kilimanjaro or the shrinking of the ice cover on the Arctic Ocean, which has been reduced by 30 percent in thirty years (Gillis 2011).

But the impacts of the current planetary transformation could also occur earlier and be more dramatic. According to the main global change research programs, earth system dynamics are "characterized by critical thresholds and abrupt changes." Human activities could "inadvertently trigger such changes with severe consequences for Earth's environment and inhabitants." Over the last half million years, the earth system has operated in different states, with abrupt transitions sometimes occurring between them. Human activities now "have the potential to switch the Earth System to alternative modes of operation that may prove irreversible and less hospitable to humans and other life" (Amsterdam Declaration 2001).

According to some scientists, major disruptions in the earth system could occur even within this century (Steffen, Sanderson, et al. 2004). The last two million years have been characterized by a highly interrelated climate system that evidenced substantial variability and sensitivity to forcing. Ocean circulation, for instance, has experienced substantial changes in the past. We cannot rule out future circulation changes, with possibly very adverse effects on our vulnerable social systems (Rahmstorf and Sirocko 2004, 168–169). Within the last 400,000 years, the most recent 12,000 years are the longest, and rather unusual, period of relatively stable climate and sea levels. So-called Dansgaard/Oeschger events that occurred at times in the last 100,000 years, for example, involved temperature changes of up to 10 degrees Celsius within decades. What is today the harsh desert of the Sahara was a green savanna only 6,000 years ago. The dramatic desertification of this savanna is likely to have occurred rather abruptly, due to small, subtle changes in the Earth's orbit, which pushed the earth system over a threshold that triggered a series of biophysical feedback reactions. At that time, the cause was solar radiation (Steffen, Sanderson, et al. 2004). Yet human influences on biogeochemical cycles could cause similar transitions. As argued by Steffen, Andreae, and other leading scientists (2004, 319), "such evidence of instabilities ...

gives a warning that human activities could trigger similar or even as-yet unimagined instabilities in the Earth system."

This insight has led to intense research in recent years on the "tipping points," or "tipping elements," in the earth system. Tipping elements are defined as subsystems of the earth system that can be switched under certain circumstances into a qualitatively different state by small perturbations (Lenton et al. 2008, 1786). In other words, climate change and other planetary transformations are not linear but might occur abruptly, determined by thresholds and tipping points in the system (Scheffer et al. 2009). Some of the most widely discussed tipping elements are the potential collapse of the Atlantic thermohaline circulation (which might cool off Europe); the dieback of the Amazon rainforest or of the boreal forest; the meltdown of the Greenland ice sheet; and alterations in the Indian summer monsoon, the Sahara/Sahel and West African monsoon, or the El Niño-Southern Oscillation. For some tipping elements, threshold values could be reached within this century (Lenton et al. 2008). For both summer and winter Arctic sea ice, the area covered by ice is declining already. The ice has become significantly thinner. The melting of the Greenland ice sheet alone—which is expected to occur rather slowly over centuries and millennia (Robinson, Calov, and Ganopolski 2012)—might raise sea levels by 2–7 meters (Lenton et al. 2008, 1788; IPCC 2014a).

Finally, our knowledge of the earth system is still very limited. It is likely to be full of further "surprises," that is, (possibly abrupt) changes based on system parameters that we do not yet fully understand. The history of earth system research points to the need for humility concerning the accurateness of the science. At the first major global environmental governance conference—the 1972 Stockholm Conference on the Human Environment—none of the major earth system challenges that we discuss today were on the agenda. Hardly anybody talked then about ozone depletion, climate change, desertification, and the mass extinction of species. This was only forty years ago! In the case of stratospheric ozone depletion, we have already had a "near miss," that is, a sudden transition in a tipping element of the earth system that was only recognized at a late stage in the process. To quote Nobel laureate Paul Crutzen, one of the lead scientists to discover stratospheric ozone depletion, "Do not assume that scientists always exaggerate; the ozone loss over Antarctica was much worse than originally thought" (Crutzen and Ramanathan 2004, 280).

Societal Impacts

In our current interdependent, partially highly developed and industrialized times, any major event related to earth system transformation will have significant impacts on human societies. Environmental changes have been related to the collapse of civilizations from time immemorial (Diamond 2005). The falls of the Indus valley civilization, the Mayas, the Khmer Empire, and many other cultures have been linked to changes in environmental parameters. The little ice age in Europe between the thirteenth and eighteenth century also caused much human suffering. Of course, modern societies have more means to adapt to changing natural systems than did the Mayas or the Greenland Vikings. Yet our societies are also highly vulnerable in quite different ways. About half of us live today in cities, many of which are megacomplexes of tens of millions of inhabitants. Many rely on international trade in food, or on long-distance transportation of water. Modern civilization, especially in the rich industrialized countries, might seem unaffected by the forces of nature that so plagued our ancestors. Yet this might well be a fatal fallacy.

Outside the rich refugia of Europe, North America, or East Asia, vulnerabilities to earth system disruptions are even higher. About 842 million people are today undernourished. This "bottom billion" of humanity is extremely vulnerable to any changes in their natural environment. Drought, floods, sea level rise, tropical storms, as well as economic decline and increased food competition due to global environmental change are severe threats to this segment of humanity (Jerneck and Olsson 2010; World Bank 2012). Current climate change is already showing more negative impacts on crop yields than positive (IPCC 2014a). Up to 1.5 billion people could suffer from water stress by 2085 even if we assume a temperature rise of only 1–2 degrees and low population growth (Warren et al. 2006, 20). Diseases might spread, such as malaria. All impacts are interlinked, and earth system changes will further increase interdependencies. Increased water stress, as one example, could reduce international food supply due to land degradation. Food and water shortages could trigger millions of people to migrate, or lead to conflicts over natural resources (German Advisory Council on Global Change 2007; Gleditsch, Nordås, and Salehyan 2007). The US-based CNA Corporation concluded in 2007 that climate change will "seriously exacerbate already marginal living standards in many Asian, African and Middle Eastern countries, causing widespread political instability and the likelihood of failed states" (CNA Corporation 2007). According to the UK government's Development, Concepts and Doctrine Centre (2010, 26), climate change could lead to "significant increases in environmentally-induced migration," in which much of the migration will be "uncontrolled and generate significant social and economic impacts wherever it occurs. States and cities that are unable to cope are likely to seek international humanitarian assistance of unprecedented scale and duration."

Toward Earth System Governance

In short, it is time to act. The scientific findings about the earth system and its current transformation become more confident every day. As Nobel laureate Paul Crutzen and Veerabhadran Ramanathan warn, "[w]ithout major catastrophes …, humankind will remain a major geological force for many millennia, maybe millions of years, to come. To develop a worldwide accepted strategy leading to sustainability of ecosystems against human-induced stresses will be one of the great tasks of human societies" (Crutzen and Ramanathan 2004, 286). In 2001, the four main global change research programs urged that an

ethical framework for global stewardship and strategies for Earth System management are urgently needed. The accelerating human transformation of the Earth's environment is not sustainable. Therefore, the business-as-usual way of dealing with the Earth System is not an option. It has to be replaced—as soon as possible—by deliberate strategies of good management that sustain the Earth's environment while meeting social and economic development objectives. (Amsterdam Declaration 2001)

Ten years later, a comprehensive Foresight Process organized by the United Nations Environment Programme (UNEP) identified "Aligning Governance to the Challenges of Global Sustainability" as the most urgent emerging issue related to the global environment (UNEP 2012a).

There is no dearth of political responses from decision makers at all levels. In 1988, the United Nations General Assembly declared the changing climate a "common concern of humankind" and called upon all countries to limit emissions. The 1992 United Nations Conference on Environment and Development was at that time the largest diplomatic gathering in human history, later surpassed only by similar megaevents in Johannesburg in 2002 and in Rio de Janeiro in 2012. More than one thousand international agreements on environmental protection are now in force (Mitchell 2013).

Yet there remains a serious mismatch between the research and recommendations of earth system analysts and the actions of political decision makers, who still operate within the parameters of a nation-state system inherited from the twentieth century. Policymakers in the twentieth century gained much experience in managing confined ecosystems, such as river basins, forests, or lakes. In the twenty-first century, they are faced with one of the largest governance challenges humankind has ever had to deal with: protecting the entire earth system, including most of its subsystems, and building stable institutions that guarantee a safe transition process and a coevolution of natural and social systems at planetary scale.

I call this the challenge of earth system governance. I define earth system governance here (following Biermann, Betsill, et al. 2009) as the sum of the formal and informal rule systems and actor networks at all levels of human society that are set up to steer societies toward preventing, mitigating, and adapting to environmental change and earth system transformation. The normative context of earth system governance is sustainable development, that is, a development that meets the needs of present generations without compromising the ability of future generations to meet their own needs (World Commission on Environment and Development 1987).

About This Book

This book attempts to contribute to a better understanding of earth system governance as an empirical reality and a political necessity. The book advances both an analytical and a normative perspective on earth system governance.

The *analytical theory* of earth system governance studies this emerging phenomenon as it is expressed in hundreds of international regimes, international bureaucracies, national agencies, local and transnational activists groups, expert networks, and so forth. The analytical perspective is, in short, about how the current governance system functions. I assess five elements of earth system governance, following a conceptual framework that I first advanced in 2005 (Biermann 2005a and 2007) and that has been further developed in the science plan of a global research program (Biermann, Betsill, et al. 2009; see also www.earthsystemgovernance.org). These five dimensions of effective governance—which are interrelated yet can be studied individually as well—are:

• the analytical problem of *agency* in earth system governance, including agency that reaches beyond traditional state actors;

- the overall *architecture* of earth system governance, from local to global levels;
- the *accountability* and *legitimacy* of earth system governance;
- the problem of (fair) *allocation* in earth system governance; and
- the overall *adaptiveness* of governance mechanisms and of the overall governance system.

Each analytical problem is investigated in detail in chapters 3–7.

The effectiveness of governance is not conceptualized in this framework as a separate analytical problem. Instead, it is seen as an underlying dependent variable in studying all five governance dimensions. In other words, I assume that the analysis of all five governance dimensions, in their totality and complexity, will lead toward a better understanding and explanation of the prevailing lack of effectiveness in the current overall system of earth system governance. Governance effectiveness is understood, in this book, as changes in social behavior due to the influence of the governance process in question, as well as related positive changes in environmental parameters (on concepts of governance effectiveness and performance see Mitchell 2007, 2008, and 2009; Stokke 2012). Studying the actual effectiveness of current earth system governance lays the basis, I argue, for the development of a normative theory.

This *normative theory of earth system governance* is the critique of the existing systems of governance in light of the exigencies of earth system transformation in the Anthropocene. The normative theory understands earth system governance as a political project that engages more and more actors who seek to strengthen the current architecture of institutions and networks at local and global levels. Here lies the second contribution of this book: In chapters 3–7, I not only analyze current governance and assess its potential, but also propose potential reforms. I develop policy proposals to make current earth system governance better equipped to deal with the challenges that lie ahead.

Some of these policy proposals might not seem realistic in the short term. But realism in the short term is not my aim. Instead, I offer proposals that could provide a long-term vision and long-term development trajectory for earth system governance. Major changes are required if humankind is to cope with earth system transformation and keep key parameters of our system within ranges that are sustainable. As pointed out by leading earth system scientists, what are needed now are strategies for earth system governance that can generate a new level of effectiveness, legitimacy, and overall performance. World politics in the Anthropocene cannot be business as usual.

As such, this book is directly related to the larger effort of the global research network Earth System Governance Project. This research alliance has put forward a science plan that has a structure similar to this book, notably in the identification of five analytical themes of agency, architecture, accountability and legitimacy, allocation, and adaptiveness (Biermann, Betsill, et al. 2009). Nonetheless, there are also substantial differences. While the science and implementation plan of the Earth System Governance research alliance proposes a scientific agenda that involves hundreds of scientists from all over the globe, this book is a much more modest undertaking as it presents my own vision and analysis of the current processes of earth system governance, with a particular focus on reform options that could contribute to an integrated system of earth system governance over the next decade or two. While most colleagues in the Earth System Governance research alliance would agree with my overall research motivation to identify more effective forms of earth system governance, many will disagree with one or more of the particular analytical propositions and policy reform proposals that I advance. Such differences in point of view of close colleagues, to the extent that they are published, I have cited in the analytical and policy reform sections of chapters 3–7. This book is hence by no means a comprehensive assessment of the state of the art from the perspective of the entire community of earth system governance researchers. It is rather an individual contribution to the overarching program of the Earth System Governance research alliance.

In addition, within the larger context of earth system governance theory I concentrate in this book on international, or transnational, politics. Earth system governance is not, as I point out in detail in chapter 2, restricted to global institutions. Earth system governance is a process that must involve, and be based on, local actors and national policies. Earth system governance needs to draw on the engagement of cities, the energy of civil society organizations, the support of local authorities, the social responsibility of corporations, and the support of citizens. Strengthened policies are needed at the local and national levels to energize societies and strengthen the worldwide transition to sustainability. Global multilateral institutions, intergovernmental cooperation, and the UN system are thus only one part, and one dimension, of earth system governance. Yet strong and legitimate international cooperation and institutions remain in my view a critical component of earth system governance, without which failure is guaranteed. I have focused in this book thus on the global level of earth system governance. Most of my reform proposals target multilateral institutions and the United Nations system as well.

This does not imply that I believe that the *current* United Nations system will be a solution to all problems of earth system governance. Most likely it will not. Instead, my policy discussions rather aim at a *new* United Nations: a new United Nations that is substantially different from the current system that follows in many ways the trodden paths of the twentieth century. Effective earth system governance and planetary stewardship require *new types of multilateralism* and *new forms of global governance* that are better aligned with the exigencies of the Anthropocene. I have laid out elements of such new types of multilateralism in more detail in the policy reform sections of chapters 3–7.

The remainder of this book is organized in seven chapters.

Chapter 2 presents my conceptualization of earth system governance. I elaborate upon this concept based on existing literature in earth system science and global governance studies, and distinguish earth system governance from traditional environmental policy studies. I identify key elements of the earth system governance problem structure that make it particularly challenging and complicated, and lay out the normative frame for earth system governance.

Chapters 3–7 present my analysis of each of the five dimensions of earth system governance. Each chapter has a similar structure: First, I introduce and conceptualize the analytical problem at hand. Next I provide an assessment of the current state of governance, drawing on existing research and focusing on aspects of international governance that I see as particularly relevant and important. Drawing on this assessment, each chapter will then develop a set of policy reforms.

In line with this general structure, chapter 3 addresses the *agents* of earth system governance. I distinguish here between agents and actors, and argue that agents are actors who have authority to set standards and rules that govern human interactions. I discuss four types of agents of earth system governance: first, the state; second, nonstate agents, with special focus on the increasing number of transnational public policy networks that bring actors together from different parts of society; third, transnational networks of scientists; and fourth, international bureaucracies.

Chapter 4 discusses the overall *architecture* of earth system governance. I conceptualize architecture as the overarching system of intergovernmental and nonstate institutions operating in a governance domain. It is, in other words, the institutional framework within which agents operate. I look at the increasing institutional fragmentation within earth system governance, and between earth system and economic governance, and outline a number of reform options to increase the overall consistency and coherence of earth system governance.

Chapter 5 develops further an important dimension that is touched upon briefly in chapters 3 and 4: the *accountability* and *legitimacy* of earth system governance. I argue in this chapter that questions of accountability and legitimacy are becoming ever more important. All key elements of the problem structure of earth system governance, as outlined in chapter 2, pose particular and often novel challenges for the accountability and legitimacy of governance. I discuss these challenges in some detail, and outline political reform options to cope with them.

Chapter 6 addresses another key element of effective and legitimate earth system governance: the question of *allocation*, or differently put, of justice, fairness, and equity. This chapter places earth system governance within the context of a highly divided world, with huge differences in resources and vulnerabilities, where one-tenth of humankind consumes sixty percent of global wealth. I distinguish here between three ways of distributing costs and benefits of earth system governance. These are, first, direct allocation through multilateral agreement, such as through international funds; second, allocation through markets established under international agreements, such as emissions trading; and third, allocation through environmentally motivated restrictions of global trade and investment.

Chapter 7 addresses the *adaptiveness* of governance arrangements. This chapter reflects the increasing thinking among scientists that current efforts in earth system governance are too little, too late. While much timely and relevant research has discussed adaptation at local and national levels, my analysis addresses the requirements of *global* adaptation governance. I discuss core dilemmas such as adaptability versus stability, effectiveness versus legitimacy, and effectiveness versus fairness in global governance arrangements. As one example of global adaptation governance, I analyze governance of climate-related migration and propose a system of global governance that could cope with substantially increased numbers of migrants due to earth system disruptions, notably sea level rise and more frequent or more severe droughts and extreme weather events.

Chapter 8 presents my conclusions. I summarize the political proposals that I develop in chapters 3–7, and reflect on the realistic utopianism that runs as a leitmotif throughout this book.

Über das Frühjahr

Lange bevor

Wir uns stürzten auf Erdöl, Eisen und Ammoniak

Gab es in jedem Jahr

Die Zeit der unaufhaltsam und heftig grünenden Bäume.

Wir alle erinnern uns

Verlängerter Tage

Helleren Himmels

Änderung der Luft

Des gewiß kommenden Frühjahrs.

Noch lesen wir in Büchern

Von dieser gefeierten Jahreszeit

Und doch sind schon lange

Nicht mehr gesichtet worden über unseren Städten

Die berühmten Schwärme der Vögel.

Am ehesten noch sitzend in Eisenbahnen

Fällt dem Volk das Frühjahr auf.

Die Ebenen zeigen es

In alter Deutlichkeit.

In großer Höhe freilich

Scheinen Stürme zu gehen:

Sie berühren nur mehr

Unsere Antennen.

Bertolt Brecht, 1928

Concerning Spring

Long before

We swooped on oil, iron and ammonia

There was each year

A time of irresistible violent leafing of trees.

We all remember

Lengthened days

Brighter sky

Change of the air

The certainly arriving Spring.

We still read in books

About this celebrated season

Yet for a long time now

Nobody has seen above our cities

The famous flocks of birds.

Spring is noticed, if at all

By people sitting in railway trains.

The plains show it

In its old clarity.

High above, it is true

There seem to be storms:

All they touch now is

Our aerials.

2

Conceptualization

"Long before / We swooped on oil, iron and ammonia / There was each year / A time of irresistible violent leafing of trees," wrote Bertolt Brecht almost one hundred years ago, and continued: "High above, it is true / There seem to be storms: / All they touch now is / Our aerials." This poetic line of 1928 captures well the emergence as well as the current political challenge of the Anthropocene. The storms are maybe not yet raging, but fundamental transformations of planetary systems are predicted by science if no action is taken—not the least a rapid withdrawal from our societal addiction to "oil, iron and ammonia." And yet these storms, predicted as they be, still merely touch "our aerials"; they largely remain within the confines of the reports and assessments of our scientific research communities. They have not yet led to fundamental adjustments in how our societies and the international political system inherited from the twentieth century still function.

In a nutshell, this is the challenge of earth system governance, which stands at the center of this book. In this chapter, I further develop the conceptual foundation of earth system governance as a research field. I first discuss the theoretical basis and academic ancestry of earth system governance, with a focus on its two main components: the emergence of an integrated and increasingly sophisticated understanding of the earth as a system, and the recent discourse on governance, which describes steering processes in modern societies that differ, in particular, from traditional concepts of government. I will also differentiate earth system governance from competing concepts that are found in the literature, notably the notion of "earth system management."

Based on this conceptual foundation, I discuss the normative goal of earth system governance. If health governance seeks to improve human health, and economic governance to raise living standards, what is the normative goal of "earth system" governance? I will especially focus here on a discussion of earth system boundaries as it has emerged in recent years.

Finally, the chapter outlines the fundamental problem structures that make earth system governance one of the most complex and difficult political challenges of our time. Based on this problem structure, I then sketch basic governance principles for effective earth system governance. The concluding part of this chapter draws the discussion together and relates it to the five analytical chapters that follow.

The Earth as a System

The notion of earth system governance follows the paradigmatic shift in environmental sciences from a place-based understanding of environmental pollution to an emerging conceptualization of the planet as an interdependent integrated social-ecological system. This paradigmatic shift toward an earth system perspective has been pioneered by the natural sciences. Increased scientific efforts in global research programs, generally supported by vastly increased computing power available to researchers, has led to an improved understanding of both the complex interdependencies in the earth system and the rapidly growing planetary role of the human species. Scientific research has brought ever-increasing evidence about past developments in planetary history, including the nonlinearity of processes, potentials for rapid system turns, and complex interrelationships between components of the system. The relative stability of the global climate during the Holocene—the last 12,000 years that brought about the development of human civilization—can be seen almost as a fortunate exception. The earth system appears more and more to be interconnected and fragile.

The vast global impact of the human species has also become highly visible. While first mass extinctions of larger mammals might be related to early hunter societies, human influences have grown since the Neolithic revolution with the development of agriculture and husbandry. Today, at the height of industrialization, humanity has fully evolved as a geological force, able to influence global geobiophysical systems (Steffen et al. 2011). This development has been aptly symbolized by Paul Crutzen and Eugene Stoermer's (2000) call to declare the Holocene ended and a new epoch in planetary history begun—the Anthropocene.

Scientifically, the Anthropocene has motivated the development of numerous novel concepts of scientific integration and reorganization in order to cope with this new situation. Four clusters of novel concepts are most important: global change, earth system analysis, sustainability science, and resilience theory. These concepts are not mutually exclusive but reflect instead different intellectual trajectories, institutional traditions, and research topics.

The globalization of environmental pollution, for one, transformed this notion in the twentieth century into the broader concept of *environmental change*, which encompasses all sorts of processes from air pollution to land degradation. From the 1990s onward, this concept has been further broadened to global environmental change, nowadays mostly shortened to *global change*. The deletion of the word "environmental" denotes the all-encompassing nature of the global changes of human-nature interaction and coevolution that can no longer be seen as merely problems of the environment and environmental pollution. The term global change is now widely in use, both for research programs and research institutions.

A second research trajectory is integrated *earth system analysis*, or *earth system science*. The call for an earth system science follows from the complexities of earth system transformation that require the involvement of most academic disciplines at multiple spatial and temporal scales. Its conceptual origins are computer-based modeling programs that have become better integrated in recent years. The aim of these efforts has been to combine and integrate models of different strands of research to gain understanding not of isolated elements of global change but of the totality of processes in nature and human civilization. Hans-Joachim Schellnhuber, a pioneer of this concept, ascribes earth system analysis the status of a science *in statu nascendi*, because, as he writes (with Volker Wenzel), it has "1. a genuine subject, namely the total Earth in the sense of a fragile and 'gullible' dynamic system, 2. a genuine methodology, namely transdisciplinary systems analysis based on, i.a., planetary monitoring, global modelling and simulation, 3. a genuine purpose, namely the satisfactory (or at least tolerable) coevolution of the ecosphere and the anthroposphere (vulgo: Sustainable Development) in the times of Global Change and beyond" (Schellnhuber and Wenzel 1998, vii; see also Schellnhuber 1998 and 1999).

Institutionally, the idea of an integrated earth system science led in 2001 to the creation of the Earth System Science Partnership. This Partnership was meant to serve as the overarching alliance, or network, of the four main global change research programs: Diversitas (the biodiversity sciences program); the International Geosphere-Biosphere Programme; the World Climate Research Programme; and the International

Human Dimensions Programme on Global Environmental Change (Leemans et al. 2009). The Earth System Science Partnership was loosely organized, with a small secretariat in Paris and a scientific steering committee that combined the chairs of the four global change programs and a few other leading scientists. Conceptually, the Partnership adopted a holistic concept of the earth as a complex and sensitive system regulated by physical, chemical, and biological processes and influenced by humans. The focus was on anthropogenic change, including through integrated analytical approaches and advanced modeling techniques. To this end, the Partnership sponsored four integrated joint projects of the global change research programs: the Global Carbon Project, the Global Environmental Change and Food Systems Project, the Global Water System Project, and the Global Change and Human Health Project.

In recent years, however, it was felt by many actors, notably the funding agencies, that the Earth System Science Partnership did not achieve the integration that was required and desirable. For this reason, in 2012 the Earth System Science Partnership was transformed into a more integrated global initiative, called Future Earth: Research for Global Sustainability. Future Earth is described as a ten-year international research initiative to mobilize thousands of scientists to develop the knowledge for responding effectively to the risks and opportunities of global environmental change and for supporting transformation toward global sustainability, while strengthening partnerships with policymakers and other stakeholders (Future Earth Transition Team 2012).

Thirdly, related to earth system science yet with a different ancestry, is *sustainability science*. The conceptual foundation of sustainability science is the notion of sustainable development as advanced in 1987 by the World Commission on Environment and Development. Like earth system science, sustainability science also seeks to create a new scientific discipline by integrating disciplines in the larger quest for a transition to sustainability (Kates et al. 2001; Clark, Crutzen, and Schellnhuber 2005; Schellnhuber et al. 2004). As Robert Kates and colleagues argue (2001), the challenge of sustainable development is so complex that it requires sustainability science as a new integrative field of study. Such a sustainability science can improve collaboration of natural and social scientists as well as deliver research designs that better integrate local and global scales. It would also imply modifications to the traditional model of knowledge generation and a new way in which sustainability science, as a science, is conducted.

Like earth system science, sustainability science is also reflected in various recent attempts at reorganizing global change research. There is a Sustainability Science Program run by Harvard University that seeks to build a global community of affiliated researchers; four journals and one book series with "sustainability science" in the title; and various education programs where young scholars can obtain doctoral or master's degrees in sustainability science. Numerous universities have set up specialized organizational units, such as a Faculty of Sustainability Sciences (University of Lüneburg, Germany), a School of Sustainability (Arizona State University), or the Lund University Centre for Sustainability Studies.

A fourth conceptual trajectory is *resilience theory*, which has evolved in the last twenty years as a major integrative paradigm in environmental research. The resilience perspective emerged from ecology in the 1960s and 1970s through studies of interacting populations, such as predators and prey, in relation to ecological stability theory (Folke 2006, 254). The current resilience literature includes also human actors in the notion of coupled social-ecological systems. Resilience is then defined as the degree of change a social-ecological system can undergo while retaining control of function and structure as well as sufficient options to further develop (Berkes, Colding, and Folke 2003; Folke 2006; Galaz et al. 2008; Lebel et al. 2006; Nelson, Adger, and Brown 2007). The notion of "social-ecological" systems necessitates an integrated understanding of social and ecological factors; social and ecological systems cannot be considered in isolation from one another but must be analyzed as coupled systems (Folke 2006; Olsson et al. 2006). So far, the resilience framework has largely been applied to local and regional social-ecological systems, such as Swedish lakes or Thai river basins. Theoretically, however, the planet as such can also be seen as a coupled social-ecological system, which opens up the resilience literature to the study of earth system governance.

Yet there are also differences. While much of resilience theory argues for example against top-down and centralized management, and for polycentric and multilayered systems of governance, this has never been a problem in *global* governance. International politics are almost by definition polycentric and multilayered. Top-down and centralized bureaucratic approaches that were common at local levels in the last century are essentially absent at the global level. Internationally, the question is rather a matter of degree: In the polycentric, multilayered *global* governance context, what is the optimal distribution of authority between global institutions and national or local governments? What is the optimal level of diversity and integration? I will address these questions in chapter 4 on the architecture of earth system governance.

Like sustainability science and earth system science, resilience theory has also found expression in the creation of new research units, or the reorganization of existing ones. A central actor here is the Stockholm Resilience Centre, funded by a major grant from the Swedish MISTRA foundation, and the global Resilience Alliance that brings together various institutions and researchers from around the globe in this field.

All four of these lines of research share a number of core characteristics.

First, all focus on the analysis of interlinked *systems*. This is obvious in the case of earth system science, yet equally important for resilience theory, which concentrates on the analysis of coupled social-ecological systems. The eventual unit of analysis of all these approaches is the earth as an interdependent system with interlinked subsystems and shaped by human and nonhuman agency.

Second, all approaches study the *coevolution* of humans and nature. They see humanity as an agent of earth system transformation, one that shapes natural systems just as natural systems influence human systems. Boundaries between natural and social systems are broken down, as in the notion of coupled social-ecological systems at different scales.

Third, all approaches seek *to break down disciplinary boundaries*. In the cases of earth system science and sustainability science, this is integral to creating a new science that combines existing disciplines in a joint effort to study coupled social-ecological systems (Leemans and Solecki 2013). Also, resilience theory cuts across traditional disciplines and seeks their integration. Such approaches are founded on the conviction that integrated studies of coupled human and natural systems can reveal new and complex patterns and processes that may not be evident when they are studied by social or natural scientists separately (Liu et al. 2007, 1513). Accordingly, resilience theorists have long argued that "it is no longer fruitful to separate humans and nature, nor is it useful to fight endless disciplinary battles between 'social' and 'natural' sciences" (Folke et al. 1998, 4).

Fourth, all these approaches seek to integrate research *across all scales*. The analysis of the earth system naturally depends on an advanced understanding of its subcomponents. Sustainability science and resilience theory thus integrate research from the local level—for instance, studying a Swedish lake area as a coupled social-ecological system—to the global level, either with a view to the entire earth system or with a focus on global coupled subsystems. Boundaries between local and global are systematically broken down in both theory and research practice.

Fifth, in terms of methods, *computer-based modeling* is important, if not central, to most of the new integrated approaches. Earth system science has directly evolved from the integration of different models of earth system subcomponents, such as ocean and atmosphere models (e.g., Uhrqvist and Lövbrand 2013). Sustainability science and resilience theory also include study programs that build on computer modeling. Related to this is the ancestry of most of these approaches in the natural sciences. Earth system science, sustainability science, and resilience theory have all been developed by natural scientists. Most core publications that have been influential in setting up these communities are authored by natural scientists, and have appeared in the standard outlets for conceptual advancement in natural sciences, such as *Nature* or *Science*.

Finally, these concepts are largely overlapping rather than mutually exclusive. Some core institutions adhere to several concepts simultaneously, such as Arizona State University with its focus on sustainability and its participation in the Resilience Alliance. Some leading scholars combine different terms, for example in book titles such as *Earth System Analysis for Sustainability* (Schellnhuber et al. 2004) or in the International Council for Science (ICSU) initiative described in *Earth System Science for Global Sustainability: The Grand Challenges* (ICSU 2010), which has evolved into the current new global research alliance Future Earth: Research for Global Sustainability (Future Earth Transition Team 2012).

Yet so far, the role of the *social* sciences in these endeavors is poorly defined. Social sciences are in demand, yet their input lacks well-understood contours, strength, and assertiveness.

Earth system governance is, I argue, a response to the emergence of this multitude of integrative science programs in the last decades. The notion of earth system governance accepts the core tenet of these new approaches, that is, the understanding of the earth as an integrated, interdependent system transformed by the interplay of human and non-human agency. The focus of earth system governance is not "governing the earth," or the management of the entire process of planetary evolution. As I lay out in the next section, earth system governance is different from technocratic visions of what is sometimes referred to as "earth system management" or even earth system "engineering."

Instead, earth system governance is about the *human impact on planetary systems*. It is about the societal steering of human activities with regard to the long-term stability of geobiophysical systems. As such, earth system governance is essentially a *social science research program* related to the larger strand of governance theory in the social sciences. Cooperation and, at times, integration with natural science programs is useful and important. Yet the foundation of earth system governance needs to be firmly within the social sciences. I will later elaborate on this grounding of earth system governance research in the social sciences, its relationship to the theory of governance, as well as its links to the natural sciences. Before that, however, it is important to differentiate earth system governance from the concept of *earth system management*.

Earth System Governance versus Earth System "Management"

The notion of *earth system management* first appeared in the 1990s. It has mostly been used in relation to natural science programs and organizations, for example when it comes to providing data on earth system parameters that are influenced by human action. The first time the term was used—to my knowledge—was at the 7th International Remote Sensing Systems Conference in Melbourne in 1994 by a representative of the UN Environment Programme, Noel J. Brown, in his presentation "Agenda 21: Blueprint for Global Sustainability, New Opportunities for Earth System Management" (personal communication, Heiner Benking, August 2005).

In 1994–1996, ICSU held a series of discussions to establish a standing committee on Science and Technology for Earth Management. This standing committee was envisaged as serving as the "conscience of ICSU" and would have functioned as an early warning system, drawing attention to new and emerging issues and initiating new scientific research. Yet the committee was also expected to issue "recommendations for the legal and administrative infrastructure needed to achieve results." Eventually, the ICSU executive board abandoned the idea of such a standing committee, seeing it as an unnecessary duplication given the parallel establishment of a number of global change research programs (SCOSTEP 1997). The idea of managing the earth lived on in ICSU. For example, at the 1999 World Conference on Science "Science for the Twenty-First Century," hosted jointly by UNESCO and ICSU, the notion of earth system management was used in relation to the achievements of the International Geoscience Programme (a purely natural science effort with no role for social science research), which was applauded for its efforts in the area of "earth sciences, earth system management, and natural disaster reduction" (UNESCO 2002, 24).

Among other groups, the Potsdam Institute for Climate Impact Research in Germany adopted the idea of earth system management in its research strategy, identifying earth system analysis as the "integrated global-scale studies of the coupled ecosphere-anthroposphere complex," and earth system management as "inquiries into the nature and processes of key relevant human actions and reactions" (Schellnhuber and Tóth 1999, 201). Yet the Potsdam Institute did not develop a strong profile in the study of governance processes, and its social science program focused rather on the economics of climate change. Some central publications related to this program remain close to managerial, technocratic visions. One example is Schellnhuber's vision of a large-scale reallocation of resources in the form of "a global redesign [that] could aim at establishing a more 'organic' distribution of labour, where the temperate countries are the main producers of global food supplies, the sub-tropical zones produce renewable energies and high technology, and the tropical zones preserve biodiversity and offer recreation" (Schellnhuber 1999, C23).

The management concept is also often associated with engineering, notably geoengineering (Hamilton 2013). In some civil engineering communities, a concept of "earth systems engineering and management" seems to emerge as a research program on interventions in the earth system, notably the climate system. A newly founded Centre for Earth Systems Engineering Research at the University of Newcastle, for example, seeks to explore engineering interventions at a range of scales, in subsystems including cities, river basins and coasts, as well as at a global scale.

The term "earth system management" was most prominently used in the Amsterdam Declaration (2001) that "urgently" called for "an ethical framework for global stewardship and strategies for Earth System management." Formally, this declaration bears the signature of the (then) chair of the scientific committee of the leading social science program, the International Human Dimensions Programme on Global Environmental Change. Yet it is doubtful whether this should be interpreted as an overall endorsement of this rather managerial notion by the social science community.

Instead, I argue that the term earth system *management* is not usable for social science research. For social scientists, the notion of management would be seen, in this context, as closely related to hierarchical steering, planning, and controlling of social relations. Earth system management brings connotations of technocratic interference in social processes: the manager who controls, plans, and decides. From a social science perspective, earth system management as an analytical or normative concept is both infeasible and—in its connotation of hierarchical planning—undesirable. Global stewardship for the planet is different from centralized management. Instead, global stewardship must be based on cooperation, coordination, and consensus building among actors at all levels. It must include state and nonstate actors. It must include complex architectures of interlinked institutions and decision-making procedures, but also different forms of collaboration, such as partnerships and networks. In a world of diversity and disparity, earth system *management* is no option. Instead, I argue, we observe the emergence of a new and different paradigm: earth system governance.

An Earth System Perspective in Governance Theory

Earth system governance is thus part of the larger academic effort centered on governance studies and governance theory, to which it adds an earth system perspective as normative goal and analytical issue area. The notion of governance is widely used in the social sciences, yet—as with other conceptual innovations in the social sciences—it has no consensus definition. All usages of the term share certain characteristics that are also fundamental for the understanding of earth system governance. Most importantly, governance differs from government, even though governments are often part of governance processes. Yet governance is not confined to states and governments as sole actors, but is marked by the participation of myriad public and private actors at all levels of decision making, ranging from networks of experts, environmentalists, and multinational corporations to new agencies set up by governments, such as intergovernmental organizations. Governance also often implies notions of self-regulation by societal actors, private-public cooperation in the solving of societal problems, and new forms of multilevel policy (e.g., van Kersbergen and van Waarden 2004; for environmental governance see Adger and Jordan 2009; Jordan 2008; Kanie et al. 2013; Lebel et al. 2006).

The concept of governance encompasses institutions but is also broader. Institutions are commonly defined as clusters of rights, rules, and decision-making procedures that give rise to social practices, assign roles to participants in these practices and govern interactions among players of these roles (IDGEC 1999; Young 2002). Governance transcends this concept of institutions through a dynamic perspective that looks at processes of governing; that focuses on governance systems and integrates research on linkages among institutions; and that brings a stronger emphasis on actors and especially on nonstate actors.

Earth system governance can thus be seen as part of the broader field of governance studies, seeking to advance understanding of the governance processes by which to steer human behavior in a way that maintains stable and safe conditions for human well-being on planet earth. Earth system governance is thus no unified, top-down endeavor: it is characterized instead by a multitude of layers and clusters of rule making and rule implementing, fragmented both vertically between supranational, international, national, and subnational layers of authority, and horizontally between parallel rule-making systems comprising often different sets of public and private actors.

Broadly speaking, there are two ways of theorizing about earth system governance: analytically and normatively.

The *analytical theory of earth system governance* seeks to explain processes and outcomes in this field. This is traditional social science. It is about the effectiveness of institutions and policies, about their interlinkages, and about the diagnostics of specific institutional and policy designs. The analytical theory of earth system governance also involves other core problems of the social sciences, such as the role of power, ideas, norms, different legitimacy claims, and the distributive outcomes of governance.

Given the breadth of its domain, earth system governance research is inherently interdisciplinary within the social sciences. First, earth system governance research transcends traditional concepts of environmental policy or nature conservation. The anthropogenic perturbation of the earth system encompasses more puzzles and problems than scholars have traditionally examined in environmental policy studies, now ranging from changes in biogeochemical systems to the global loss of biological diversity. Key questions—such as how Bangladesh could adapt to rising sea levels, how deterioration of African soils could be halted and climate migrants resettled, or how land use changes in Brazil could be analyzed— have barely been covered by traditional environmental policy research. Yet they are inevitably part of the study of earth system governance.

Second, earth system governance transcends levels of analysis. It is more than a problem of the regulation of the "global commons" through global agreements and conventions. It is also about decisions that different actors take in their daily lives or in their professional positions. Consequently, the analysis of earth system governance covers the full range of social science disciplines across scales, from anthropology to international law (Biermann, Betsill, et al. 2009; Mattor et al. 2013; on law in the Anthropocene see Kotzé 2013). It covers local regulatory systems to address problems ranging from air pollution to the preservation of local waters, waste treatment, or desertification and soil degradation. It also includes the study of international treaties seeking to regulate the environmental behavior of governments and multinational corporations. Earth system governance requires the integration of these strands of research at multiple scales from global to local.

As laid out in chapter 1, I focus in this book on the *global level of decision making*, that is, on the new challenges of world politics in the Anthropocene. The book thus seeks to contribute also to the general theory of "global governance," as it tries to explain institutions and governance processes beyond the confines of the nation-state. The concept of global governance is often described in very broad terms, even encompassing processes at the local or individual level that impact on global issues. For example, the Commission on Global Governance (1995, 2–3) has described global governance broadly as

the sum of the many ways individuals and institutions, public and private, manage their common affairs. It is a continuing process through which conflicting or diverse interests may be accommodated and cooperative action taken. It includes formal institutions and regimes empowered to enforce compliance, as well as informal arrangements that people and institutions either have agreed to or perceive to be in their interest.

(For other foundational definitions see for example Young 1999, 11; Finkelstein 1995, 369; Overbeek et al. 2010; Rosenau 1995, 13, and 2002, 4.)

With a view to global decision making, the analytical theory of earth system governance can build therefore on long-standing research on international environmental cooperation (comprehensive overviews in Dauvergne 2012; Falkner 2013). This tradition dates back at least to the 1972 Stockholm Conference on the Human Environment that led to a first wave of academic studies on intergovernmental environmental cooperation (for example Kennan 1970; Johnson 1972; Caldwell 1984). One important precursor to current earth system governance research is for example the debate on international environmental regimes of the 1980s (Young 1980, 1986, 1989a, and 1989b) and 1990s, including the discussions on the creation of such regimes, their maintenance, and their effectiveness (for instance, Bernauer 1995; Brown Weiss and Jacobson 1998; Haas, Keohane, and Levy 1993; Keohane and Levy 1996; Young 1994, 1997, and 1999; Young, Levy, and Osherenko 1999). Added to this is important earlier work on intergovernmental environmental organizations (Bartlett, Kurian, and Malik 1995) and nonstate environmental organizations (Conca 1995; Wapner 1996), both of which are important to current earth system governance analysis as well.

The *normative theory of earth system governance*, for its part, is the critique of the current systems of governance. Normative theory does not ask what is, but what should be. It juxtaposes the findings and insights from analytical theory—for instance on the effectiveness of international regimes—with the needs and necessities of earth system stability. Normative theory is essentially critical theory, focusing on the reform and reorganization of human activity in a way that helps us "to navigate the Anthropocene" (Biermann, Abbott, et al. 2012).

At the global level, the normative theory of earth system governance relates also to a broader tradition in global governance research that seeks to critique and reform multilateral institutions. Marie-Claude Smouts (1998, 88), for instance, has argued that global governance should be seen not as an "analytical reflection on the present international system [but as a] standard-setting reflection for building a better world." Leon Gordenker and Thomas G. Weiss (1996, 17) defined global governance as "efforts to bring more orderly and reliable responses to social and political issues that go beyond capacities of states to address individually." The UN's Commission on Global Governance (1995) elaborated shortly after the end of the Cold War a plethora of far-reaching reform proposals to deal with problems of modernization, some of which I discuss in the following chapters with a view to earth system governance.

In this sense, effective earth system governance will necessarily be transformative. Given current scenarios and trends, business as usual is unlikely to prevent critical transitions in the earth system. Technological revolutions and efficiency gains might provide partial solutions within the current systems of production, distribution, and consumption; yet this seems inadequate at present. Instead, earth system governance, to be effective, will need to address directly key causes of social change. Notably, in a highly divided world, earth system governance poses fundamental questions of allocation within and among countries (see chapter 6). Earth system governance also raises important questions about the legitimacy and accountability of public and private action and the exercise of power, and eventually about how we conceive effective mechanisms of democratic earth system governance (see chapter 5). Earth system governance is therefore as much about environmental parameters as about social practices and processes. Its normative goal is not purely environmental protection on a planetary scale—this would make earth system governance devoid of its societal context. Environmental targets in earth system governance—such as control of greenhouse gases at a certain level—can be pursued through different global and local governance mechanisms that bring unequal costs for actors in different countries and regions. Earth system governance is thus about social welfare as well as environmental protection; it is about effectiveness as well as global and local equity.

Earth System Governance Research beyond the Social Sciences

For these reasons, earth system governance research is interdisciplinary within the social sciences. Yet it also reaches beyond social science. It is an integral part of the overarching context of sustainability science or earth system science, in which social scientists work with natural scientists to advance integrated understanding of the coupled social-ecological system that our planet has become. Both social and natural sciences, and scientists, need to be open to collaboration, including the collective assessment of research findings.

Even so, earth system governance research needs to remain grounded in the particular theoretical, epistemological, and methodological approaches of the social sciences and the humanities. Integrated research thus needs to combine academic communities with rather different theoretical and methodological traditions (Biermann 2007). One is driven by an integrated computer-based approach that brings together most natural sciences and those social sciences that are able to contribute models and quantified data. Most of earth system governance research, however, will continue to employ (often) qualitative, case-based and context-dependent methodologies and approaches in order to analyze the organized human responses to earth system transformation, in particular the institutions and agents that cause earth system transformation and the institutions that are created to steer human development in a way that guarantees a safe coevolution with natural processes. Both communities need then to find ways of collaborating in joint programs, for example on the global carbon cycle.

Some scientists believe in the development of computer-based modeling tools that will eventually provide a true integration of *all* sciences, including social sciences. The physicist John Schellnhuber, for example, has formalized, in his attempt of a mathematical description of sustainability, the notion of a "global subject" S, which he conceptualizes as part of the human civilization H together with the anthroposphere A (the totality of human life, actions, and products that affect other components of the earth system). Translated into social science language, this "global subject" S could be seen as the global political system including its national and subnational subparts, all of which share the collective ability to bring the "human impact" in line with the needs of the ecosphere (Schellnhuber 1999, C20–C22).

In practice, however, it is still unclear to what extent institutional and governance research can contribute to, and be integrated with, the more model-driven research programs, apart from problem-oriented, issue-specific collaboration. Computer-based modeling is problematic for most students of institutions and governance—and likely to remain so (Young et al. 2006). Qualitative modeling projects, partially organized by the Earth System Governance Project, to analyze for example international governance processes and institutions are in their infancy (for example, Biermann, Berséus, et al. 2011; Eisenack, Kropp, and Welsch 2006; Dellas et al. 2011; de Vos et al. 2013; Dellas and Pattberg 2014). Some major problems in modeling earth system governance remain: to name a few, the complexity of variables at multiple levels, human reflexivity, and difficulties in conceptualizing key social concepts such as power, interest, or legitimacy.

Given these inherent difficulties, social science is at times easily viewed as less scientific than the natural sciences. One example is the conceptualization of social science in the 23 questions that the Global Analysis, Integration and Modeling task force of the International Geosphere-Biosphere Programme put forward as overarching questions for the earth system analysis community a decade ago (Schellnhuber and Sahagian 2002). Some of these questions relate to the social sciences. However, these social science questions are not viewed as part of the "analytical" questions (which are exclusively related to the natural sciences), but as part of the "strategic" questions (for example question no. 23, "What is the structure of an effective and efficient system of global environment and development institutions?") or "normative" questions (for example, question no. 18, "What kind of nature do modern societies want?"). The value of institutional research as an *analytical* program of inquiry is relegated to its policy-oriented, advisory dimensions.

Arguably, this is a logical outcome of a conceptualization of earth system analysis that is solely motivated by the needs of computer modeling and quantification. One cannot, however, subject governance analysis to epistemological uniformity and to methods from the natural sciences that it is infeasible to implement and impossible to trust in social research. Instead, earth system governance researchers will need to continue to develop research programs that are interdisciplinary across the social sciences—for example, linking international relations and international law—and that follow the internal logic, methods, and metatheories of social science.

On the other hand, there is no doubt that earth system governance research will be a central part of the overarching effort of earth system analysis and sustainability science. One leading example is the current formation of a worldwide alliance of all scientific projects and programs in this field, called Future Earth (Future Earth Transition Team 2012). This alliance is an example of new and intensified collaboration of natural and social scientists in an institutional setting that breaks down disciplinary boundaries and creates new space for fresh ideas and engagement. In such global multidisciplinary research alliances, earth system governance research will need to maintain its critical stance as a social science program, yet it will also integrate, to the extent feasible, with all other research communities, including from the natural sciences, in the joint effort to advance a more holistic understanding of planetary processes.

Earth System Governance: What on Earth For?

As I laid out above, earth system governance is not about managing the entire process of planetary evolution, but rather about the societal steering of human activities with regard to the long-term stability of geobiophysical systems. But the latter is nontrivial: What *precisely* are the goals of earth system governance? In what *concrete* directions should human agency develop? What are the normative assumptions that underlie earth system governance?

One obvious response is to name sustainable development as the final goal of governance. The concept of sustainable development is so broadly in use today that there is no resistance to it, partially since the notion has few contours (Robinson 2004; Olsson, Hourcade, and Köhler 2014).

The core idea was defined by the World Commission on Environment and Development in the 1980s: "Humankind has the ability to make development sustainable—to ensure that it meets the needs of the present without compromising the ability of future generations to meet their own needs" (World Commission on Environment and Development 1987). Yet this definition is broad, and was meant to be broad. As aptly summarized by Kates, Parris, and Leiserowitz (2005, 10), "[t]his malleability allows programs of environment or development; places from local to global; and institutions of government, civil society, business, and industry to each project their interests, hopes, and aspirations onto the banner of sustainable development."

To provide more focus, it is common to distinguish three pillars of sustainable development. For example, the Johannesburg Declaration adopted at the 2002 World Summit on Sustainable Development posited a "collective responsibility to advance and strengthen the interdependent and mutually reinforcing pillars of sustainable development—economic development, social development, and environmental protection—at local, national, regional, and global levels." The European Union has also enshrined the notion of sustainable development with its broad, multipillar understanding within its policymaking system (Adelle and Jordan 2009). Yet how these three pillars are to be weighted and defined in concrete cases of earth system governance—for example climate change or biodiversity depletion—remains undefined, and there is hardly any consensus about this in either academic or political communities.

One way forward is to conceptualize the normative goal of earth system governance holistically as the preservation of human development and well-being within the confines of certain boundary conditions in the earth system. Rockström and colleagues (2009), for example, have defined nine "planetary boundaries" that could, if crossed, result in a major disruption in (parts of) the system and a transition to a different state, with disastrous consequences for humanity. The threshold values are, to use a related concept, the "tipping points" in the system. Rockström and colleagues suggest boundaries for nine earth system processes: climate change; biodiversity loss; the nitrogen cycle; the phosphorus cycle; stratospheric ozone depletion; ocean acidification; global freshwater use; land use change; atmospheric aerosol loading; and chemical pollution. Eventually, this approach should allow for the quantification of threshold parameters, which is then expected to guide political responses.

For some of these boundaries, our current knowledge is still too uncertain to allow for quantification. For others, however, Rockström and colleagues (2009) feel confident enough to suggest a numeric threshold value. In this endeavor, they err on the side of caution and a strict interpretation of the precautionary principle: where they see remaining uncertainties, they suggest the lower values for the boundary that they identify. Taken together, the nine earth system boundaries define what Rockström and colleagues describe as a "safe operating space for humanity."

An important insight is that three threshold values have been crossed already. Regarding climate change, we have reached atmospheric carbon dioxide concentrations of 400 ppm (compared to 280 ppm in preindustrial times), whereas the threshold value proposed by Rockström and colleagues (2009) would lie at 350 ppm. Regarding biodiversity, the current extinction rate is over 100 extinct species per million species per year, while the suggested threshold is 10 extinctions. As for the nitrogen cycle, humans remove about 121 million tons of nitrogen per year from the atmosphere today, while a safe rate, according to Rockström and colleagues, is a maximum of 35 million tons. In these three areas, therefore, humankind has pushed the earth system past tipping points into a new—and unknown—world.

The approach by Rockström and colleagues (2009) is part of a broader line of research in the earth system sciences. The approach is similar, for example, to the earlier notion of "guardrails" and "tolerable windows" that was developed in the late 1990s by the German Advisory Council on Global Change (1997 and 2000) in collaboration with the Potsdam Institute for Climate Impact Research. As argued then by the German Advisory Council (2000, 135), the

concept of tolerable windows ... is characterized by the normative stipulation of non-tolerable risks, termed guard rails. ... The purpose of limiting tolerable developments of climate change by means of guard rails is to prevent the climate system from moving dangerously close to possibly unstable states, which, considering the extremely high potential for damage, could lead to dramatic climatic hazards.

One quantified guardrail had been the target of a maximum average global temperature increase of 2 degrees Celsius, which is today accepted by most governments.

More broadly, all current work on critical transitions and tipping points in the earth system closely relates to the approach of earth system boundaries. Tipping elements are defined as parts of the earth system that can be switched by small perturbations under certain circumstances into a qualitatively different state (Lenton et al. 2008, 1786). Tipping points refer to the critical values at which the state of the system is qualitatively changed. At present, our knowledge about such tipping points is preliminary at best, and substantial research is directed at the identification of early warning signals for such critical transitions in the earth system (Scheffer et al. 2009).

Despite some differences in approach, perspective, and research trajectory, all of these notions of earth system boundaries, guardrails, tipping points, and critical transitions come down to the same basic idea: the attempt at a quantified suggestion of the boundaries of the earth system that need to be observed in order to maintain the potential for human development and well-being.

Importantly, within this overall target corridor, the concept of earth system boundaries leaves human societies ample space for different political choices and socioeconomic development trajectories (Biermann 2012b; Galaz et al. 2012a, 2012b, and 2013b). These socioeconomic development trajectories—within the safe operating space set by the earth system boundaries—are not defined by scientists. They are left open to the democratic political process and intergovernmental negotiation. In this sense, the notion of earth system boundaries is just one element of the overall policy objective of sustainable development. They define the broad limitations and guardrails for human development. They are in principle neutral toward human values and aspirations. The earth system boundaries do not determine any "limits to growth," but set limits to the total human impact on planetary systems.

In fact, many political trajectories for societies are conceivable that stay within the safe operating space as defined by earth system boundaries. In theory, staying within the earth system boundaries could be achieved by Malthusian, totalitarian, plutocratic, or oligarchic political systems, or any combination of them. Yet such political systems would conflict with other important policy goals such as democracy, human rights, and freedom. In such circumstances, therefore, environmental effectiveness would be incompatible with human development and social justice, which are part of the broader notion of sustainable development. In short, the *concept of earth system boundaries defines the safe operating space for humankind within the larger context of sustainable development, and serves as policy target only within this broader social context.* (A related question that cannot be expanded here is whether democratic deliberation and the protection of human rights are *an essential prerequisite* for effective environmental protection, which would make them an *inherent part* of staying within earth system boundaries; see here for example Dryzek and Stevenson 2011.)

The core idea of the concept of earth system boundaries is quantification and (increasing) precision. This has raised concerns among some social scientists who argue that definition of precise targets is impossible and that Rockström and colleagues mistake the planet for a machine with a dashboard of switches and steering devices. This constructivist critique is correct inasmuch as clear-cut quantifiable boundaries do not exist in the earth system, or at least remain beyond human understanding. Yet such resignation does not help in shaping a normative vision for earth system governance and the concrete rules and standards that are needed to steer human behavior. What counts for governance is not absolute precision on boundaries but broad agreement among scientists and policy networks about the goals we should strive for. And these goals will likely be more powerful if they are clear and convincingly quantified. Thus, even though quantification of earth system boundaries will always be based on scientific research that may become more certain but never fully certain, quantification of earth system boundaries has the potential of creating powerful political narratives. The 2-degree Celsius target for global warming, for example, surely defies precise calculation and reasoning (and may even be too high anyway), but it has become a powerful narrative for change and for galvanizing action. Other simple indicators, for instance the presence of certain species as indicators of healthy ecosystems (tigers, salmon), have become powerful symbols that have oriented political action toward resolving much more complex underlying issues, such as river pollution or ecosystem degradation.

Consequently, the nine earth system boundaries identified by Rockström and colleagues (2009) offer an important conceptual framework for a research and assessment program. Rockström and colleagues readily admit that the science behind the quantification of target values for earth system boundaries is still contested, and several boundaries are identified but not quantified. The boundaries will thus remain a moving target, to be defined and refined as scientific research and political discourse develop.

Why political discourse? Are earth system boundaries not defined by purely scientific efforts? They are not. While the concept of earth system boundaries is normatively neutral, its implementation is not. The scientific determination of earth system boundaries is, like most scientific assessments (Mitchell et al. 2006; Jasanoff and Martello 2004), a political process. It has to be understood, and analyzed, as such. I discuss two examples.

First, the exact definition of earth system boundaries depends on normative assumptions about the risks that we, as humankind, are taking. Earth system boundaries assume that the human species is a collective that is able and willing to take joint action. Yet the human species, as main driving force of the Anthropocene, is starkly divided in wealth and living standards. According to the World Bank (2008, 4), the richest 20 percent of humanity account for 76.6 percent of total private consumption, while the poorest 25 percent still have no access to electricity (UNDP 2007) (see chapter 6, on "Allocation"). It is in this global context of large inequalities in resource use and entitlements that the parameters of earth system boundaries need to be agreed upon.

Global inequalities could translate, for example, into conflicting perspectives on the underlying uncertainties and risks. Richer societies might prefer a risk-averse approach, conserving the world as it is and preventing any harm. Poorer societies, for their part, might be more risk-taking, prioritizing economic development to alleviate poverty. Yet the interest constellation, if differently framed, could also be the other way round. Conservative threshold values—such as the 350 ppm threshold in atmospheric carbon dioxide concentration that Rockström and colleagues (2009) suggest—will require most efforts first from those who pollute most, that is, the richer societies in the North. On the other hand, system disruptions because of violated earth system boundaries will cost poorer societies most in relative terms, that is, those who are most vulnerable and have the least means to adapt. It is thus the poorer island developing countries that are the most demanding in international climate negotiations, pushing for the lowest possible concentration targets for greenhouse gases. In sum, the definition of the goals in earth system governance is inevitably influenced by the risks that governments and societal actors are willing to take.

As a second example, the definition of boundaries is more complex, and politically more problematic, in some areas than in others. Stratospheric ozone depletion gives societies relatively little freedom; here, the scientific assessment should lead, and in fact has led, directly to political action. Yet in the case of land use change, for example, the value that Rockström and colleagues (2009) suggest—at most 15 percent of global land cover can be converted to cropland—could be more debatable, given that 842 million people suffer from chronic hunger, 98 percent of whom live in developing countries (FAO, IFAD, and WFP 2013). Also the earth system boundaries for global freshwater use raise questions of sufficient access and fair allocation. Today, one billion people lack sufficient access to water and 2.6 billion people have no basic sanitation (UNDP 2006). The definition of the acceptable earth system boundaries needs to be seen in this light, too.

Given that the translation of the concept of earth system boundaries from assessment to action needs to be done in political negotiations and agreements, the role of scientists is implicated in this as well (see also chapter 3, on "Agency"). Since the assessment of earth system boundaries is inherently political, scientists involved in this process become inadvertently also political actors. This raises fundamental questions about the legitimacy and accountability of scientific assessment processes (see the contributions in Mitchell et al. 2006). The history of the Intergovernmental Panel on Climate Change, which evolved from a small group of mainly natural scientists from industrialized countries into a vast, highly institutionalized network of thousands of experts, is the best-known example, one where science becomes intermeshed with governmental oversight, geographic quotas, political conflicts, and fundamental questions about what science is and who may count as a scientist (Siebenhüner 2002a and 2002b; Berkhout 2010).

In short, the exact earth system boundary in any of the nine domains identified by Rockström and colleagues (2009) is not simply a matter for scientists to negotiate—it is also a *political* boundary that needs to be negotiated by political actors who have to weigh scientific evidence and degrees of uncertainty with their own assessment of the risks to be taken and the costs to be endured. Despite all accuracy in attempts at measurement, the earth system boundaries are in the end a social construct. Yet this does not take away from their value for the larger purpose of earth system governance. The concept of earth system boundaries provides a framework for scientific research and political negotiation to define jointly the safe operating space for human development, and is hence an important element in the study and practice of earth system governance.

Outline of a Normative Theory of Earth System Governance

As laid out above, I distinguish between an analytical and a normative theory of earth system governance. While the first studies and explains how governance is conducted, the latter critiques the status quo with a normative vision of effective earth system governance. It confronts the ideal with the reality. In this section, I lay out elements of a normative theory of earth system governance (drawing on Biermann 2007). These consist of six functions that effective earth system governance needs to deliver, which I derive from five core elements of the overall problem structure in this governance domain. This normative theory forms the background for the detailed chapters 3–7 on agency, architecture, accountability, allocation, and adaptiveness in earth system governance.

Problem Structure

I first discuss the specific problem structure of earth system governance, since governance must be tailored to the specific characteristics of a problem. This causes particular difficulties for earth system governance. The anthropogenic transformation of the earth system is diverse in its causes, consequences, and possible responses, which renders it impossible to design universal, one-size-fits-all solutions. Earth system governance must cope with at least five problem characteristics.

Analytic and normative uncertainty. First, anthropogenic earth system transformation is marked by persistent uncertainty regarding the causes of earth system transformation, its impacts, the interlinkage of various causes and response options, and the effects of possible response options. Most transformations, such as global climate change, are nonlinear and might accelerate, or slow down, at any time. Surprises in system behavior can be expected, but are by definition unforeseeable. The history of the belated and partially accidental scientific discovery of stratospheric ozone depletion and its man-made causes has been particularly well documented in the literature, with its intriguing story of computer systems that excluded high ozone depletion as measurement errors, of scientists who first did not report their findings, and of politicians who first refused to act (Litfin 1994; Parson 2003). Uncertainty has found its institutional response in repeated rounds of global environmental assessments that have brought together the world's leading scientists in complex institutional settings, with the IPCC as a prime example. Yet these scientific assessment and research institutions cannot fully resolve the persistent uncertainty that complicates earth system governance (see chapter 3, on "Agency").

Uncertainty is not only analytical but also normative. Most problems of earth system transformation are unprecedented. The adequacy of policies, polities, and modes of allocation remain uncertain, initially always contested, and require agreement by societies over time (see chapter 6, on "Allocation"). Uncertainty hence poses particular governance challenges. It requires governance to be stable over several decades to withstand sudden changes of earth system parameters (or changes in our knowledge about these parameters), but also to be flexible enough to adapt to changes within the larger stable framework (see chapter 4, on "Architecture"). Governance must be oriented toward the long term, but must also provide solutions for the short term. Normative uncertainty requires the development of new norms and conceptual frameworks for collective action in uncharted territory. The global allocation of emissions entitlements in climate governance, which oscillates between the extremes of equal per capita allocation and allocation according to existing use, is a prime example (see chapter 6, on "Allocation"). Analytical and normative uncertainty is part of any collective decision making. In earth system governance, it is extreme.

Temporal interdependence. Second, the anthropogenic transformation of the earth system creates intergenerational dependencies that pose further exceptional governance challenges. Causation and effect of earth system transformations are usually separated by decades, often by generations. The same holds for the decoupling over decades of the costs of mitigation and the benefits of avoided harm. Sea level rise, for example, is expected within a time range of a hundred years. Such planning horizons exceed the tenure and even the lifetime of present decision makers and stakeholders. Among other things, this poses the challenge of international credibility and trust that future governments will comply with commitments taken on by present ones, and the problem of securing democratic legitimacy of policies in the intergenerational context (see chapter 5, on "Accountability and Legitimacy"). What rights and responsibilities do present generations, and their representatives in parliaments, have vis-à-vis their unborn successors? Intergenerational equity and responsibility are not confined to earth system governance but are also, for example, part of many social security systems. Yet in earth system governance, intergenerational interdependence is at the core.

Functional interdependence. Third, earth system governance must respond to the functional interdependence of earth system transformation and of potential response options. Functional interdependence relates to the interdependence of natural subsystems—linking, for instance, climate change to biodiversity or land degradation—as well as to the interdependence of social systems and policy areas. Response strategies in one problem segment or one policy domain are likely to have repercussions for many others. Functional interdependence also relates, in many problem segments, to the mutual substitutability of response options, which poses particular problems of international allocation. In climate governance, for example, for every global policy target there are an unlimited number of possible combinations of local responses across countries and time frames with similar degrees of effectiveness. Functional interdependence requires policy coordination to the extent possible. It lies at the heart of the discourse on national environmental policy integration as well as of attempts to cluster the plethora of international regimes into core groups, such as a "chemicals cluster" or "biodiversity cluster" (von Moltke 2005; Fauchald 2010). Functional interdependence is also a key concern in addressing the current fragmentation of the overall architecture of earth system governance, and of earth system governance and economic governance (see chapter 4, on "Architecture").

Spatial interdependence. Fourth, the anthropogenic transformation of the earth system creates new forms and degrees of (global) spatial interdependence. This relates to both natural (direct) and social (indirect) interdependencies. Natural interdependencies are functions of the earth system that transform local environmental pollution into changes in the global system that affect other localities. Prominent examples are climate change, stratospheric ozone depletion, the global distribution of persistent organic pollutants, and the global spread of species with potential harm to local ecosystems. Social interdependencies are functions of the (global) social system that transform local environmental degradation into transregional or global social, economic, and political crises. These include negative influences on the world economy, for example from large-scale flooding, drought, or disease. They also include negative influences on the material security of human populations, for example when regional climatic change causes decreases in food production or increases in global food prices. Eventually, these social interdependencies will also affect global and regional security. Economic crises or mass migration due to transformations of the earth system will not be confined to some countries; they will affect all. Spatial ecological interdependence binds all countries. This creates a new dependence of even the most powerful states on all others. This is a defining characteristic as well as a key challenge of earth system governance that requires an effective institutional framework for global cooperation (see chapter 3, on "Agency"; and chapter 4, on "Architecture").

Extreme impacts. Fifth, earth system governance has to cope with, and gains its particular relevance from, the extraordinary degree of harm that is possible, and that current governance systems are not fully prepared for. Sea level rise, food shortages, drought, storms, land degradation, reproductive disorder, and many other consequences of earth system transformation—if unchecked—are conceivable. Some might be catastrophic, such as changes in monsoon patterns or in the thermohaline circulation, the large-scale breakdown of ecosystems, or rising sea levels in low-lying countries. Developing countries, in particular, will be ill prepared to adapt to these changes, which might in some cases require large-scale domestic migration or transnational food assistance (see chapter 7, on "Adaptiveness"). The likelihood of extreme impacts challenges earth system governance in many ways. Extreme impacts could exceed the regulatory capacity of individual states, both in affected regions and in less affected potential donor regions. Global assistance is needed, including globally coordinated planning and preparation. Large-scale assistance programs will test emerging norms of global solidarity to an unprecedented extent. Global solidarity led states and private citizens to transfer substantial funds to victims of disasters in the past, from the flood assistance to the Dutch in 1953 to the tsunami aid programs in Southeast Asia in 2005. Yet the extent of potential impacts of earth system transformation will require continually evolving norms of global solidarity (see chapter 7, on "Adaptiveness").

Governance Functions

These problem characteristics of earth system transformation through human action—high analytic and normative uncertainty, high temporal, functional, and spatial interdependence, and potentially extreme impacts—are unprecedented in the governance of human affairs. From these characteristics of earth system transformation, I derive six core functions of earth system governance (drawing on Biermann 2007).

Credibility. First, effective earth system governance requires governments to commit resources both domestically and through transnational transfer mechanisms for mitigation and adaptation policies. Given the uncertainty and temporal and spatial interdependence of anthropogenic earth system transformation, governments will need to commit these resources based on the assumption that other governments will reciprocate when it is their turn—including in the future. Earth system governance must thus produce the necessary credibility for governments and others to believe in this reciprocity of interaction over time and space. Importantly, governments need to agree on basic notions of fairness and equity in implementing their long-term obligations toward earth system governance (see chapter 6, on "Allocation").

Stability. This requires that earth system governance be stable enough over decades to withstand political changes in participating countries or changes in the world political system. Governments that commit resources within a global normative framework in the present must rely on the perseverance of this framework over time, yet effective transnational institutions and governance systems with a time horizon of many decades or centuries are rare. It will be a key task for analysts to chart ways toward such stable architectures of earth system governance in the twenty-first century (see chapter 4, on "Architecture").

Adaptability. Within this stable framework, actors must have the ability, based on collectively agreed procedures and principles, to change governance elements to respond to new situations, without harming both credibility and stability of the entire system. The tension between stability and credibility, on the one hand, and the need to respond quickly to new scientific findings and new interest constellations is one of the key challenges for earth system governance. Governing has always implied a degree of social learning and adaptation to changed circumstances—at least for those political systems that have survived for some generations. Earth system transformation brings with it new challenges regarding the degree and speed of potential change. The conditions for effective and equitable *adaptive governance* are increasingly discussed at the local and regional levels, for example concerning water governance. The conditions for effective global adaptive governance of large-scale earth system transformations during the twenty-first century within a stable global institutional order are less understood (see chapter 7, on "Adaptiveness"). One important element is modes of decision making, which I discuss in chapter 4.

Inclusiveness. The interdependence of earth system governance, as well as the complexity and uncertainty of the entire system that may change the overall interest constellation within a few years, require the governance system to be as inclusive as possible regarding the number of stakeholders involved. Both for mitigation and adaptation efforts, it is important to include weaker states that might lack influence in world politics. In particular, developing countries are significantly more relevant, and hence more powerful, in key issue areas of earth system governance, from climate change to biodiversity governance, and this needs to be reflected in multilateral governance architectures. Added to this comes the challenge of involving nonstate stakeholders in local and global decision making (see chapter 3, on "Agency"). The complexity and uncertainty of earth system governance cannot be resolved through action by governments and public agents alone. However, this inclusion of nonstate actors and civil society also requires methods and mechanisms that are seen by all stakeholders as legitimate, effective, and fair (see chapter 5, on "Accountability").

Differentiation. Inclusiveness requires earth system governance also to allow for different standards within the overall common commitment of all actors. Norms must be differentiated according to the capabilities and responsibilities of countries. This has been recognized in principle 23 of the Stockholm Declaration (1972) on the Human Environment and in principle 7 of the Rio Declaration (1992), which stated:

In view of the different contributions to global environmental degradation, States have common but differentiated responsibilities. The developed countries acknowledge the responsibility that they bear in the international pursuit of sustainable development in view of the pressures their societies place on the global environment and of the technologies and financial resources they command. (Rio Declaration 1992, principle 7)

This rationale is the basis of many issue-specific regimes in earth system governance. For example, the 1987 Montreal Protocol on Substances that Deplete the Ozone Layer differentiates obligations between industrialized countries, which must comply in full with treaty provisions, and certain developing countries, to which exemptions apply (Biermann 2002a). A similar differentiation became part of the climate convention in its distinction between industrialized and developing countries, along with a number of further, often merely vaguely defined exemptions and special rights for groups of countries. Yet while the general principle of differentiation is widely agreed, its implementation is not, especially since the traditional distinction between developed and developing countries is becoming blurred given the rapid economic growth in many Southern countries, notably China. The concrete implementation of the principle of differentiation thus remains a key challenge for the long-term institutional architecture of earth system governance (see also chapter 4, on "Architecture").

Solidarity. Norm differentiation, however, cannot resolve fundamental earth system challenges that require all countries to take action. The corollary function is hence international solidarity, that is, the need for richer countries to assist others so that they can also contribute to earth system governance. In 2000, governments agreed in their Millennium Declaration on the "fundamental value" of solidarity as being "essential to international relations in the twenty-first century," stating that "[g]lobal challenges must be managed in a way that distributes the costs and burdens fairly in accordance with basic principles of equity and social justice. Those who suffer or who benefit least deserve help from those who benefit most" (UNGA 2000, para. I.6).

By adopting national policies to protect global commons, developing countries will assume considerable financial burdens. Environmentally sound production methods will remain out of reach in poorer regions where most recent and sophisticated technologies are unavailable. As early as the 1980s, several conferences, including the Tokyo Conference on the Global Environment and Human Response toward Sustainable Development (1989) and the Cairo World Conference on Preparing for Climate Change (1989), called for "dramatic addition and innovative new approaches to international funding ... to achieve environmentally sound and sustainable development." Since then, industrialized countries have agreed to provide additional financial assistance to developing countries to allow them to implement programs relating to the protection of the global climate, the earth's ozone shield, biological diversity, or the emission of persistent organic pollutants. Unlike earlier instances of North-South cooperation, those commitments have often been established in legally binding treaty provisions governed by decision-making mechanisms in which developing countries hold equal voting power. However, even though the principle of solidarity is formally accepted by all governments, the concrete principles of fair allocation in earth system governance still remain contested (see in detail chapter 6, on "Allocation").

Conclusion

I conceive of earth system governance in this book as an emerging domain of political cooperation and conflict, similar to more established governance domains such as health governance or economic governance. The subject that is addressed here is the entirety of the planetary systems as shaped by human action. The need for earth system governance is linked to the advent of the Anthropocene, an epoch in which the planet is being transformed by the myriad activities of its most dominant species. While the last two hundred years were marked by human ignorance with regard to the changes we were bringing about, the twenty-first century differs. Humans now understand our impact on the planet and the transformative force that our systems of production and consumption have become. Earth system governance is the response to this state of affairs, enshrined in numerous intergovernmental treaties, national laws, or local regulations along with thousands of specialized agencies, organizations, programs, and actors.

Earth system governance is, as such, also one of the most fascinating areas of research in the social sciences. Such research necessarily transcends numerous boundaries in the social sciences, between different disciplines as well as between local studies and the analysis of global decision making. It also transcends the boundary between natural and social sciences, being part of new integrative research communities such as sustainability science, resilience theory, or earth system analysis.

This book seeks to contribute to this research program. It is inevitably limited. Importantly, I focus here on international and transnational governance. This does not by any means imply that earth system governance is only a matter of international decision making. Without strong local institutions, earth system governance will surely fail, even though local governance is not part of this book.

A second focus in this book is on policy reform at the international level. It is evident that current earth system governance is not sufficient to keep within specific earth system boundaries. Carbon dioxide emissions alone increased in 2010 by 5.9 percent, leading to an overall atmospheric concentration not previously recorded in the last 800,000 years (Peters et al. 2012; see also IPCC 2014b). Change is needed.

Hence the following chapters focus on proposals for change—for a fundamental reform of the international architecture of earth system governance that we have essentially inherited from the twentieth century. My discussion will address the role of the state, public-private policy networks, science institutions, and international organizations (chapter 3); the overall global institutional architecture of earth system governance, with a focus on the current fragmentation of the system (chapter 4); the accountability, legitimacy, and democratic quality of earth system governance and possible reform options (chapter 5); the equity implications and allocative effects of governance (chapter 6); and, finally, policy options to deal with adaptation to earth system transformation (chapter 7).

Prometheus

Bedecke deinen Himmel, Zeus,
Mit Wolkendunst!
Und übe, Knaben gleich,
Der Diesteln köpft,
An Eichen dich und Bergeshöhn!
Musst mir meine Erde
Doch lassen stehn,
Und meine Hütte,
Die Du nicht gebaut,
Und meinen Herd,
Um dessen Glut
Du mich beneidest.
[...]
Hier sitz' ich, forme Menschen
Nach meinem Bilde,
Ein Geschlecht, das mir gleich sei,
Zu leiden, weinen,
Genießen und zu freuen sich,
Und dein nicht zu achten,
Wie ich.

Johann Wolfgang von Goethe, 1777

Prometheus

Cover your heaven, Zeus,
With foggy clouds,
And try yourself, like a boy
Who beheads thistles,
On oak trees and mountaintops;
You still must leave
my Earth to me,
And my hut,
which you did not build,
And my stove,
Whose glow
You envy me.
[...]
Here I sit, forming humans
In my image;
A people to be like me,
To suffer, to weep,
To enjoy and to delight themselves,
And to not attend to you—
As I.

3

Agency

The myth of Prometheus marks the beginning of the Anthropocene. Prometheus brought the secret of fire to early humans, thus launching the perpetual process of fossil-fuel-based industrialization and modern civilization. Prometheus was hence one of the first, and most powerful, agents in anthropogenic earth system transformation. Earth system governance—the collective attempt at bringing our societal development paths in line with the exigencies of earth system boundaries—enlists many more agents today. Agents in earth system governance range from governments to science networks, environmentalists, industry associations, faith-based organizations, farmer unions, and intergovernmental organizations, to name just a few.

Agents are at the center of earth system governance: they create, shape and maintain the institutions and overall architecture of earth system governance. They need to ensure the accountability and legitimacy of the decisions that are taken and the rules that are established. Agents are also responsible for the allocation of costs and benefits in any governance system. Eventually, agents guarantee the adaptiveness of governance systems to ensure their fit with changing circumstances. The role of agents and agency in earth system governance is hence the focus of this third chapter. Chapters 4–7 will build on this analysis in addressing the themes of architecture, accountability, allocation and adaptiveness in earth system governance.

Importantly, not all actors are agents in governance processes, making it necessary to distinguish between actors and agents (Biermann, Betsill, et al. 2009; Dellas, Pattberg, and Betsill 2011). Actors include all individuals, organizations, and networks that participate in decision making related to the earth system. Agents differ from actors insofar as they have been granted authority by other actors. This includes the authority to set standards, to request and expect compliance with these standards, and to allocate costs and benefits. In other words, an agent is an authoritative actor. Authority here is the legitimacy and capacity to exercise power. Legitimacy is conferred through social consent, given formally or informally (see chapter 5). Whether authority may be claimed unequivocally by an agent is an open question; here the concepts of power and authority come together.

To analyze agency in earth system governance, we need first to consider how actors become authoritative. What is the source of authority, especially outside the public sphere? Authority is not based solely on the apparatus of the state. Nor can we assume that public actors have authority and private actors do not. Organizational theory from sociology helps to shed light on how collective actors acquire agency within specific institutional environments (Barnett and Finnemore 2004; Dingwerth and Pattberg 2009). This research is embedded in the much broader structure-agent debate in the social sciences. From Weber and Durkheim to the present, social scientists have debated whether social outcomes are primarily a product of individual actions by agents or shaped by broader social structures within which agents are situated. Structure and agency are often seen as two sides of the same coin, with agents both constituting and being constituted by structures within which they operate.

States have traditionally been central agents in world politics. Earth system governance is not fundamentally different in this respect. Here, too, states are the key actors that have authority to rule, to enforce, and to allocate. The authority of states varies in line with their power, which may derive from military might, economic strength, or diplomatic and cultural domination; yet all states are agents in earth system governance, perhaps the most important agents still.

Yet, as this chapter will show, many other agents are active in earth system governance today. These include a variety of nonstate actors that range from networks of environmental groups and business organizations to scientific assessment institutions, indigenous alliances, and city networks (see below on partnerships and on science; on indigenous alliances, see Schroeder 2010; on cities see Bulkeley and Betsill 2003; Betsill and Bulkeley 2004; Bulkeley and Schroeder 2011 and 2012). These nonstate agents are often also referred to as "nongovernmental," in contrast to national governments, and thus include subnational public actors, or "private actors," in contrast to public actors. The latter distinction, however, is increasingly becoming blurred in many policy fields, including earth system governance. For instance, several governance institutions formed by nonstate actors have a clear intention to fulfill a public purpose, such as protecting marine biodiversity or preserving tropical forests. These institutions are nongovernmental, but not necessarily private in purpose.

Assessment

I discuss in this chapter three nonstate agents of earth system governance that have been the focus of my research in recent years: transnational policy networks; science networks; and international bureaucracies. The main question that I explore is the extent to which such agents beyond the state fulfill a complementary, or even alternative, governance role vis-à-vis states. But first I briefly discuss how the role of the state has come under increased pressure from earth system transformation.

The State

States have undergone tremendous transformations over the last two centuries, from the liberal state of the nineteenth century to the modern welfare state of the late twentieth. Recent scholarship has emphasized the environmental challenges that states are increasingly facing (Barry and Eckersley 2005), and has explored the requirements for an effective and democratic "green state" (Dryzek et al. 2003; Eckersley 2004b) or "ecostate" (Meadowcroft 2005). This is not the place to review this extensive literature, which has provided important insights into the transformations of the (mainly Western, highly industrialized) state over the last decades. Instead, I highlight three elements of earth system transformation that place particular burdens on the state, and that directly relate to the discussions in the subsequent chapters (drawing in part on Biermann and Dingwerth 2004).

First and foremost, earth system transformation increases the *interdependence of states*. The guarantee of security and the protection of citizens is now possible only in a governance context that transcends state boundaries. For one, earth system transformation creates new forms of systemic interstate interdependence that were unknown in the heyday of the Westphalian system. All countries are affected, for example, by the depletion of the stratospheric ozone layer or by global climate change and are hence bound to suffer from environmental harm that has been caused largely by actors outside their own territories. While some adaptation to climate change may seem feasible—though costly—in rich countries, poorer countries are faced with increasing vulnerability to a global environmental problem that has only marginally been caused by their own emissions. Beyond this direct interdependence, earth system transformation creates new indirect interdependencies through increased stress on the adaptive capacity of states. A vast literature on the relationship between environmental degradation and security has pointed to conflicts that could result from extended environmental stress and the failure of states to cope with such problems. Economic crises, migration, or local environmental problems associated with earth system transformation are not confined to particular states or regions, but will affect all states (see chapter 7, on "Adaptiveness").

Studies on the causes and consequences of international interdependence date back to Hirschman's *National Power and the Structure of Foreign Trade* (1945), Keohane and Nye's *Power and Interdependence* (1977), or in a more general sense to Kant (1795), who maintained that international trade could prevent war. Earth system transformation adds a new dimension to global interdependence. Unlike the economic interdependence that was extensively debated in the 1960s and 1970s, ecological interdependence is indissoluble and inescapable even for the most powerful countries. Ecological interdependence binds all countries, which creates a new dependence of each state on the community of all others (Biermann 1998). This is a defining characteristic as well as key challenge of earth system governance, which must provide for an effective institutional framework for global cooperation and collaboration (see in more detail chapter 4, on "Architecture").

Second, earth system transformation places additional burdens on *state capacities*. The more environmental change puts stress on societies—for instance through drought, regional climate change, or sea level rise, but also through mitigation requirements—the more state capacities will be overstretched, with local and regional governance crises as a possible consequence. Given the uneven geographical distribution of adverse consequences of earth system transformation, some states will face more demands for adaptation than others. For some societies, adaptation will come at significant costs. Developing countries will suffer most from a lack of capacities to address the social, economic, and environmental problems within their boundaries. The added stress that earth system transformation places on states may limit their options to fulfill other functions, such as guaranteeing political participation and human well-being. Where additional capacities to solve the impacts of earth system transformation—such as droughts or regular flooding—are needed, decision making may become more hierarchically structured to save time and resources. Likewise, the guarantee of minimal social conditions will become more difficult to fulfill as the demands on the capacities of states became more numerous and complex. Earth system transformation requires states to prepare for and adapt to its consequences and thus increases the demand for administrative, organizational, technological, and financial capacity of the "adaptive state"—a demand that some states will find easier to meet than others (see in more detail chapter 7, on "Adaptiveness").

Third, spatial and temporal interdependence as well analytical and normative uncertainty create new problems for the *legitimacy* of state action. Mitigation actions taken today to reduce harm will mainly benefit future generations, which will suffer less from floods, droughts, or breakdowns of ecosystems. In addition, beneficiaries of a state's actions might live outside its borders. The legitimacy of such actions thus remains difficult to foresee. This is complicated by the persistent uncertainty inherent in earth system governance, with key parameters of the planetary system remaining poorly understood. Normative uncertainty requires current generations to work toward a model of earth system governance and, implicitly, toward a future earth system whose contours and desirability for future generations remain unknown. What are known are the costs for present generations, which need to be legitimized if drastic actions are taken. This places new burdens on the legitimacy of state action (see in more detail chapter 5, on "Accountability").

Given these challenges, it seems imperative that states make every effort to mitigate and adapt to earth system transformation. States can react either on their own by devising or adapting national environmental policies, or by coordinating their efforts through bilateral or multilateral environmental policies. Since in practice states do both, two specialized fields within political science have emerged to analyze them: comparative environmental politics and international environmental politics. Many researchers from comparative law and politics, innovation studies, and environmental policy have asserted that the role of the state remains central and that the globalization of national environmental policies and horizontal policy diffusion, rather than international institutions, have been responsible for environmental successes of the last decades. Environmental research would thus need to focus on processes of diffusion of innovative environmental policies around the world (Busch and

Jörgens 2005; Busch, Gupta, and Falkner 2012; Falkner and Gupta 2009; Jänicke and Jörgens 2000; Kern, Jörgens, and Jänicke 2001).

In contrast to this comparative approach, researchers trained in international politics focus on international environmental institutions as agents of environmental governance in the global realm (overviews in Mitchell 2003; Young, King, and Schroeder 2008; Andresen and Hey 2005; Biermann and Pattberg 2012). The key premise of this literature is that the global environmental crisis requires intergovernmental institutions to constrain the behavior of states and help states to cooperate. Without any constraints, states would seek to maximize benefits for themselves while neglecting the potential damage of their action vis-à-vis the greater good, such as preventing alterations in earth systems. The political motive driving this stream of research is how to (re)design such intergovernmental institutions in a way that makes them more effective, legitimate, and fair. Most of the following chapters are devoted to this question.

In sum, the state remains important, as, in the words of Eckersley (2004b, 12), the "social institution with the greatest capacity to discipline investors, producers, and consumers ... [and] capacity to redistribute resources and otherwise influence life opportunities to ensure that the move toward a more sustainable society is not a socially regressive one." Yet the state is also put under tremendous new challenges to adapt to the changed context of the Anthropocene and earth system transformations. While much past research has focused on the role of the state in the advancement of public goals and public goods—economic development, individual freedom, democracy, and so forth—a key question for earth system governance is the adaptive capacity of the state in the Anthropocene: whether it is able to adapt internally and externally to large-scale transformations of its natural environment and planetary systems (see also in more detail Compagnon, Chan, and Mert 2012).

There are several fundamental questions regarding the role of the state vis-à-vis earth system governance that will be discussed in more detail in the following chapters. The overall role and relevance of the global governance architecture, and related to this the sovereignty of states to object to collective decisions, stands at the center of chapter 4. Questions of the accountability and legitimacy of state action in the Anthropocene are discussed in chapter 5. Chapter 6, on allocation, focuses on another increasingly central element of state functions: negotiating an international (re)distribution of assets in order to support countries that cannot take sufficient mitigating or adaptive action on their own. Finally, the role of the state in global adaptation governance is discussed in more detail in chapter 7.

Transnational Governance by Nonstate Agents

For the remainder of this chapter, I turn to nonstate agents in earth system governance, which have given rise to much fruitful scholarly debate in the 1990s and 2000s. Many have argued that the role of nonstate actors has increased substantially in global environmental governance, leading to what Paul Wapner two decades ago called a "world civic society" (Wapner 1996; see also Arts 1998; Betsill and Corell 2001; Newell, Pattberg, and Schroeder 2012; Princen, Finger, and Manno 1995; Raustiala 1997; Tamiotti 2001). Carefully orchestrated campaigns of environmentalists have changed the foreign policy of powerful states, initiated new global rules, or influenced global norm-setting processes (Alcock 2008; Gulbrandsen and Andresen 2004; Humphreys 2004; Keck and Sikkink 1998; Skodvin and Andresen 2003; Wapner 2002). Business actors have taken a more prominent direct role in international decision making as well (Arts 2002; Clapp and Fuchs 2009; Falkner 2003; Levy and Kolk 2002; Levy and Newell 2000 and 2002; Tienhaara, Orsini, and Falkner 2012; Vormedal 2008; van der Woerd, Levy, and Begg 2005). One example is the Global Compact that the United Nations has concluded with numerous corporations, which commit to support in their operations and strategies ten principles of corporate social responsibility in the areas of human rights, labor, environment, and anticorruption (Hall and Biersteker 2002; Tienhaara, Orsini, and Falkner 2012).

A new development is the influence of environmental consultants, who have a major impact on the design and implementation of novel types of earth system governance arrangements, such as the Clean Development Mechanism or emissions trading. According to Bouteligier (2011), global environmental consultancy firms exercise agency in earth system governance by contributing to the development of new policies and norm-setting processes and assisting in evaluating compliance of other actors with these. Agency can also lie with individual actors, such as social entrepreneurs (Partzsch and Ziegler 2011), policy entrepreneurs (Brouwer and Biermann 2011; Huitema and Meijerink 2009), or participants in local social networks (Benecke 2011).

Nonstate agents increasingly participate in norm setting and implementation of earth system governance (e.g., Andonova, Betsill, and

Bulkeley 2009; Bulkeley, Hoffmann, et al. 2012; Bulkeley and Jordan 2012; Okereke, Bulkeley, and Schroeder 2009; Pattberg and Stripple 2008). Schroeder, Boykoff, and Spiers (2012) and Schroeder and Lovell (2012) have studied for instance the participation of nonstate actors in climate negotiations and found a dramatic increase in such participation, both within and beyond national delegations. Nonstate actors have also joined governments to put international norms into practice, for example as quasi-implementing agencies for development assistance programs administered by the World Bank or bilateral agencies.

In recent years, a growing number of nonstate actors have chosen to develop their own governance mechanisms, creating myriad trans-national governance experiments that are the subject of increased academic scrutiny (Abbott 2012; Bulkeley, Andonova, et al. 2012; Hoffmann 2011). Hundreds of transnational partnerships now bring together civil society organizations, business associations and corporations, and a host of other public and private actors, in what Steve Waddell (2011) describes as "global action networks." Many nonstate actors have also established institutions to set a variety of global standards, such as the Forest Stewardship Council, the Marine Stewardship Council, the Aquaculture Stewardship Council, the Global Aquaculture Alliance, and many other standard-setting bodies created by major corporations and environmental advocacy groups without direct involvement of states (Pattberg 2005b, 2007, and 2012; Gulbrandsen 2004 and 2010; Kalfagianni and Pattberg 2013a and 2013b; Visseren-Hamakers and Pattberg 2013). Some institutions even deliberately exclude states. At times, traditional intergovernmental policymaking through diplomatic conferences is replaced by such transnational institutions, which some view as being more efficient and transparent. Yet serious questions regarding the accountability and legitimacy of such nonstate standard-setting institutions remain as well, as I will discuss in chapter 5.

The involvement of nonstate agents and institutional mechanisms in earth system governance can be broadly explained by the latter's problem structure (see chapter 2 above). Analytical and normative uncertainty ensures that traditional forms of state-led policymaking based on formal representation of the states' domestic constituencies no longer suffices. Functional and spatial interdependencies create policy deadlocks that make space for nonstate rule setting, as has happened in the case of global policies on fisheries or forests. Earth system governance therefore requires engagement from nonstate agents. At the same time, however, this gives these agents new degrees of autonomy from intergovernmental or single-state decision making.

Transnational public policy networks, in particular, have been hailed as an important complement to what is often seen as ineffective state action. Such networks received much attention at the 2002 Johannesburg World Summit on Sustainable Development, with its focus on "multistakeholder" partnerships of governments, nongovernmental organizations, and corporations—the so-called Partnerships for Sustainable Development (Andonova and Levy 2003; Bäckstrand et al. 2012; Glasbergen, Biermann, and Mol 2007; Pattberg et al. 2012; Wapner 2003). These partnerships were formally supported in the implementation plan agreed in Johannesburg, with over 220 partnerships with US$235 million committed before the summit. Just a few of their titles illustrate the broad scope of these transnational public policy networks, including the African Union Initiative on Promotion and Development of Agenda 21 in Africa; the Network of Regional Governments for Sustainable Development; the Partnership for Water Education and Research; the Partnership for Learning from Best Practices, Good Policies and Enabling Legislation in Support of Sustainable Urbanization; the partnership National Capacities for Up-scaling Local Agenda 21 Demonstrations; the Millennium Cities Partnership; the partnership Strengthening Human Rights Measures and Policies for Sustainable Development; and the Sustainable Agriculture and Rural Development Initiative.

Yet the role and relevance of transnational public policy networks in securing effective earth system governance remains contested. Many observers of the 2002 World Summit on Sustainable Development viewed the summit's emphasis on such networks as problematic (Ottaway 2001; Corporate Europe Observatory 2002; IISD 2002; SDIN 2002), since voluntary arrangements might privilege the aims of more powerful actors, in particular industrialized countries and major corporations, and consolidate the privatization of governance and dominant modes of globalization. In addition, some argue that transnational public policy networks lack accountability and legitimacy. Yet others see transnational public policy networks as an innovative form of governance that addresses deficits of interstate politics by bringing together key actors of civil society, governments and business (for example Reinicke 1998; Benner, Streck, and Witte 2003; Streck 2004). In this perspective, transnational public policy networks are important new mechanisms to help resolve a variety of current governance deficits.

Together with several colleagues—including Sander Chan, Ayşem Mert, and Philipp Pattberg in the core team—I have conducted a large-*n* empirical assessment of several hundred partnerships for sustainable development that were agreed upon around and after the 2002 World Summit on Sustainable Development. This analysis drew on a meta-analysis of empirical studies of the performance of such networks as well as on data from a Global Sustainability Partnership Database that we developed, which covers all partnerships registered with the United Nations (see in more detail Biermann, Chan, et al. 2007; Pattberg et al. 2012).

One claim in support of transnational public policy networks has been that they fill *regulatory gaps* in earth system governance, that is, that they function where governments fail. When governments cannot agree on effective international agreements, or when these agreements are too general to elicit any meaningful action, nonstate actors step in with the creation of transnational public policy networks. We reformulated this claim in two hypotheses. First, if transnational public policy networks fill a regulatory deficit, they will be more prominent in areas where public regulation is largely nonexistent. Alternatively, if this were not the case, then such networks would at least be spread rather equally over a wide range of problems.

Our analysis showed that networks are unequally spread over issue areas, with some areas, such as water, energy, and natural resource management receiving most attention. Other areas of equal importance for earth system governance—mining, desertification, drought, or toxic chemicals—are relatively neglected by networks. A comparison of the distribution of networks with that of intergovernmental agreements per issue suggests that issues that are less regulated also attract very few networks. Relatively many networks exist in areas that are already heavily regulated by states, such as marine resources and oceans and seas. It thus seems that high institutionalization and high density of intergovernmental agreements facilitate network entrepreneurship, whereas areas with governance gaps have been less popular for networks. This can be explained by networks picking the low-hanging fruit in highly regulated areas, since they do not necessarily view problems in terms of urgency but in terms of manageability. Public policy networks also tend to emerge in areas that receive abundant funding from governments, especially from the European Union and the United States, notably climate change, air pollution, energy, and water. This pattern indicates that the emergence of networks is more supply-driven rather than responsive to regulation deficits in earth system governance.

A second core claim in support of transnational public policy networks is that they fill an *implementation deficit* in sustainability governance, that is, they help implement existing intergovernmental regulations that are currently poorly implemented, if at all. In the official texts from the World Summit on Sustainable Development, strengthened implementation is seen as a key rationale for partnerships (Kara and Quarless 2002), given their focus on public-private cooperation and voluntary action of environmental leaders (Bruch and Pendergrass 2003).

Although some studies have addressed implementation (Witte, Streck, and Brenner 2003; Speth 2004; Streck 2004), measuring the effectiveness of transnational public policy networks in promoting the implementation of international programs remains difficult. Our research raised doubts about whether networks have the capacity and financial and personnel means to reach their goals. To start with, we found 37 percent of all partnerships registered with the United Nations to be nonoperational (Pattberg et al. 2012). This percentage is even higher in some areas. Of the 46 partnerships that seek to address the energy sector, 21 are not functional. Five of these 21 partnerships were launched but stopped working after an agreed period. The other 16 nonoperational partnerships have either not started yet or were never operational (Szulecki, Pattberg, and Biermann 2011). Partnerships that do not operate or never operated at all are kept in the UN register, and nonoperational partnerships can even become partners of other partnerships, as seems to have happened with the Pacific Islands Energy for Sustainable Development partnership and Renewable Energy and Energy Efficiency Partnership (Szulecki, Pattberg, and Biermann 2011).

Overall, partnerships are largely underfunded and spend substantial efforts not on policy implementation but on fundraising (Pattberg et al. 2012). A related question is whether such networks create new sources of funding in addition to what governments and UN agencies provide. If networks generate substantial new resources, this would be a positive indicator of their effectiveness in helping to implement sustainable development goals. At the conclusion of the World Summit on Sustainable Development, all networks initiated around the summit had less than US$250 million in resources (Hale and Mauzerall 2004, 235). In the larger context, this sum is a trifle, only slightly more than the official development assistance provided by Luxembourg. The overall sum has increased somewhat since Johannesburg. For example, by the end of 2006, US$1.28 billion had been committed. This sum is nonetheless small compared to the US$133.5 billion net official development assistance that OECD countries provided in 2011.

It is difficult to estimate the percentage of funds generated by partnerships that is genuinely new and had not been allocated for sustainable development before (Bäckstrand 2006). Partnerships were often presented to developing country representatives as a more reliable source of funding, as they do not depend on the uncertain process of negotiations. This partially explains why developing countries agreed to the partnerships concept at the World Summit on Sustainable Development, but it also supports suspicion that a substantial component of the network funds are in fact reclassified public development assistance.

Another proxy for the question of whether networks address the implementation deficit is the number of networks that monitor their progress in implementing the Millennium Development Goals. An OECD survey (2006) states that many networks that focused on environmental protection had no monitoring mechanism in place. While 81 percent of the sampled cases planned an evaluation of the effectiveness of the network, only 56 percent declared that they would evaluate their contribution to the Millennium Development Goals. If networks contributed to filling the implementation deficit in state-led governance, one would expect them to focus on regions where implementation is most urgently needed. One can analyze this by looking at where networks registered with the United Nations were intending to operate. Interestingly, it is not the least developed countries but OECD countries that are the most frequent countries of implementation. If networks exist to further the implementation of the Millennium Development Goals, such as bringing food and education to the poorest, it is striking that there is no bias in the network universe in favor of least developed countries as countries of implementation.

In sum, the general perception of networks as a response to the implementation gap seems overly optimistic. A number of indicators point to the conclusion that networks currently do not contribute significantly to filling an implementation gap in earth system governance (Biermann, Chan, et al. 2007; Pattberg et al. 2012). The suspicion arises that a sizable part of current network activity is not implementation per se, but rather the construction of a bureaucratic procedural universe in parallel to the existing intergovernmental processes. These activities may lay the foundation for effective implementation in the future—but this is far from certain.

A third core claim in support of transnational public policy networks is that they assist in solving a *participation deficit* in earth system governance. In this view, intergovernmental negotiations are dominated by powerful governments and international organizations, while networks can facilitate participation of less privileged actors, including voices from youth, the poor, women, indigenous people, and civil society at large. Increased participation from such groups is seen as necessary to improve implementation of international agreements and strengthen the legitimacy, accountability, and democratic quality of earth system governance.

Proponents of transnational public policy networks argue that national governments and intergovernmental agencies have limited resources, information, and skills and thus need to collaborate with other sectors to ensure effective governance (Reinicke et al. 2000; Ruggie 2002; Streck 2004). Networks are believed to bring together a variety of sectors in a manner that can facilitate more democratic decision making. Increased participation through networks is often related to their assumed bridge functions between state and nonstate actors (Martens 2007, 33). This assumed positive effect of networks also relates to their role in bridging the differences of understanding between industrialized and developing countries.

For networks to be effective in strengthening participation, they would need to have balanced distribution of lead partners from the global North and South and actors from developing countries in general; balanced distribution of lead partners from state and nonstate actors; and sufficient participation of traditionally marginalized actors. Our empirical research shows, however, that the overall representation and distribution of leadership roles between North and South is hardly balanced in the partnerships that we studied (Pattberg et al. 2012; Chan 2014). In more than a quarter of all partnerships registered with the United Nations, industrialized countries are the only state partners involved. Developing countries are underrepresented; 56 percent of all networks have no state partner from the developing world. Also, the leadership of networks lies predominantly with industrialized countries.

It has also been argued that transnational public policy networks create new opportunities for nonstate actors and marginalized stakeholders in global politics. Again, this is hardly supported by data on current network practice (Biermann, Chan, et al. 2007; Pattberg et al. 2012). Across all issue areas, state actors and intergovernmental organizations dominate partnerships for sustainable development. Public actors run almost 60 percent of all partnerships that have emerged from the Johannesburg process. Nongovernmental organizations lead 8.2 percent of all UN-registered partnerships, with research and science organizations and networks (12 percent) and collective actors such as partnership fora or stakeholder councils and others (18.6 percent) accounting for the rest. This picture of partnerships contradicts the optimistic idea that they can serve as a means to ensure the participation of groups that are otherwise marginalized in global politics. Rather, transnational public policy networks seem to have created mechanisms to select state and nonstate actors that are already part of the game, and to exclude others.

In sum, there is empirical support for the claim that transnational public policy networks reproduce or even intensify existing unequal relationships in the international system (Martens 2007). This is not restricted to the UN-registered partnerships for sustainable development. Similar patterns are visible in other governance arrangements (for example partnerships established through the Global Compact) and other issue areas (for example health partnerships). Partnerships for sustainable development remain dominated by states and international organizations, and are predominantly led and populated by Northern actors. Participation is limited to stakeholders that have certain competitive advantages or useful resources, and traditional patterns of political exclusion of weaker groups tend to be reproduced within transnational partnerships as well.

What is the overall role and relevance, then, of the entire system of the hundreds of transnational public policy networks that have emerged in recent years to advance sustainable development in areas such as water, energy, health, agriculture, and biodiversity? Does this system of transnational public policy networks help resolve deficits in earth system governance? The analysis of the available data leads to a rather sober conclusion (Biermann, Chan, et al. 2007; Pattberg et al. 2012; Szulecki, Pattberg, and Biermann 2011). While some UN-registered partnerships surely help address the regulation, implementation, and participation deficits, this does not seem to be the case for the system of transnational public policy networks as a whole. Networks are most frequent in those areas that are already heavily institutionalized and regulated. They are predominantly not concerned with implementation, but rather with further institution building, and for many it is doubtful whether they have sufficient resources to make any meaningful contribution toward implementation in the first place.

In short, transnational multistakeholder networks will be useful in certain specific cases, but this governance innovation is less effective than its proponents believe it to be. As recent research suggests, the partnership approach has not met the high expectations placed on these new mechanisms to contribute to the Millennium Development Goals and to enhance stakeholder participation (Bäckstrand 2008; Bäckstrand et al. 2012; Meadowcroft 2004 and 2007; Pattberg et al. 2012; Szulecki, Pattberg, and Biermann 2011). Many public-private partnerships seem to represent "symbolic politics" rather than serious efforts to engage with sustainable development. A lack of funding, underdeveloped organizational structures, an absence of quantitative targets and goals, and poor accountability systems often further limit effectiveness. Transnational public policy networks cannot substitute for effective state action in earth system governance. Their contribution depends a lot on their specific institutional design, which can be improved based on the manifold experience that has been gained (for instance, Waddell 2011). Yet overall, the role of transnational public policy networks remains limited, and would need strengthening through careful reform efforts (on reform proposals, see further below).

Transnational Networks of Scientists

In addition to environmentalist organizations and business associations, networks of scientists have assumed a new role in providing complex technical information that is indispensable for policymaking on issues marked by high analytic and normative uncertainty. While the new role of experts in world politics is evident in many policy areas, it is particularly prevalent in earth system governance. Given the tremendous complexities of the earth system, effective governance must rely on scientific information on the nature of the problem and options for decision makers to cope with it. Some global environmental problems, notably climate change and biodiversity protection, have thus sparked formidable increases in scientific research.

Over the last two decades, this research has been increasingly institutionalized in global programs and alliances, notably the World Climate Research Programme, the International Geosphere-Biosphere Programme, the International Human Dimensions Programme on Global Environmental Change, and the biodiversity sciences program Diversitas. All these programs have dozens of long-term "projects," which are usually major research programs in their own right and include several "joint projects" that are sponsored by all global change programs, for instance the Global Carbon Project, the Global Environmental Change and Food Systems Project, the Global Water System Project, or the Global Change and Human Health Project. All these programs and projects have been collaborating since 2001 in the Earth System Science Partnership (Leemans et al. 2009; Leemans and Solecki 2013) and are set to merge by 2014–2015 into the more integrated global initiative called Future Earth: Research for Global Sustainability, which is designed as a new 10-year international research initiative to mobilize thousands of scientists while strengthening partnerships with policymakers and other stakeholders (Future Earth Transition Team 2012).

This global research institutionalization is an essential precondition for effective earth system governance. Research on earth system processes must adopt a holistic analytical perspective that synthesizes a mosaic of local, national, regional, and global processes. This again requires a global approach to the organization of research. As Kates and colleagues argued in their blueprint of an integrated "sustainability science," "a comprehensive approach to [scientific] capacity building will have to nurture … global institutions in tandem with locally focused, trusted, and stable institutions that can integrate work situated in particular places and grounded in particular cultural traditions with the global knowledge system" (Kates et al. 2001, 642). The globalization of problems can be countered only by the globalization of research. Furthermore, earth system research needs to be inherently interdisciplinary, bringing together the entire breadth of natural and social sciences along with health sciences and professional fields of study such as law.

Along with the global institutionalization of research programs, major science networks have emerged for the policy-relevant *assessment of scientific findings*. Again, this is related to the complexity inherent in earth system governance. The indeterminateness of scientific knowledge in this field often results in different assessments by different experts. What information is accepted or rejected, and what weight is given to different and often contrary readings of the science, can bear heavily on the political process by influencing decision makers in governments and nongovernmental groups and decisions by individual actors. The literature on science and technology studies speaks here of an area of trans-science—a zone of knowledge that is not entirely political, since it is only partly based on political modes of interaction such as bargain, but that is also no longer entirely scientific because scientific claims to truth, such as empirical proof, do not suffice to solve the problem with which the policymaker is faced. In transscience, science and politics inevitably intertwine (Jasanoff 1987 and 1996). Within states, governments authoritatively determine methods of coping with the societal construction of, and engagement with, science. Politicians set rules that determine boundaries between science and policy in different issue areas and assign competencies to different actors, including competence to delimit accepted truth from other claims.

In the international realm, however, given a lack of authoritative governmental power, competence and legitimacy are allocated in decentralized, nonhierarchical processes, in which state and nonstate actors establish mutually agreed procedures for determining an acceptable reading of knowledge and for assigning competence on delimiting accepted truth from other claims. The most prominent example is the UN-sponsored Intergovernmental Panel on Climate Change (IPCC). The IPCC was initiated not by governments but by international organizations—the World Meteorological Organization (WMO) and the United Nations Environment Programme (UNEP). It comprises private actors—experts, scientists, and their autonomous professional organizations—which are nonetheless engaged in a constant dialogue with representatives from governments. The final summary conclusions of IPCC reports are drafted by scientists, but are submitted to line-by-line review by governmental delegates. The reports from the IPCC are partially commissioned by public institutions—the UN climate convention—but are structured and organized by the expert community itself. There are numerous global assessments that follow the IPCC example in other areas, most recently the Intergovernmental Science-Policy Platform on Biodiversity and Ecosystem Services.

These immense networks of scientists, experts, national governments, private bodies, and international organizations are powerful agents in earth system governance (A. Gupta, Andresen, et al. 2012). This is mirrored in the substantial academic interest in global scientific networks over the last two decades (Haas 1990; Siebenhüner 2002a and 2002b; Biermann 2002b and 2006; Mitchell et al. 2006; Jasanoff and Martello 2004; Rietig 2013 and 2014).

Many of these networks have been transformed from purely scientific endeavors into highly political activities. This is not surprising. If governments need to decide under uncertainty while relying on highly interpretable scientific knowledge, those better able to structure, generate, support, maintain, and use this accepted truth are likely to have a greater influence. In some cases, certain dominant scientific assessments may affect the interests and strategies of actors and even the outcome of international negotiations, leading to political conflict about the processes of generating scientific assessments.

In particular, the long history of the IPCC has been marked by a variety of conflicts, from the definition of what a "scientific source" is (for instance, whether it covers gray literature) to the demarcation of what constitutes an "expert" in the first place. Political conflicts over the representation of experts from developing countries and inclusion of knowledge from the South (which is often not published in OECD-based academic journals) have long persisted. Continuous complaints from developing countries about their exclusion have led to a number of reforms. For example, IPCC rules of procedure now require each working group of scientists to be chaired by one developed and one developing country scientist. Each chapter of the assessment report must have at least one lead author from a developing country. Participation of developing country scientists in the IPCC thus appears to be much more visible than previously. The IPCC's governance structure now has a quota system that rather resembles public political bodies of the UN system (see Biermann 2002b and 2006).

Yet despite the increasing role of networks of scientists in environmental decision making, their influence is perceived to be limited. This became apparent again at the 2012 United Nations Conference on Sustainable Development (also known as the Rio+20 summit). The scientific community had invested substantial resources in preparing for this conference, and numerous assessments had been published with particular reference to this event, bringing together the state of knowledge in the natural and social sciences in the field. In particular, more than 3,000 scientists had gathered in March 2012 in London for a major science congress, "Planet under Pressure," that was meant to synthesize the state of earth system science and to contribute this knowledge to the Rio+20 conference. Yet this growing consensus among scientists about dangers of large-scale earth system transformation was hardly reflected in governmental discussions.

It would be simplistic to explain this lack of political influence by pointing to an insufficient "speaking truth to power." On the other hand, there is also widespread agreement that the current integration of scientific knowledge into intergovernmental decision making needs to be improved. In the preparations for the 2012 Rio+20 conference, the High-Level Panel on Global Sustainability recommended that the

Secretary-General should lead a joint effort with United Nations agencies, international financial institutions, the private sector, and other stakeholders "to prepare a regular global sustainable development outlook report that brings together information and assessments currently dispersed across institutions, and analyses them in an integrated way" (High-Level Panel on Global Sustainability 2012, 75). The panel also suggested that "the Secretary-general should consider naming a chief scientific adviser or establishing a scientific advisory board with diverse knowledge and experience to advise him or her and other organs of the United Nations" (High-Level Panel on Global Sustainability 2012, 75). Two months after the panel's report, the congress "Planet under Pressure" concluded similarly that "[t]he international scientific community calls for a framework for regular global sustainability analyses that link existing assessments that build on the foundations of the IPCC, Intergovernmental Platform on Biodiversity and Ecosystem Services and other ongoing efforts. Such analyses can be designed to bring coherence to the science-policy interface" (State of the Planet Declaration 2012).

The 2012 Rio conference made some progress in strengthening scientific input. For instance, it called for a "universal intergovernmental high level political forum" to replace the current UN Commission on Sustainable Development (discussed in chapter 4 below), which would also "strengthen the science-policy interface through review of documentation bringing together dispersed information and assessments, including in the form of a global sustainable development report, building on existing assessments" (The Future We Want 2012, para. 85.k). Yet this is not enough. A more ambitious integration of scientific advice into intergovernmental decision making is required. I will elaborate on these reform proposals later in this chapter.

Intergovernmental Bureaucracies

I now turn to a fourth core agent in earth system governance: international bureaucracies. International bureaucracies are agencies set up by governments or other public actors for the support of public policies in the international arena, with some degree of permanence and coherence and a mandate that places them beyond the direct control of single governments (see Biermann and Siebenhüner 2009 for more detail). This definition includes a wide array of actors, ranging from the United Nations Organization and its specialized agencies to its many semiautonomous subsidiary bodies, such as treaty secretariats or specific programs. They can also include regional bodies, for example river basin organizations (Mukhtarov and Gerlak 2013). The notion of international bureaucracies is independent of the status of a body under international law and different also from the concept of institutions, which can be more broadly understood as a set of norms, rules, and decision-making procedures in specific issue areas. The notion of international bureaucracies also differs from international organizations, which are broader institutional arrangements that combine a normative framework and an assembly of member states with a bureaucracy as organizational core (Biermann and Siebenhüner 2009).

The role of international bureaucracies in earth system governance has received renewed interest in recent years (Bartlett, Kurian, and Malik 1995; Biermann and Siebenhüner 2009; Biermann, Siebenhüner, and Schreyögg 2009; Elliott 2005). It has been shown, for example, that international bureaucracies influence the knowledge and belief systems of actors: through the funding and administration of research, the synthesis of scientific findings, the development of policy proposals, problem frames, and policy assessments, and eventually through the distribution of this knowledge and problem framing to stakeholders, from national governments to individual citizens (Kanie et al. 2013; Bauer, Andresen, and Biermann 2012; Widerberg and van Laerhoven 2014).

International bureaucracies also influence earth system governance through the creation, support, and shaping of norm-building processes. In the early 1980s, for instance, the UN Environment Programme pushed stratospheric ozone depletion onto the international agenda while governments lacked interest (Benedick 1998). International bureaucracies are also important in the implementation of treaties. This is the role of the treaty secretariat staff in particular, who organize meetings, set agendas, and report to the conferences of the parties. International bureaucracies are crucial in shaping procedures, providing arenas for negotiations, and framing inter- and transnational processes of bargaining (Biermann and Siebenhüner 2009).

Finally, international bureaucracies shape earth system governance by helping countries to implement international agreements, which reshapes national interests. It is often international bureaucracies that raise administrative capacity in many countries, especially in the developing world. In the ozone regime, for example, three international bureaucracies (the World Bank, the UN Development Programme, and the UN Environment Programme) organized an international campaign to install small administrative offices in each capital in the developing world. These offices were linked to the national environment ministry, with staff trained and financed by international bureaucracies to draft and implement national programs on the phase-out of ozone-depleting substances (Bauer 2009a). Even though states paid for these programs, it was the staff of the international bureaucracies that developed and shaped them, setting the stage for emission control policies in more than one hundred countries. Without the substantive input of these bureaucracies, the positive outcome of the regime in phasing out ozone-depleting substances worldwide would hardly be conceivable.

In short, international bureaucracies are important agents in earth system governance (also Kanie et al. 2013; see generally on the agency of international organizations Abbott and Snidal 1998; Barnett and Coleman 2005; Hawkins et al. 2006a and 2006b). However, recent research indicates that international bureaucracies fall short of their potential in this domain. For one thing, the community of international bureaucracies in earth system governance is highly fragmented, with most major international agencies running their own environmental programs, along with several hundred larger or smaller convention secretariats, all of which work with little effective coordination (see also chapter 4, on "Architecture").

In addition, earth system governance does not draw on one major international bureaucracy that is solely devoted to supporting governance processes in this area. This situation has led to a debate in academia and policy circles on the need for a "World Environment Organization" or "UN Environment Organization." Proposals to create such an international agency have been debated for over forty years now (overviews in Biermann and Bauer 2005; Lodewalk and Whalley 2002; Vijge 2010 and 2013). The first proposal for such an organization came from US foreign policy strategist George F. Kennan (1970), who argued for an International Environmental Agency encompassing "a small group of advanced nations." As one outcome of this early debate, the United Nations established UNEP in 1973, following a decision adopted at the 1972 Stockholm Conference on the Human Environment. UNEP is not an intergovernmental organization, however, but a subsidiary body of the General Assembly reporting through the Economic and Social Council. Its secretariat is located in Nairobi, Kenya, making it the first major UN body to be hosted by a developing country. UNEP is financed by the general UN budget, with an additional small "Environment Fund" supported by voluntary government contributions for specific projects.

The creation of UNEP was a more modest reform than the strong international environmental organization that some observers had called for at that time, and most studies argue that UNEP lacks standing and influence (see with further references Andresen 2007a and 2007b; Andresen and Rosendal 2009; Bauer 2009b and 2013; Ivanova 2010). In the late 1990s, some governments came forward with concrete initiatives for establishing a new global environmental agency. At the 1997 Special Session of the UN General Assembly on environment and development, Brazil, Germany, Singapore, and South Africa submitted a joint proposal for a "global umbrella organization for environmental issues, with the United Nations Environment Programme as a major pillar."

Starting in the 1990s, more skeptical voices and critics of a new organization also came forward. The former head of the secretariat of the Convention on Biological Diversity, Calestous Juma, argued that advocates of a central authority divert attention from more pressing problems and fail to acknowledge that centralizing institutional structures is an anachronistic paradigm. Sebastian Oberthür and Thomas Gehring (2005) supported these concerns based on institutional theory. Konrad von Moltke (2005) argued in favor of decentralized institutional clusters to deal with diverse sets of environmental issues rather than entrusting all problems to one central organization (similarly Oberthür 2002).

In recent years, the debate has been given new impetus by the diplomatic effort of France to create a UN Environment Organization. In 2003, the French government advanced a proposal to transform UNEP into an "Organisation spécialisée des Nations Unies pour l'environnement," which followed up on earlier French initiatives. This proposal has been emphasized by the 2007 Paris Call for Action during the Citizens of the Earth Conference for Global Ecological Governance, and supported by an intergovernmental "Group of Friends of the UN Environment Organization" (Vijge 2013).

A consultative process within the UN, with strong backing from the European Union and African countries, further explored the possibility of a more coherent institutional framework for the environmental pillar of the UN system. In 2010, a Consultative Group of Ministers or High-Level Representatives on International Environmental Governance (2010, para. 13) identified three "potential options for strengthening the form of the environmental pillar in the context of sustainable development and achieving effective international environmental governance": enhancing UNEP; a specialized UN agency such as a World Environment Organization; and enhanced institutional reforms and streamlining.

A High Level Dialogue on the Institutional Framework for Sustainable Development hosted by Indonesia concluded that there is now "a greater willingness by all groups of countries to explore the question of a specialized agency status [for UNEP]" (High Level Dialogue on Institutional Framework for Sustainable Development 2011).

Developing country positions varied in this debate. These countries initially feared that strong international environmental governance could be a threat to economic development. The influential Founex Report of 1971, for example, argued that the environmental problems of developing countries are "predominantly problems that reflect the poverty and very lack of development of their societies." Among other things, the location of UNEP headquarters in Nairobi has increased support from developing countries. Overall, the position of developing countries has gradually evolved from opposition to participation and then to active engagement in discussions about environmental governance, which is demonstrated by their increased involvement in proposals for reform.

At the 2012 UN Conference on Sustainable Development, a specialized-agency status for UNEP was strongly supported by the member states of the African Union, the European Union, and a number of other countries (Biermann 2013). The European Union submitted to the conference that,

Pursuant to Articles 57 and 63 of the UN charter, a Specialized Agency of the UN (a "World Environment Organization" or "United Nations Environment Organization") would be established as the global body for the environment with its seat in Nairobi. It would be based on the models of some of the existing, medium-sized UN specialized agencies such as the International Labour Organization (ILO), the World Meteorological Organization (WMO), or the World Intellectual Property Organization (WIPO). (European Union 2011)

The upgrade of UNEP to a World Environment Organization was also included in a number of policy statements by research institutions in the run-up to the 2012 conference (e.g., Institute for Global Environmental Strategies 2011; Biermann, Abbott, et al. 2012).

Resistance remained strong, however, from the United States, Japan, Russia, and even Brazil, which had earlier been a supporter of a World Environment Organization but now seemed afraid of an imbalance in favor of the environmental pillar of sustainable development. These countries argued that such institutional reform required further debate and analysis. In *The Future We Want*, the concluding document of the 2012 conference, governments in Rio merely committed to strengthening the role of the United Nations Environment Programme as the leading global environmental authority that sets the global environmental agenda, that promotes the coherent implementation of the environmental dimension of sustainable development within the United Nations system and that serves as an authoritative advocate for the global environment. (The Future We Want 2012, para. 88)

"Within the United Nations system" was inserted here at the request of the United States to block interference of UNEP beyond the United Nations; the United States also insisted on describing UNEP's role as "an authoritative advocate" instead of "the authoritative advocate" (Bastos Lima 2012). Governments agreed that UNEP should have "secure, stable, adequate and increased financial resources," yet added the qualifier "from the regular budget of the UN and voluntary contributions to fulfill its mandate."

One concrete reform agreed upon in Rio is universal membership in the governing council of UNEP. To date, 58 governments were represented in this council, elected by the General Assembly based on regional representation. From now on all countries will be represented in the council, similar to UN specialized agencies that include all member states in their general assemblies. Yet this universal membership for the UNEP governing council is only a rather small step that consolidates reforms that had been agreed upon over a decade ago. In 1999, governments established the Global Ministerial Environment Forum with universal membership to meet annually to discuss important and emerging policy issues, and decided that the UNEP governing council would constitute this forum. In other words, this reform of 1999 has now merely been formalized and further institutionalized. UNEP also received in Rio the mandate to develop a system-wide environmental strategy, yet not to effectively coordinate the activities of the multilateral environmental agreements, notably the climate, biodiversity, and desertification conventions. In sum, the reforms agreed in 2012 in Rio de Janeiro fall short of the creation of a full-fledged international organization for the environment.

Toward Reform

As this assessment of the various agents in earth system governance suggests, agency in earth system governance can be further strengthened. In this section I discuss such reform options, from a more effective system of transnational public policy networks and a better standing of scientific assessment bodies in the international system to the creation of a World Environment Organization.

Institutionalization and Oversight of Transnational Partnerships

To start with, transnational public policy networks are less effective and influential than often claimed, as laid out earlier in this chapter. Yet this relatively weak performance can be improved both at the level of the individual partnership and at the systemic level.

Regarding individual partnerships, for example, an analysis of 46 energy partnerships suggests that the degree of institutionalization and the internal organization of networks make an important difference in their effectiveness (Szulecki, Pattberg, and Biermann 2011). Effective partnerships are usually those that have been institutionalized into real organizations that enable them to work toward their goals, often with an executive board that includes representatives of major stakeholders and a permanent administrative secretariat dedicated to the goal and mission of the initiative. The involvement of powerful actors can help by bringing in necessary resources and is crucial in the case of large-scale partnerships established to perform difficult and costly activities. The examples of relatively effective partnerships show that this organizational form often differs little from the standard structure of intergovernmental organizations (Szulecki, Pattberg, and Biermann 2011). Funding levels also matter, depending on the type of activities. Partnerships that focus on knowledge dissemination, training, or advocacy require fewer resources than those that aim for broader implementation or technology development (Bäckstrand et al. 2012).

At the systemic level, it seems important that, to strengthen public-private partnerships as a tool for effective earth system governance, the United Nations need a stronger mandate and better methodologies for the verification and monitoring of progress (Biermann, Abbott, et al. 2012). Similarly, a meta-analysis of private governance mechanisms has suggested that the role of governments is crucial for the success of these schemes, through regulations that create incentives for firms to seek certification, focused procurement policies, legitimation of measures, and involvement in monitoring their broader sustainability effects (Biermann, Abbott, et al. 2012, based among others on Bernstein and Cashore 2007; Cashore et al. 2007; Chan and Pattberg 2008; Pattberg 2006; Clapp 1998 and 2009; Usui 2003). International organizations, too, can play a powerful role here in catalyzing and "orchestrating" novel and more effective forms of private and public-private governance (Abbott and Snidal 2009 and 2010).

A Global Environmental Assessment Commission

Second, it is vital to strengthen the input from science into political decision making, as laid out above. Existing scientific assessment institutions such as the IPCC are issue-specific and largely react to governmental mandates. In addition, large areas of concern are not covered by such assessment institutions, nor are the linkages between issue areas. Broad-scope expert commissions have been temporary—like the commissions headed by Brandt or Brundtland or the High-Level Panel on Global Sustainability—or have remained technical commissions, such as the specialized commissions that determine the safety of food or medicine. A continuous and stable integration of knowledge on the environmental state of the planet with high authority in the UN system is currently missing.

One option to strengthen the authoritative voice of the scientific community in the intergovernmental system is through establishing a permanent United Nations Global Environmental Assessment Commission (first proposed in Biermann 2012a). This commission would consist of a limited number of experts of high esteem. Its function would be to synthesize the state of scientific knowledge on vital planetary systems, with a particular view to assessing the effectiveness of international policymaking. The commission would operate independently from governments as an autonomous (warning) voice with a view to planetary stability and security. In formulating its advices, it would draw on the integrated assessment of a variety of existing scientific assessment institutions, such as the IPCC, UNEP's Global Environmental Outlook, or the Sustainable Development Outlook proposed by the government of Mexico (Laguna-Celis 2012).

National political systems provide various examples of a strong, authoritative role for independent expert bodies. These include constitutional (or supreme) courts, which serve in some countries as the highest arbiter for the legality of acts from legislative and executive bodies; the boards of central banks, which in many countries guarantee currency stability independently of parliamentarian influences; or various types of ombudspersons or chambers of appointed senators. Despite all differences in detail and political function, what all of these bodies have in common is technical expertise, independence from direct political influence, long terms of office, a mandate to protect a specified public good often with a long time horizon (such as currency stability or the national constitution), and generally a high public esteem and respect.

These criteria would also apply to the Global Environmental Assessment Commission. Unlike temporary high-level commissions, the Global Environmental Assessment Commission would be permanent and firmly institutionalized in the UN system, similar to the International Court of Justice, which is provided for by the UN Charter (UN 1945). The Commission would have the mandate to ascertain the state of knowledge regarding core parameters and boundary conditions of the earth system, as well as the broad effectiveness of political responses. The Commission would rely on widely supported scientific evidence, such as reports by the IPCC. Like international courts, the Global Environmental Assessment Commission could also hold public hearings that would be open to submissions by governments and civil society representatives.

Given the overall structure of the intergovernmental system, the decisions by the Global Environmental Assessment Commission would remain largely hortatory. They would need to weigh on political processes through the scientific and moral standing of its members as well as the underlying evidence. This function would need to be supported by giving the Commission a strong functional role in the UN system, for instance by allowing the Commission to place items on the agenda of functional UN commissions and in special cases even of the UN General Assembly, and to request international bodies to respond to its conclusions. Also, members of the Commission could become, as chief scientists, part of the bureau or executive boards of international institutions, conferences, and agencies.

The selection criteria for the members of the Global Environmental Assessment Commission would be key to its success. The selection would need to be based first and foremost on individual expertise and excellence. In this way, again, the commission would resemble international institutions such as courts and ombudspersons. Members of the International Court of Justice, for example, are elected "regardless of their nationality from among persons of high moral character, who possess the qualifications required in their respective countries for appointment to the highest judicial offices, or are jurisconsults of recognized competence in international law" (ICJ 1945, article 2). For the Global Environmental Assessment Commission, one could think for example of Nobel laureates or winners of the Volvo prize for environmental sciences. Geographic representation would need to be another broad criterion, again similar to the International Court of

Justice that needs to represent all world regions and systems of law. The commission would be broadly interdisciplinary and link key expertise on human societies with knowledge of the planetary system. Similar to the selection of international judges, members of the Global Environmental Assessment Commission would be selected by governments in open and transparent processes.

Formalized rights of expert commissions in public policy raise important challenges of accountability and legitimacy. One might feel reminded of Plato's idea of governance by philosophers instead of by the people. For this reason, the mandate of the UN Global Environmental Assessment Commission would need to be clearly defined. Instead of detailed policy advice, its mandate would be identification of state-of-the-art scientific knowledge about earth system boundaries and critical states of planetary systems. In addition, commission members would need to develop a practice of "expert restraint," similar to the practice of judicial restraint common to court systems in many countries (that is, when courts limit the exercise of their power by deferring as much as possible to the legislative branch of government).

A World Environment Organization

Finally, as I laid out above, the policy domain of earth system governance lacks a strong pillar in the system of UN specialized agencies. The UN Environment Programme was set up in 1972 to serve as a catalyst for environmental action in the international system, yet failed to fully live up to the requirements of current, more complex governance situations. For this reason, a variety of observers and increasingly also governments, including the members of the African Union and the European Union, have called for the upgrading of UNEP to a full-fledged international organization, on a par with other specialized agencies.

I have argued in favor of such an upgrading of UNEP for over a decade (see in particular Biermann 2000), and continue to believe that a World Environment Organization, or a "United Nations Environment Organization" as it is sometimes referred to, would indeed improve earth system governance in a variety of ways. Upgrading UNEP to a specialized UN agency would follow the long-standing policy of functional specialization within the UN system, with the World Environment Organization as the focal point among numerous independent organizations for specific issues, such as food and agriculture (FAO, established in 1945); education, science, and culture (UNESCO, 1945); health (WHO, 1946);

civil aviation (ICAO, 1944); or meteorology (WMO, 1947/1950). While some specialized organizations are much older than the United Nations itself (for instance the Universal Postal Union, created in 1874), most were founded simultaneously with the United Nations, since it was felt at that time that the vast number of issues in the economic, social, or technical fields would overstretch the world body. Environmental problems, however, were not a major concern in 1945, with the term "environment" not even appearing in the UN Charter. It was only in 1972 that UNEP was set up as a mere program, without legal personality, without budget, and—according to its founding instruments—with only a "small secretariat." UNEP thus is institutionally much weaker than the other specialized UN organizations that can avail themselves of more resources and hence influence.

The establishment of a UN specialized agency on environmental issues could strengthen, first, global norm building and institutionalization. One example of how this could work is the International Labor Organization (ILO). ILO has developed a comprehensive body of "ILO conventions" that come close to a global labor code. In comparison, current earth system governance is far more disparate and cumbersome in its norm-setting processes. The general assembly of a World Environment Organization—a World Environment Assembly with universal membership—could adopt draft treaties that have been negotiated by subcommittees under its auspices. A World Environment Organization could also further the subsequent ratification and implementation of new agreements. The ILO Constitution, for example, requires its parties in article 19.5 to submit within one year all treaties adopted by the ILO General Conference to the respective national authorities (such as the parliament) and to report to the organization on progress in the ratification process. This goes much beyond the powers of the UNEP Governing Council, which can initiate intergovernmental negotiations but cannot adopt legal instruments on its own.

A World Environment Organization could also be enabled to approve by qualified majority vote certain regulations which would then be binding on all members, comparable to article 21 and 22 of the World Health Organization (WHO) Constitution. Within the WHO system, certain regulations—for instance on various sanitary and quarantine requirements, nomenclatures, or safety or labeling standards—enter into force for all states after adoption by the World Health Assembly, with the exception of states that have notified the organization of rejection or reservations within a certain period.

Apart from regime building and norm setting, a World Environment Organization could also improve implementation of earth system governance, for example by a common reporting system on the state of the environment and on the state of implementation in different countries, as well as by stronger efforts in raising public awareness of environmental issues. At present, several multilateral environmental regimes require their parties to report on their policies, and a few specialized organizations collect and disseminate valuable knowledge and promote further research. Yet there remains a sizeable lack of coordination, bundling, processing, and channeling of this knowledge in a policy-oriented manner. Most conventions still have different reporting needs and formats, with a certain amount of duplication. The current system is burdensome especially for developing countries, since the myriad reporting systems siphon off administrative resources that governments could use for other purposes. All reporting requirements could be streamlined into one single report to be dispatched to one single body, such as a World Environment Organization. Instead of adding another layer of bureaucracy, a World Environment Organization could provide a degree of streamlining and harmonizing that would reduce the administrative burden in particular for developing countries. Importantly, an organization, as opposed to a program, could allow for a system of regular, predictable, and assessed contributions of members, instead of voluntary contributions generated at unpredictable "pledging conferences," as is currently the case with UNEP.

A World Environment Organization could help smaller developing countries in particular in making their participation in earth system governance stronger and more effective. One problem is that the current organizational fragmentation and inadequate coordination cause special problems for developing countries. Individual environmental agreements are negotiated in a variety of places. Recent conferences on climate change, for example, were hosted in a circular movement covering four continents, from Berlin in 1995 to Geneva, Kyoto, Bonn, Buenos Aires, The Hague, Marrakech, New Delhi, Milan, Buenos Aires, Montreal, Bali, Poznań, Copenhagen, Cancún, Durban, Doha, and in 2013 in Warsaw. Smaller developing countries lack the resources to attend all these meetings with a sufficient number of diplomats and experts. Even larger countries often need to rely on their local embassy staff to negotiate highly complex technical issues. India, for example, entrusted the task of negotiating the adjustments and amendments of the highly technical lists of chemicals controlled under the Montreal Protocol in Helsinki 1989 to its local ambassador to Finland (Rajan 1997). This system of a "traveling diplomatic circus" distinguishes earth system governance from many other policy fields, where negotiations are held within the assembly of an international agency at its headquarters. The creation of a World Environment Organization could thus help developing countries to build up specialized "environmental embassies" at the seat of the new organization. This would reduce their costs and increase their negotiation influence. The same could be said for nongovernmental organizations, which could participate in global negotiations within the World Environment Assembly and its committees at lower costs. Decision-making procedures based on qualified majority voting—as developed later in chapter 4, on "Architecture"—could ensure that the World Environment Organization would not evolve into a new form of ecocolonialism, as many Southern actors and observers may fear.

In addition, a World Environment Organization would not only advance earth system governance by providing a powerful new *agent* to initiate and support transformative change—which was the focus of this chapter—but would substantially help to address problems of the institutional *architecture* of earth system governance. This final important aspect I will further elaborate in chapter 4.

Conclusion

Agents are at the core of earth system governance. In this chapter, I have discussed four important agents: nation-states; transnational public policy networks; science networks; and international bureaucracies.

There is no doubt that states remain crucial agents in earth system governance. However, the nation-state is challenged by earth system transformation in a variety of ways. The legitimacy and accountability of state activities are becoming more complex through the temporal interdependence in earth system governance that requires action today for the benefit of future generations, and possibly the accountability of current generations for the activities of past generations. In addition, the state has to increase its adaptive capacity, evolving from a purely welfare or security-oriented state toward an "adaptive state." Externally the state is forced by processes of earth system transformation to cooperate with others. The fundamental spatial and functional interdependence that has been created, or reinforced, by earth system transformation no longer allows for completely independent action. International collaboration is the necessary, although not sufficient, condition for effective earth system governance. This raises, among other things, the question of the over-arching architecture of earth system governance, which I discuss in the next chapter. It also affects the question of equity and allocation in earth system governance, which I discuss in chapter 6.

Nonstate agents also play an increasingly important role in earth system governance. As my analysis of transnational public policy networks has shown, the effects of such mechanisms are discernible, yet unlikely to resolve effectively the pressing problems of earth system governance by themselves. Nonstate governance can be, at most, a complement to effective state action. It is unlikely to be a substitute, or even alternative, to intergovernmental collaboration. In addition, nonstate governance, even more than state action, raises various legitimacy and accountability challenges in earth system governance. In chapter 5, I discuss such challenges in more detail and develop proposals to address them.

Scientists, too, are important agents in earth system governance through their global networks for research and for the assessment of this research. In this process, scientists have become political actors, and their networks are increasingly politicized, for example in order to account for different cultural backgrounds, political interests, and disciplinary perspectives in earth system governance. Yet overall, the link between science networks and political decision making remains weak. For this reason, I have proposed to better institutionalize advice from scientific assessment processes within the intergovernmental system, along the lines of many national advisory systems. One way forward could be the institutionalization of a permanent Global Environmental Assessment Commission within the United Nations.

Finally, even though international organizations and bureaucracies play important roles in earth system governance, the current system lacks effectiveness. This is partially due to a lack of a core agency in this respect. I have laid out in this chapter a proposal for upgrading UNEP to a World Environment Organization. The establishment of a World Environment Organization would improve coordination of earth system governance; pave the way for the elevation of environmental policies on the agenda of governments, international organizations, and private entities; assist in developing capacities for environmental policy in African, Asian, and Latin American countries; and strengthen the institutional environment for the negotiation of new conventions and action programs as well as for the implementation and coordination of existing ones. Clearly, a World Environment Organization as outlined here cannot simply solve the problems of environmental degradation. It is no silver bullet. Such an organization can, however, initiate new and stronger international agreements, help implement existing agreements, and strengthen the capacity of countries in terms of both mitigation and adaptation.

Overall, however, international bureaucracies, stronger public-private partnerships, and better science institutions are no alternative for effective state action. Nonstate agents can play an important role in advancing earth system governance, but they still need to be able to rely on the support of states and their multilateral institutions.

Morgendliche Rede an den Baum Griehn

1.

Griehn, ich muss Sie um Entschuldigung bitten.

Ich konnte heute nacht nicht einschlafen, weil der Sturm so laut war.

Als ich hinaus sah, bemerkte ich, dass Sie schwankten

Wie ein besoffener Affe. Ich äußerte das.

2.

Heute glänzt die gelbe Sonne in Ihren nackten Ästen.

Sie schütteln immer noch einige Zähren ab, Griehn.

Aber Sie wissen jetzt, was Sie wert sind.

Sie haben den bittersten Kampf Ihres Lebens gekämpft.

Es interessierten sich Geier für Sie.

Und ich weiß jetzt: einzig durch Ihre unerbittliche

Nachgiebigkeit stehen Sie heute morgen noch gerade.

3.

Angesichts Ihres Erfolgs meine ich heute:

Es war wohl keine Kleinigkeit, so hoch heraufzukommen

Zwischen den Mietskasernen, so hoch herauf, Griehn, dass

Der Sturm so zu Ihnen kann wie heute nacht.

Morning Address to a Tree Named Green

1.

Green, I owe you an apology.

I couldn't sleep last night because of the noise of the storm.

When I looked out I noticed you swaying

Like a drunken ape. I remarked on it.

2.

Today the yellow sun is shining in your bare branches.

You are shaking off a few tears still, Green.

But now you know your own worth.

You have fought the bitterest fight of your life.

Vultures were taking an interest in you.

And now I know: it's only by your inexorable

Flexibility that you are still upright this morning.

3.

In view of your success it's my opinion today:

It was no mean feat to grow up so tall

In between the tenements, so tall, Green, that

The storm can get at you as it did last night.

Bertolt Brecht, *Hauspostille*, 1927, in the version revised by Brecht in 1956

4

Architecture

Institutions do not operate in a void. They interact, can be in conflict with each other, and are usually embedded in clusters with other institutions in complex webs of rules and claims to authority. This overall institutional arrangement within an issue area I describe in this book as *governance architecture*.

The study of architecture is fundamental to all other dimensions of earth system governance. Architecture describes the framework in which agents shape processes of earth system governance (chapter 3). It sets the rules for the accountability of those who govern toward those who are governed (chapter 5), defines the context in which distributive conflicts and power politics shape the allocative outcomes (chapter 6), and determines the degree of adaptability of the overall system (chapter 7). In short, architecture describes the overall institutional framework of governance, including all relevant intergovernmental and nonstate institutions, organizations, and other types of steering mechanisms and rule systems (the following draws on Biermann 2008; Biermann, Pattberg, et al. 2009).

The notion of governance architecture stands between two other concepts frequently used in international relations research: "regimes" and "order."

The notion of architecture is broader than that of international regimes, which are usually defined as sets of implicit or explicit principles, norms, rules, and decision-making procedures around which actors' expectations converge in a given area of international relations (Krasner 1983, 2). Regimes are in most cases distinct institutional elements of a larger governance architecture, which is sometimes described by terms such as a regime complex (Raustiala and Victor 2004; Keohane and Victor 2011) or regime cluster (Gehring and Oberthür 2006; Young 1996). While substantial research on regime interlinkages has analyzed dyadic relations between institutions and linkages across issue areas (for instance Oberthür and Gehring 2006a and 2006b), the notion of governance architectures focuses on the overall institutional setting in which distinct institutions exist and interact. The notion of architecture is thus broader than mere institutional interaction, which is one element in the research program on architecture.

On the other hand, through its focus on a particular issue area, the concept of governance architecture is narrower than the notion of order. Both architecture and order share a concern with overarching governance structures that reach beyond single regimes. Yet while international order reflects the organization of the entire system of international relations (Bull 1977), architecture is a more appropriate concept for distinct areas of international relations. Moreover, the concept of international order often implies an optimistic bias regarding the coherence and internal coordination of the international system. Architecture, in my understanding, is more neutral and accounts for dysfunctional and unintended effects, too. Architecture does not presuppose order in a normatively loaded sense.

Importantly, the notion of governance architecture allows for typologies of architectures (climate governance architecture, biodiversity governance architecture, etc.) and the comparison of the overall effectiveness and efficiency of different types of architecture. It allows us to analyze situations of both synergy and conflict between different elements of an architecture, such as regimes or other types of institutions, in a specific domain. It also allows us to study synergy and conflict between the overarching norms and principles that govern these interactions, and to analyze overarching norms and principles that run through distinct regimes, for example the principle of common but differentiated responsibilities and respective capabilities that is common to many modern institutions in earth system governance. This implies that the notion of architecture should be seen as value-free. There is neither an a priori existing state of universal order nor a universal trend toward order. In most empirical cases, international governance architectures result from incremental processes of institutionalization that are decentralized and hardly planned. The concept of architecture does not assume the existence of an architect.

Assessment

Architecture has many facets. In this chapter, I concentrate on the tension between fragmentation and integration within earth system governance (here drawing on Biermann 2005b; Biermann, Pattberg, et al. 2009; and Biermann 2010), and between fragmentation and integration within the larger context of economic and earth system governance.

Fragmentation within Earth System Governance

The fragmentation of governance architectures is common in today's world politics. Many policy domains are marked by a patchwork of international institutions that are different in their character (organizations, regimes, and implicit norms), their constituencies (public and private), their spatial scope (from bilateral to global), and their subject matter (from specific policy fields to universal concerns). The notion of institutional fragmentation relates to earlier debates in the 1970s on interlocking institutions, which were followed by more recent studies on institutional "interlinkages," "overlaps," "interactions," or "interplay" (see the literature reviews in Biermann, Pattberg, et al. 2009; Zelli 2011b; Zelli, Gupta, and van Asselt 2012; Zelli and van Asselt 2013; van Asselt 2014).

The term fragmentation is widely employed especially in international legal literature (van Asselt 2014; ILC 2006). Increasingly, scholars in international relations and international economics also refer to the fragmentation of arrangements, especially regarding environmental governance (for example, Andresen 2001; Bernstein and Ivanova 2007; Biermann 2008, 287–290; Kanie 2007; Najam 2005). Similar phenomena are captured at times under different terminology, including the "decentralization" or "multiplicity" of global governance (Ivanova and Roy 2007), "division of labor" among international norms and institutions (Haas 2004, 8), or, with a more negative connotation, "treaty congestion" (Brown Weiss 1993).

Like many areas of world politics today, earth system governance is also marked by a fragmentation of its governance architecture, both vertically and horizontally. The global institutionalization of earth system governance does not uniformly cover all parts of the international community to the same extent.

Degrees of fragmentation. This is not surprising. All governance architectures are fragmented to some degree; that is, they consist of distinct parts that are hardly ever fully interlinked and integrated. Unfragmented, "universal" architectures are theoretically conceivable: an architecture would be universal if all countries in an issue area were subject to the same regulatory framework, participated in the same decision-making procedures, and agreed on a core set of common commitments. Empirically, however, such a situation is difficult to trace in current world politics. Fragmentation, in other words, is ubiquitous. Yet the degree of fragmentation *varies* from case to case. The concept of architecture allows for the comparative analysis of issue areas and policy domains and for the study of overarching phenomena that the more restricted concept of regimes cannot capture. Important variables to assess the degree of fragmentation within governance architectures are the degree of institutional integration and overlaps between decision-making systems, the existence and degree of norm conflicts, and the type of actor constellations (see in more detail Biermann, Pattberg, et al. 2009).

For example, fragmentation is limited when the core institution includes (almost) all countries and provides for effective and detailed general principles that regulate the policies in distinct yet substantially integrated institutional arrangements. An example is the 1985 Vienna Convention and its 1987 Montreal Protocol on Substances that Deplete the Ozone Layer and its amendments from London (1990), Copenhagen (1992), Montreal (1997), and Beijing (1999). Each amendment to the protocol adds new substances to the regulative system, including decision-making procedures on further policies on these substances. Each amendment requires ratification by governments. Since not all governments have ratified all amendments, and since only parties to an amendment can participate in the respective decision making, the governance architecture on ozone depletion comes close to a system of five concentric circles, with the 1987 Montreal Protocol having the most parties and each later amendment a more restricted reach. However, the overarching treaties govern all amendments in every important aspect, serving as integrative umbrella and authority in linking the different amendments and political processes. No significant institutions on this issue exist outside the framework of the Montreal Protocol, which shows a high degree of institutional integration.

Fragmentation in earth system governance is higher when an issue area is marked by different institutions and decision-making procedures that are more loosely integrated; when the relationship between norms and principles of different institutions is ambiguous; and/or when the core institution does not comprise all countries that are important in the issue area. Policies in the same area are then defined, decided, and monitored through different institutions, or through core institutions, on the one hand, and individual countries that are not part of this institution, on the other. However, overall integration within the governance architecture in the issue area is sufficient to prevent open conflicts between different institutions.

One major example of such fragmentation is climate governance. The institutional core of the governance architecture is the United Nations Framework Convention on Climate Change, ratified by almost all countries. The convention lays down a number of fundamental principles, such as its ultimate objective to prevent dangerous anthropogenic interference with the climate system, the principle of common but differentiated responsibilities and respective capabilities, and a precautionary approach. The convention provides also for a sizeable international bureaucracy for administrative support, data collection, and policy development as the organizational nodal point of the governance architecture in this area (Busch 2009). Yet beyond this core, fragmentation is substantial. The Kyoto Protocol under the climate convention provides for quantified emission reduction obligations only for industrialized countries, and includes several new institutional mechanisms (such as international emissions trading, the Clean Development Mechanism, and various funding arrangements) that go beyond the convention. Importantly, one of the world's largest greenhouse gas emitters, the United States, is party only to the climate convention and not to the protocol, which creates a high degree of fragmentation within the regime (Zelli 2011a; van Asselt and Zelli 2014).

There are also an increasing number of additional institutional governance arrangements, such as public-private partnerships, high-level ministerial dialogues, several regional emissions trading schemes, as well as numerous private institutions that try to regulate issue areas relevant for climate governance, such as the Carbon Disclosure Project (Pattberg and Stripple 2008). One recent study has counted more than sixty transnational institutions with some role in climate governance (Bulkeley, Andonova, et al. 2012; also Abbott 2012). Many of these arrangements explicitly relate to the institutional core, and most initiatives acknowledge the UN process, even though many do not provide for a coordination mechanism that ensures mutual compatibility. Climate governance is thus an example of what one could call *cooperative fragmentation*, where overlaps are sizeable yet all actors intend to cooperate and collaborate.

Fragmentation of earth system governance architectures can also be *conflictive*. This is the case when an issue area is marked by different institutions that are hardly connected and/or have different, unrelated decision-making procedures; have conflicting sets of principles, norms, and rules; or have different memberships and/or are driven by actor coalitions that accept, or even advance, these conflicts. One prominent example is the regulation of access to and benefit sharing of plant genetic resources (see Zelli 2010 and Rosendal 2006 in more detail). Here, two regimes try to regulate this issue, the Convention on Biological Diversity and the Agreement on Trade-Related Aspects of Intellectual Property Rights (TRIPS) under the World Trade Organization. The Convention on Biological Diversity seeks to strengthen and harmonize systems of intellectual property rights, whereas the TRIPS agreement reaffirms sovereign rights of states over biological resources (Zelli 2010; Zelli and van Asselt 2010).

Climate governance also has a few signs of conflictive fragmentation. For example, the now defunct Asia-Pacific Partnership on Clean Development and Climate from 2005 departed from key features of the UN climate regime, notably in its lack of consideration of climate change impacts and differentiation between industrialized and developing countries. Though not comparable to the UN regime in terms of financial endowment or membership, the Asia-Pacific Partnership provided an alternative to international climate action that may have reduced incentives for complying with, or signing up to, international legally binding commitments (Karlsson-Vinkhuyzen and van Asselt 2009; McGee and Taplin 2006; van Asselt 2014).

Consequences of fragmentation. Different degrees of fragmentation in earth system governance are likely to show different degrees of governance performance. More integrated earth system governance may promise a higher effectiveness in terms of solving the core problems in an issue area. Yet this claim is contested, and several authors emphasize the potential benefits of having a multitude of agreements, institutions, and approaches within an overall fragmented architecture (see in more detail Biermann, Pattberg, et al. 2009).

First, proponents of fragmentation in governance architectures argue that agreements that encompass only a few important countries may on average be negotiated and brought into force more quickly. Fragmentation could thus be a positive quality, or at least not a reason for concern. Concerning climate governance, Victor for instance favors a "club" approach that involves few countries that would negotiate and review climate policy packages (Victor 2007). Others have suggested that the United States should conclude regional agreements with like-minded countries, for example in Latin America or with China and other key developing countries (Stewart and Wiener 2003; Bodansky 2002). Such regional or small-*n* agreements could cover only the world's largest greenhouse gas emitters and allow for experimentation with alternative international regulatory frameworks. Likewise, Barrett argues for a "multi-track climate treaty system, with protocols for research and development into mitigation technologies; the development and diffusion of these technologies; funding for adaptation; and geo-engineering" (Barrett 2007). Barrett and Toman (2010) argue that an approach consisting of loosely coordinated smaller-scale agreements, each addressing a different aspect of the challenge and being enforced in its own way, would likely sustain more actual abatement than would the establishment of targets and timetables for countries to limit their aggregate greenhouse gas emissions. Sugiyama and Sinton (2005) suggest an "orchestra of treaties" that would complement the climate convention with a focus on mitigation and adaptation technologies, clean development in developing countries, and carbon markets. Countries could apply a pick-and-choose strategy and sign only those treaties that promote their interests.

However, it is doubtful whether the speed of reaching small-*n* initial agreements may indeed improve overall governance performance. A highly fragmented institutional architecture produces solutions that fit the interests only of the few participating countries. There is no guarantee that other countries will join. A quick success in negotiating small-*n* agreements might run counter to the long-term success if important structural regime elements have not sufficiently been resolved. A certain degree of instant problem solving through small-*n* agreements might provide disincentives for third countries to engage in joint action and could further disintegrate the multilateral negotiation system. Regional agreements between a few like-minded players, in the hope that others will later follow, do not promise to bring the long-term trust and regime stability that is needed in earth system governance. Also, sectoral institutions, for example international organizations dealing with energy, "are often captive to their constituencies and tend to acquire a 'booster-club mentality'" (van de Graaf 2013a, 30; see also van de Graaf 2013b).

As a second proposed benefit, some strands of cooperation theory suggest that small-*n* agreements within a fragmented architecture might prove more progressive and far-reaching. While a universal architecture might include all countries and ideally even reach full compliance, its norms and standards might be rather lax and modest.

A fragmented architecture could promote more stringent obligations, for instance by increasing opportunities for side payments. Bilateral or small-n agreements among countries might allow for concessions that governments would find it unacceptable to grant to a larger group of states. Such concessions could include bilateral trade concessions, the bilateral exchange of technology, or support for enhanced political influence in international organizations. Some strands in the literature on environmental policy analysis also suggest that fragmentation and regulatory diversity increase innovation and thus overall governance performance (Jänicke and Jacob 2006). In federal political systems, for instance, regulatory competition may allow for the development of different solutions in different regulatory contexts, of which the most effective will survive and be diffused to other regulatory contexts. Fragmentation may enhance innovation at the level of the firm or public agency and increase innovation in the entire system. A key notion is that of diffusion of innovation, including innovations of policies, technologies, procedures, and ideas.

When interest constellations change and new situations arise, however, it might be difficult to reach agreement within the international community without an overarching institution. In addition, smaller agreements with a few like-minded countries will decrease the opportunity for creating package deals, which will minimize overall policy acceptance and effectiveness.

Economic modeling projects that compared different hypothetical universal and fragmented climate regimes—based on criteria of environmental effectiveness, cost effectiveness, and cost distribution—also concluded that the more fragmented a regime is, the higher the costs are to stabilize greenhouse gas concentrations at low levels, because more ambitious reduction targets need to be achieved by a smaller number of countries (Hof, den Elzen, and van Vuuren 2010). Similarly, economic model calculations show that emission trading brings both higher environmental effectiveness and cost-effectiveness if based on a universal architecture. If one compares the relative costs of four possible architectures for emissions trading—global trading based on the Kyoto Protocol, formal linking of regional emission trading, indirect linkages of regional emissions trading through common acceptance of credits, and a mixed approach that combines elements of these three scenarios—one finds that an environmentally ambitious global trading approach works best to control global emissions, while formal linking of emission trading systems can be a fallback option. A more fragmented architecture, for example through indirect linking, is less likely to lead to a comprehensive and effective response (Flachsland et al. 2010).

In addition, regulatory fragmentation in combination with free trade and economic competition might result in the general decline of environmental standards, the so-called race to the bottom. Future needs of more stringent environmental policies will increase costs of regulation, which could make regulatory differentials in some sectors decisive factors in investment decisions. This problem is central to domestic complaints by energy-intensive industries in many countries (van Asselt and Biermann 2007). This is related to the concern with a general regulatory "chaos" in environmental policy, but also in areas such as energy, agriculture, or transport. For example, investors in the Kyoto Protocol's Clean Development Mechanism have emphasized the importance of clear signals regarding a long-term commitment of all actors to one stable process. In sum, fragmented governance architectures, particularly of the conflictive type that do not unite all major actors in one coherent and consistent regulatory framework and that include conflicting norms and principles, are likely to send confusing messages to all, reducing the overall performance of the system.

Third, some suggest that more fragmentation might lower the entry costs for actors, including private entities such as industry and business. The role of nonstate actors and new forms of governance beyond the state are a key concern in recent institutional scholarship on the environment (see chapter 3). A loose network of institutions, many of which might be public-private, could make it easier for business actors to engage in rule making and thus help create regulatory systems that are easy to implement and affordable from a business perspective. In addition, a fragmented institutional architecture might make it easier to broaden the coverage of relevant sectors. Fragmented architectures could help circumvent negotiation stalemates caused by the need to secure universal agreement. For example, the Kyoto Protocol does not require emission reductions from aviation and international maritime transport, whereas the European Commission has taken up aviation in the EU emissions trading scheme. Thus, particularly in cooperative fragmentation, where key norms do not conflict, diverse policy approaches could allow for the inclusion of more actors and areas than would be feasible through a more integrated but static architecture.

Yet again, serious challenges may outweigh such benefits. First, conflictive fragmentation, where different actors pull in different directions, may complicate linkages with other policy areas. There may be strong economic implications—in terms of international competitiveness—if one coalition of states adopts a stringent policy (for example binding emission ceilings) while others opt for a less rigorous way of reducing emissions (for example voluntary pledges). This, in turn, could have severe ramifications for a world trade regime that unites both coalitions under one uniform umbrella. A less fragmented architecture, on the other hand, could allow for systematic and stable agreements between the institutional frameworks of the world trade regime and environmental institutions. Since a fragmented architecture may decrease entry costs for private actors, it is also conceivable that corporations use regulatory fragmentation to choose among different types of obligation, thereby starting a race to the bottom within and across industry sectors (Vormedal 2008).

Fourth, a fragmented architecture could offer solutions that are tailored for specific regions and thus increase equity by better accounting for special circumstances. Some lawyers also argue that increased fragmentation in international law is a way of accommodating different interests of states. As a result, specialized regimes may better serve the interests of governments and have higher compliance rates. Yet fragmented architectures also raise serious concerns of equity and fairness (see also chapter 6). Cooperation theory assumes that bilateral and small-n agreements grant more bargaining power to larger and more influential countries, while large-n agreements allow smaller countries to enter into coalitions, such as the Group of 77 and China, which protect their collective interests. In the end, perceptions of inequity and unfairness are linked to policy effectiveness through legitimacy—a governance system that is not seen as fair by all is likely to lack in overall effectiveness. As stressed by Benvenisti and Downs, fragmentation "functions to maintain and even extend the disproportionate influence of a handful of powerful states—and the domestic interests that shape their foreign policies—on the international regulatory order" (Benvenisti and Downs 2007). Fragmentation allows powerful states to opt for a mechanism that best serves their interests or to create new agreements if the old ones no longer further their interests.

In this way, fragmented governance architectures often lack legitimacy as they exclude potential stakeholders from participating in decision making (Karlsson-Vinkhuyzen and McGee 2013). For example, small-n agreements by larger countries cannot rely on the support of smaller, excluded countries and hence lack legitimacy with these countries (Zelli and van Asselt 2013, 9). Many climate-related initiatives like the (now defunct) Asia-Pacific Partnership, the Carbon Sequestration Leadership Forum, or the Methane to Markets partnership include only leading developed and developing countries while excluding least developed countries (Karlsson-Vinkhuyzen and McGee 2013). The investment agendas of these initiatives hence do not reflect the immediate interests of many of those countries that are most affected by climate change (Zelli et al. 2013).

Most developing countries thus continue to support the multilateral approach in environmental policy as in other policy domains. Less fragmented and more integrated architectures allow the South to count on its numbers in diplomatic conferences and gain bargaining power from a uniform negotiating position. They allow for side payments across negotiation clusters within a policy domain and across different policies, and they minimize the risk for developing countries of being coerced into bilateral agreements with powerful countries that might offer them suboptimal outcomes (Abrego et al. 2003). For the many smaller and medium-sized developing countries, unity is strength, and multilateralism may seem its core guarantee. Since the emergence of the climate issue, the South has therefore sought to bring all negotiations under the UN framework and to frame global warming as an overarching political problem with implications far beyond mere environmental policy.

In sum, fragmentation is a ubiquitous structural characteristic of the architecture of earth system governance. Different degrees of fragmentation exist, ranging from rather synergistic to cooperative or even conflictive fragmentation. Different degrees of fragmentation are likely to yield different degrees of governance performance. While synergetic and cooperative fragmentation may entail both significant costs and benefits (Falkner, Stephan, and Vogler 2010), there is little to be gained from highly conflictive fragmentation (see Biermann, Pattberg, et al. 2009 in more detail). On balance, conflictive fragmentation of earth system governance—even if labeled as institutional diversity or pluralism—appears to do more harm than good and can generally be seen as a burden on the overall performance of the system.

This does not necessarily imply a need for major reorganization of the existing plethora of international environmental agreements, but rather the development of overarching principles and the strengthening of institutions and organizations that can authoritatively negotiate between different policy domains and governance mechanisms (Falkner, Stephan, and Vogler 2010).

One possible solution has been advanced by the Planetary Boundaries Initiative, a group of lawyers who base their reasoning on the notion of nine planetary boundaries identified by Rockström and colleagues (2009;

see also chapter 2 in this book). In this line of reasoning, each planetary boundary should be regulated by a specific institution, ensuring that violations of boundaries are made impossible. Yet from the current empirical experience in earth system governance, such planned top-down institutional reorganization seems neither feasible nor necessary. The effective governance of specific types of social behavior that may contribute to the violation of an earth system boundary can—and in many cases should—instead be limited in scope and cover only parts of the overall human impact. For example, the 1971 Convention on International Trade in Endangered Species of Wild Fauna and Flora—which is part of the overall effort to limit loss of biodiversity—has proven to be relatively effective, despite governing only a limited set of species and only one activity (that is, trade). The 1972 Convention on the Prevention of Marine Pollution by Dumping of Wastes and Other Matter was equally powerful despite its limited scope. Thus, it is unlikely that a targeted top-down approach that follows the notion of earth system boundaries—for instance, one global institution for each boundary—would prove overall more effective. Issue-specific, tailor-made solutions appear in general more promising.

This does imply, however, that specific rules are needed to address institutional interactions. One salient example is the conflict between the Kyoto Protocol under the climate convention and the various institutions that protect biological diversity, notably regarding reforestation and aforestation (Zelli 2010 and 2011a; van Asselt 2014). These normative and institutional conflicts require urgent resolution; yet they can be better addressed by the development of overarching principles, coordination policies, and the steering and orchestrating role of central international organizations than by creating new specific institutions at the interface of distinct earth system boundaries.

The distinction between cumulative and systemic problems is important here. Systemic problems often require larger actor coalitions at the outset of cooperation, stronger noncompliance management, and stronger incentives to draw in less interested actors through positive side payments. Cumulative problems can be governed, at least initially, by smaller coalitions of countries, in more fragmented governance systems, and they require less strict and powerful noncompliance mechanisms. The problem, however, is that cumulative problems often require action only, or especially, by a small group of countries. If this group of countries lacks the means or interest to take powerful action, the provision of the overall public good is threatened unless other countries increase their efforts by means of support and side payments. The governance of desertification or deforestation—both centering on relatively small groups of often poor countries—are examples.

In sum, political institutions should follow social dynamics, not necessarily earth system boundaries. In some cases, human activities are directly related to the earth system boundary, as in the case of stratospheric ozone depletion. In some cases, global interdependencies might require a global "grand bargain" and hence a strong global institution in one area, as in the case of climate change. In other cases, however, issue areas are more disparate, conflict lines overlapping, and causation diffuse. Here, as in the case of land use change, a domain-specific architecture of nested institutions might be more effective.

How then to ensure the overall integration of earth system governance? The rather unique situation in earth system governance is that international norms and standards are created by distinct and independent institutions with little respect for repercussions in and links with other fields. Coordination occurs in an ad hoc manner by means of more or less effective interplay management through governments and treaty institutions, yet there is no effective overarching coordination mechanism. According to a recent analysis by the UN Joint Inspection Unit (the independent external oversight body of the United Nations system that is mandated to conduct evaluations, inspections, and investigations systemwide), current international environmental governance is ineffective because it lacks "a common mechanism to resolve contradictions among MEAs [multilateral environmental agreements] ... [and] a framework for common administrative, financial, and technical support services to promote synergies between UN agencies and MEAs" (Joint Inspection Unit 2008, 15).

The coordination also relates to the organizational structure of multilateral institutions. Most international environmental treaties have their own secretariats—a practice that was judged by the UN Joint Inspection Unit as "rather exceptional under existing institutional arrangements for multilateral conventions within the United Nations system" (Joint Inspection Unit 2008, iv).

The attempt to network multilateral environmental institutions and international agencies has been ongoing since 1972, when a first coordinating body was set up within the United Nations. This and its successors, however, have lacked the legal authority to overcome the special interests of multilateral institutions, UN departments, programs, and convention secretariats. For earth system governance, no central anchoring point within the overall governance architecture exists that could compare, for instance, to the WTO or ILO in their fields. Instead, there is an overlap in the functional mandates of several institutions. An international institutional core with a clear strategy to ensure effective earth system governance is thus the need of the hour. As suggested by the UN Joint Inspection Unit, "[a]n overarching authority for global environmental governance is lacking within the United Nations system" (Joint Inspection Unit 2008, 30). Overarching principles are needed to govern the interaction between different institutions, to regulate norm conflicts between these institutions, and to increase efficiency and effectiveness by providing for general standards of behavior (such as the principle of common but differentiated responsibilities) or general institutions and organizations (such as integrated funding mechanisms like the Global Environment Facility, or joint mechanisms of customs control). Many issue areas of world trade law are regulated under the overarching principles enshrined in the Agreement on Establishing the World Trade Organization. Similar overarching agreements and institutions are needed for the governance of human interactions with the earth system. I will address this further below in the section on policy reforms.

Fragmentation of Economic and Earth System Governance

In addition to fragmentation within earth system governance, the broader architecture of governance for sustainable development is also fragmented. Especially the environmental and the economic pillars of sustainable development are poorly integrated, and the two are dealt with by different sets of institutions. Global economic governance is regulated largely outside the UN system through the governing bodies of the World Bank and the International Monetary Fund (IMF), the regulatory system of the World Trade Organization, and the Group of 20 major economies as an overarching informal negotiation forum. Earth system governance, for its part, relies on a decentralized system of a few hundred multilateral environmental agreements, supported by UNEP and specialized subunits in various international organizations. To better integrate different dimensions of sustainable development, a number of multilateral bodies are in theory available.

One such body is the UN Economic and Social Council (ECOSOC), which was created in 1945 as a principal organ of the United Nations and as a key institution for policy integration within the UN system. In the vision of the drafters of the UN Charter (UN 1945), this council would serve as the central forum for discussing international economic and social issues and for issuing policy recommendations directed at both governments and UN agencies. Even though environmental policy is not explicitly mentioned in the UN Charter, environmental policies and sustainable development fall today under the purview of ECOSOC. The council is based on regional representation; its 54 members include 14 governments from Africa, 11 from Asia, 6 from Eastern Europe, 10 from Latin America and the Caribbean, and 13 from Western Europe and other industrialized countries. While some larger countries are often reelected as members of ECOSOC, the council includes a large number of smaller countries with equal voting rights, unlike the governing bodies of the Bretton Woods institutions, which are based on financial contributions and hence economic power. Overall, ECOSOC has only a marginal influence on key processes of earth system governance.

In order to further integrate environment and development policies, governments established in 1992 the UN Commission on Sustainable Development (CSD) in the course of the United Nations Conference on Environment and Development in Rio de Janeiro. One task of this commission was to oversee implementation of Agenda 21, the program of action agreed upon at that conference as well. The CSD, however, did not fulfill the expectations of its founders. Its standing in the UN system remained low, the importance given to it by governments too little, and its power to influence economic or social decision making insignificant. The commission remained under the purview of the national ministries of the environment. Economic or finance ministries were hardly involved in its deliberations. Overall, the CSD did not manage to significantly influence the development of global governance in the area of sustainable development or economic policy (Andresen 2007a and 2007b; Kaasa 2007; Widerberg and van Laerhoven 2014).

The 2012 UN Conference on Sustainable Development, held in Rio de Janeiro, had thus to move forward in reforming the overall institutional architecture and integration of sustainable development policies. According to the final conference statement (The Future We Want 2012, para. 83), the UN Economic and Social Council is to be "strengthen[ed] within its Charter mandate," with a "key role in achieving a balanced integration of the three dimensions of sustainable development." In addition, governments decided "to establish a universal intergovernmental high level political forum, building on the strengths, experiences, resources and inclusive participation modalities of the Commission on Sustainable Development, and subsequently replacing the Commission." This high-level forum, which is to include all UN member states, should provide leadership and recommendations for sustainable development, enhance the integration of the environmental, economic, and social dimensions of sustainable development in a holistic manner, and provide a "dynamic platform for regular dialogue, and stocktaking and agenda setting to advance sustainable development," along with a number of related tasks (The Future We Want 2012, para. 85). Multilateral financial and trade institutions such as the World Bank or the World Trade Organization are "invited" to participate—which is far removed, however, from the major coordinating mandate that many observers had hoped for regarding a new body for sustainable development in the UN system.

It is not clear what the difference between this new body and the CSD will be, except that the new body is meant to replace the CSD. In *The Future We Want*, the forum is spelled with small first letters, indicating its informal and inconclusive standing at present. One difference between the CSD and the new body is the added qualifier "high level," which could indicate a higher commitment from governments to participate in these discussions than has been the case to date with the CSD. A negotiation process under UN General Assembly auspices will now need to sort out the organizational aspects of this forum. As I will lay out further, the decision by the 2012 conference went in the right direction, but not far enough in bringing forward meaningful reform.

In recent years, a fundamentally different multilateral forum has emerged outside the UN system for the coordination of economic policies and the preservation of global economic and financial stability: the Group of 20 major economies. Its core members are the finance ministers and central bank governors of 19 large economies (not all the 19 largest though!) plus the European Union. At present, the group includes Argentina, Australia, Brazil, Canada, China, the European Union, France, Germany, India, Indonesia, Italy, Japan, Republic of Korea, Mexico, Russia, Saudi Arabia, South Africa, Turkey, United Kingdom, and the United States of America. The group convened for the first time in 1999. The Group of 20 effectively integrates the earlier coordinating mechanism of the Group of 7 industrialized countries. The group's original focus on economic cooperation has slowly broadened, now covering issues such as energy, climate, and migration. In short, the Group of 20 meetings are evolving into attempts at policy coordination for sustainable development. However, links with the UN system—notably with ECOSOC or the United Nations Conference on Trade and Development (UNCTAD)—are weak, in contrast to the stronger cooperation with the

IMF and the World Bank, whose executive heads participate in meetings of the Group of 20.

Many observers, concerned about the slow progress of multilateral environmental governance, argue for a stronger role for the Group of 20 in sustainable development and earth system governance. For example, it is envisaged that annual meetings of the Group of 20 could include sessions for environmental ministers along with representatives of UNEP and related agencies. Proponents of such a role argue that the Group of 20 represents about two-thirds of the world's population and around ninety percent of global gross national product (including all EU members). With merely 19 countries plus the European Union, decision making can be expected to be faster than in agencies with more universal membership. Due to the inclusion of major developing countries, legitimacy problems are also likely to be less pronounced than for the Group of 7 industrialized countries (overview of the argument in Vestergaard 2011).

One major downside is that the Group of 20 excludes roughly 150 countries (if all EU member states are counted as being included). Vast regions of the world are not represented, including all of Africa (except for South Africa), most parts of Latin America (all except Brazil, Argentina, and Mexico), and most countries in Asia (except for China, India, Indonesia, Japan, South Korea, Saudi Arabia, and Turkey), while other regions are fully represented, such as North America and Europe (since most smaller countries are represented as members of the European Union). Ultimately, the Group of 20 also follows the old governance mode established by the Group of 7 in the 1970s, as an informal network of some of the most powerful presidents and prime ministers. It is doubtful whether a directorate of the powerful few can best handle the complexities of earth system governance.

Instead, a way forward would be to realign the advantages of the Group of 20 with the broad legitimacy of the United Nations within overall UN reform. This would require, however, a fundamental revision of the modes of decision making in the UN system. I address these and other reform options next.

Toward Reform

The fragmentation of earth system governance, as well as lack of integration between earth system governance and economic governance, call for several fundamental reforms in the current institutional architecture.

Integration through Interaction Management and Incremental Change

One immediate challenge for policymakers is to increase the coordination and integration of governance mechanisms and institutions, both within policy domains, such as climate governance, and across different domains, for instance between environmental and economic governance. Skillful "orchestration" of fragmented policy domains by international organizations and institutions (Abbott and Snidal 2009 and 2010) and careful "interplay management" between different institutions and regimes (Oberthür and Stokke 2011a) can help overcome problems that are often associated with institutional interaction and governance fragmentation, such as duplication of efforts and normative ambiguity. A variety of mechanisms for such orchestration and interplay management exist and have been widely studied in recent years, combining considerations both from political science (see Zelli 2010; Oberthür and Stokke 2011b; Zürn and Faude 2013; van Asselt and Zelli 2014) and from international law (van Asselt 2014).

Improved interplay management is crucial in the short term. Yet it is limited in the extent to which it can authoritatively resolve conflicts between institutions, avoid overlap, identify and resolve regulatory gaps, and provide overall guidance based on jointly agreed principles of governance.

For such higher-level coordination in many governance domains, governments have embraced umbrella agreements, such as the UN Convention on the Law of the Sea, or overarching institutions with constituting agreements, such as the Agreement on Establishing the World Trade Organization or the founding documents of the World Intellectual Property Organization. Similar overarching institutions are needed in the field of earth system governance to strengthen its overall architecture.

However, the need for overarching institutions does not imply that they have to be created *ex novo*. One likely pathway is, for example, the building block approach outlined by Falkner, Stephan, and Vogler (2010), in which separate agreements are slowly morphed by governmental agreement into a coherent global constitutional structure. The world trade system is a prime example, which can be seen

to have been fabricated out of a number of building blocks that allowed countries to adjust their expectations and identify common interests in a process of repeated negotiations. The WTO was the crowning achievement, rather than the starting point, of a regime-building process. (Falkner, Stephan and Vogler 2010, 260)

Similarly, Urpelainen (2013) argues for a dynamic approach in climate governance that would ensure progress through a series of small wins—such as technology agreements—guided by a unifying "big dream of an encompassing architecture for global climate governance," which would need to be negotiated under the climate convention and to be accepted by all major emitters (Urpelainen 2013, 113). Yet even if global coordination and integration of earth system governance is likely to follow from incremental agreements among leading governments, the eventual "crowning achievements" or "big dreams" need to be carefully identified and discussed. The following sections lay out four elements of a reformed global institutional architecture of earth system governance.

A World Environment Organization

To start with, the integration of different domains and institutions within earth system governance would be fundamentally advanced by bringing them under the overall umbrella of a World Environment Organization, comparable to the World Trade Organization. I have discussed the merits of a World Environment Organization, based on upgrading UNEP, in chapter 3 with regard to its function as an agent of earth system governance. Equally important is the institutional, architecture function of a World Environment Organization: such an entity would embody the much-needed overarching institution and decision-making system that coordinates, and hence strengthens, the hundreds of distinct multilateral environmental agreements (for a more cautious view, see Young 2008, 17–19).

The constitutive treaty of the organization could provide general principles for multilateral environmental treaties as well as coordinating rules that govern the organization and its relationship with the issue-specific environmental regimes (see also Fauchald 2010). Following WTO usage, environmental regimes covered by the World Environment Organization could be divided into "multilateral" and "plurilateral" agreements. For "multilateral" agreements, ratification would be compulsory for any new member of the organization, while "plurilateral" agreements would still leave members the option to remain outside. The multilateral agreements would thus form the "global environmental law code" under the World Environment Organization, with the existing conferences of the parties functioning under the guidance of a World Environment Assembly. This would enable the World Environment Assembly to develop a common reporting system for all multilateral environmental agreements, reducing the administrative burden for developing countries. A common dispute settlement system could strengthen the development and implementation of international environmental law and provide a stronger counterweight to the powerful dispute settlement system of the World Trade Organization, hence reducing the incentive for forum shopping in conflicts between trade and environment. An authoritative World Environment Organization could also issue detailed guidelines on various issues—based on an interagency agreement—for instance for the environmental activities of the World Bank and for environmentally related conflicts under the WTO dispute settlement system. Finally, a strong World Environment Organization could integrate efforts of other international agencies into a coordinated system of capacity building for developing countries, along with financial and technological transfer.

Some experts, including former UNEP executive director Klaus Töpfer (2003), have argued that the environment is too complex an issue area for a single organization to cover, and have hence proposed a "world organization on sustainable development" that would build on a merger and upgrade of UNEP and the United Nations Development Programme (UNDP) (at least). I view this option as problematic. It would be a marriage of unequals that is likely to harm environmental interests without strengthening development goals. First, the UNDP and UNEP are unequal in their size and resources. Taking into account that the UNDP's budget is sixteen times larger than UNEP's, merging the two programs would come close to the incorporation of UNEP within the significantly larger UNDP. This could result either in a strengthening of environmental goals within the development community or in the slow degrading of environmental goals in a larger development-oriented agency. Both UNEP and the UNDP are marked by distinct organizational cultures tuned to their respective goals. Given differences in size and resources, it is unlikely that the much smaller environmental community will prevail in changing the much larger development community within a merged organization. The strength and independence of environmental concerns may thus weaken over time.

At the national level, hardly any country has opted for the administrative merger of "economic development" and "environmental protection" as policy areas. Most countries maintain the differentiation between economic or development ministries and environmental ministries. These national experiences illustrate that environmental policy indeed can, and should, be addressed by one administrative unit. Such administrative functional differentiation should be maintained also at the international level. Most international organizations and national ministries have clearly defined mandates for their policy areas, and it is not difficult to demarcate the responsibilities of a new international organization for the environment (see also Charnovitz 2005). This would speak against a merger of UNEP and the UNDP.

If, on the other hand, a world organization on sustainable development would imply merely the upgrading of UNEP to an international organization with this name, while leaving other bodies—including the UNDP or the World Bank—untouched, it is unclear what consequences the choice of the organization's name—"sustainable development" instead of "environment"—would have. This could reduce the overarching concept of "sustainable development" to what many in the South believe to be the Northern understanding: an attractive yet deluding label for environmental protection (for instance, Agarwal, Sharma, and Narain 1999). In sum, a world organization on sustainable development would be either ill-advised if it implies the integration of UNEP and the UNDP, or misleading if it implies giving a new name to what is essentially an environmental organization.

This does not imply that a World Environment Organization should address environmental policy unrelated to the larger quest for sustainable development. A World Environment Organization would pursue environmental aims *within* the development process, not unlike the role of environmental ministries in developing countries. A World Environment Organization would thus provide a framework of environment *for* development. The constitution of a World Environment Organization would hence have to incorporate environmental aims within the broader development concerns of the South. Therefore, general principles such as the right to development, the sovereign right to natural resources within a country's jurisdiction, or the principle of common but differentiated responsibilities and capabilities would need to be integrated into the constitutive instrument of a World Environment Organization.

A High-Level UN Sustainable Development Council

While a World Environment Organization would improve institutional coherence *within* earth system governance, the overall integration of sustainable development institutions and policies, as noted above, requires further reforms, notably regarding economic and environmental governance.

The 2012 UN Conference on Sustainable Development decided to replace the rather toothless Commission on Sustainable Development by a "universal intergovernmental high level political forum." This reform is a step in the right direction, yet needs to be further transformed into the creation of a separate coordinating institution, namely a high-level UN Sustainable Development Council. Such a council has found support in a number of policy papers and assessments (among others, Hakone Vision on Governance for Sustainability in the 21st Century 2011; Biermann, Abbott, et al. 2012; Kanie et al. 2012; High-Level Panel on Global Sustainability 2012; Institute for Global Environmental Strategies 2011; State of the Planet Declaration 2012; Civil Society Reflection Group 2012; for an extensive overview of the options, see Bernstein with Brunnée 2011).

The creation of such a council would be possible by a decision of the UN General Assembly under article 22 of the UN Charter (similar to the United Nations Human Rights Council, which has been established as an independent body of the United Nations General Assembly). If the UN General Assembly decided to proceed in this manner, ECOSOC would remain unaffected by this decision, thus requiring a delineation of responsibilities between the two councils.

A second, more far-reaching proposal is to fully replace ECOSOC with a UN Sustainable Development Council (at highest level, that of heads of state or government), or to amend the functions of ECOSOC with similar effect, expanding its mandate to cover sustainable development more comprehensively. Both replacement and amendment of ECOSOC would require amending the United Nations Charter. Such an amendment would encounter substantial resistance from many countries, also because it could be linked to other long-standing reform issues, such as reorganization of the UN Security Council. Interestingly, informal meetings before the 2012 Rio conference suggested that the link with the Security Council and other nonenvironmental UN reforms might even build further support for reform: countries might back amendments of ECOSOC exactly because this might advance debates on changes to the status of the Security Council, through issue linkage and an opening for a major overhaul of the UN Charter.

A new UN Sustainable Development Council would have a broad mandate and be firmly placed at the highest level of UN decision making. It would need to be mandated to influence all types of overlap, fragmentation, and lack of coordination related to sustainable development in the UN system and beyond (Bernstein with Brunnée 2011). This would include, notably, the mandate to issue recommendations to the governing bodies of the Bretton Woods institutions.

One normative basis for the Council could be a set of internationally agreed sustainable development goals. The idea for such goals was originally advanced by the governments of Colombia and Guatemala (Colombia and Guatemala 2011) in the lead-up to the 2012 Rio Conference, to complement the earlier Millennium Development Goals to be achieved by 2015. At the 2012 UN Conference on Sustainable Development, governments decided to negotiate new "Sustainable Development Goals." Such goals should include environmental, economic, and social goals in a balanced way. They should be

action-oriented, concise and easy to communicate, limited in number, aspirational, global in nature and universally applicable to all countries while taking into account different national realities, capacities and levels of development and respecting national policies and priorities. (The Future We Want 2012, para. 246)

Unlike the Millennium Development Goals, which were targeted at developing countries, the new goals will thus also cover industrialized countries and potentially set UN-agreed "development goals" for the North also—an issue that the United States tried hard to prevent, but in vain. Also some poorer developing countries were concerned about the discussion around sustainable development goals, fearing that they could divert attention and resources from the Millennium Development Goals, especially after 2015 (Bastos Lima 2012). Governments further agreed that the sustainable development goals shall be measureable and probably quantified ("Progress towards the achievement of the goals needs to be assessed and accompanied by targets and indicators"; see The Future We Want, 2012, para. 250). However, the concrete topics to be covered by such goals—sensitive issues for both North and South—are yet to be decided. The Sustainable Development Goals will now be developed by a group of thirty representatives of countries drawn from the five UN regional groups. This group is to "ensure the full involvement of relevant stakeholders and expertise from civil society, the scientific community and the UN system in its work in order to provide a diversity of perspectives and experience" (The Future We Want 2012, para. 248). Regardless of the outcome of these ongoing negotiations of future Sustainable Development Goals, what is needed is a comprehensive body at highest level in the UN system to coordinate and integrate various sectoral policies and programs on sustainable development. A UN Sustainable Development Council, as outlined in this section, could be such overarching institution.

A Trusteeship Council for Areas beyond National Jurisdiction

In addition, a redesign of the architecture of global sustainability governance to increase policy coherence should include a stronger collective governance system for those vast areas of our planet that do not fall under the jurisdiction of any state: the high seas, Antarctica, and outer space. This could be achieved, I argue (drawing on Biermann 2012a), by a redesign of the trusteeship system of the United Nations, building on earlier ideas advanced by UN Secretary-General Kofi Annan.

The present United Nations trusteeship system was created almost one hundred years ago under the League of Nations for former colonies and territories of Germany and the Ottoman Empire that were not declared independent but placed under the "trust" of the major colonial powers of that time. To oversee these trust relationships, a Trusteeship Council was set up under the UN Charter. The council was comprised of an equal number of countries that administered trust territories and of countries that did not administer trust territories, and included the five permanent members of the UN Security Council. With the independence in 1994 of the last trust territory (the former German colony Palau), the UN Trusteeship Council became obsolete and decided in 1994 to end its regular meetings.

In the same year, the UN Commission on Global Governance (1995) proposed to reform this UN Trusteeship Council and to give it a mandate over the global commons. UN Secretary-General Kofi Annan adopted this idea in 1997 and suggested reconstituting the Council as a forum for member states to exercise their collective trusteeship for the integrity of the global environment and of common areas such as the oceans, atmosphere, and outer space (UN Secretary-General 1997, para. 85). There was not much support for this reform at that time—or for any other reform that required a change of the UN Charter—and eight years later, Annan proposed to delete the provisions on the trusteeship system from the UN Charter (UN Secretary-General 2005, paragraph 218).

The key problem with the early proposals from the Commission on Global Governance and the UN Secretary-General was the combination of different problem areas. A global trust over issues as ill-defined as a "global commons" is too complex for the concrete delimitations of a political and legal mandate. The UN trusteeship system was based on the governance of specific territories, and it is difficult to conceive a mandate for it beyond this core function. There remain, however, three vast areas upon which human activities have a major environmental impact, yet which are outside the jurisdiction of countries: the high seas, Antarctica, and outer space. A revitalized UN trusteeship system, in the framework of broader UN reform, could place these three areas beyond national jurisdiction more firmly under the oversight of the international community.

This does not imply the need for new regulations or institutions, since Antarctica, the high seas, and outer space already fall under complex regulatory systems that have evolved since 1945, namely the Antarctic Treaty system; the UN Convention on the Law of the Sea and the newly created UN Oceans; and the Committee on the Peaceful Uses of Outer Space (created in 1959 by the General Assembly as the central forum for the development of rules governing outer space, including the five main treaties on the use of outer space). Yet the governance challenges for these three areas beyond national jurisdiction are rapidly increasing, from the impacts of global warming to depleted and possibly collapsing fish stocks and unilateral initiatives in the area of geoengineering, which could involve both the high seas and installations in outer space. In this rapidly developing context, a UN Trusteeship Council for Areas beyond National Jurisdiction would imply an upgrade of the regulatory oversight of the international community over these areas, through a UN council at the highest level within a reformed and strengthened UN system.

Realigning International Decision Making

One fundamental shortcoming of the current architecture of earth system governance is its mode of decision making, which works against progressive policies and further integration. To begin with, many of the relevant intergovernmental institutions build on decision making by consensus. Consensus rules are often more a matter of practice than an explicit mandate—many treaties in fact allow for majority voting. However, consensus remains a widely accepted rule for decision making, with about 4 out of 5 environmental agreements operating by consensus (Hovi and Sprinz 2006). The climate convention, for example, has operated since 1994 without formal agreement on its rules of procedure because governments have not yet been able to agree on the voting rules that would apply; consensus decisions are hence still the default.

Consensus decisions maximize the procedural legitimacy of intergovernmental rulemaking by giving all governments an effective voice. However, by granting each government a veto, consensus requirements reduce the overall performance of the decision-making system. The country that is least interested in reform will determine the outcome of negotiations. Majority voting instead allows international negotiations to advance more quickly and to adopt decisions that are more demanding (for exceptions see Hovi and Sprinz 2006). It is a tradeoff between input and output legitimacy: the collective accountability of governments in global decision making hinges on the veto powers of a few countries that seek special benefits, pursue minority political agendas, or reap economic benefit from nondecisions and a persistence of the status quo. And, as Schroeder, Boykoff, and Spiers (2012) argue, "[c]onsensus-based decision-making … stifles progress and contributes to negotiation deadlocks, which ultimately hurts poor countries more than rich countries."

One way forward could be stronger reliance on qualified majority voting. Some international institutions already allow for decisions based on qualified majorities. For example, the International Maritime Organization has recently adopted mandatory efficiency standards for new ships against the votes of Brazil, Chile, China, Kuwait, and Saudi Arabia (Bodansky 2011). Also the International Civil Aviation Organization decides by qualified majority vote, if no consensus can be reached. The organization's 2010 climate change resolution was adopted against the objections of a few powerful developing countries (Bodansky 2011). Importantly, both maritime shipping and civil aviation regulations are usually applicable for all member states without any differentiation, putting these governance systems, with their majority-based decision making, in inherent conflict with the "common but differentiated responsibilities" principle under the UN climate convention.

Even in the practice of climate negotiations, consensus is no longer the same as unanimity. Objections of individual countries have been overruled in recent years by decisions of conference chairs who closed discussions by stating the "consensus" of parties. After even Russia's objections had been ignored in the final hours of the 2012 conference of the parties to the climate convention, Belarus, Russia, and Ukraine essentially blocked any negotiations at the June 2013 session of the Subsidiary Body for Implementation due to their dissatisfaction concerning this issue (ENB 2013a). In effect, climate governance today veers in the direction of decision making based on (very large) majorities, without clear rules on this matter. In other words, also in climate governance, the question of formal majority-based decision making will become more dominant very soon. Out of frustration with slow progress in climate negotiations, majority voting was formally proposed by Papua New Guinea in the 2009 conference of the parties, and later repeated in conjunction with Mexico with some support from the European Union, Indonesia, and a number of developing countries (UNFCCC 2011b; Vihma and Kulovesi 2012; see also European Commission 2013, 9). The question of the future decision-making rules will surely be a major conflict zone in the upcoming negotiations for the next climate agreement (ENB 2013b).

The core question is how the voting system would be organized in practice. Current proposals seem to call for majority voting on the traditional basis that grants each country one vote, regardless of its size, population, relative contribution to the problem, or relative vulnerability. The proposal by Papua New Guinea and Mexico, for example, suggests formally amending the climate convention to the effect that decisions by the conference of the parties can be adopted—after all efforts at consensus have been exhausted—by a three-fourths majority vote, except for decisions on financial support for developing countries, which shall remain under the consensus rule (UNFCCC 2011b). A precedent is the existing rules on amendments to the climate convention, which can be adopted by a three-fourths majority of its parties, each having equal voting rights. (However, amendments enter into force only for countries that later ratify them.) The 1996 draft rules of procedure of the conference of the parties to the climate convention—which were never adopted because of lack of agreement on the voting rules—stipulated two alternatives, either the requirement of a two-thirds majority vote for all decisions except for financial issues and the adoption of a protocol, or a two-thirds majority vote only for decisions on financial issues while consensus is required for all other matters of substance (UNFCCC 1996).

This traditional approach of majority decisions that grant each country one (equal) vote is widely used in the UN system, where it has granted a structural majority to developing countries since the 1970s. One outcome was a series of decisions by the United Nations General Assembly in the 1970s on the establishment of a new international economic order, which were in the end ignored by the outvoted minority of industrialized countries. In a one-country-one-vote system, countries like Liechtenstein or Monaco have formally equal voting power with major powers like China and India. China's population alone is greater than the combined populations of the 159 least populous UN member states; combined, the two votes of China and India in UN meetings represent roughly 37 percent of humankind. In the current UN system, the 100 least populous countries are able to take majority decisions although they represent only 3.9 percent of the world population and 6.4 percent of global GDP. It is doubtful whether far-reaching decisions, for example on emission reductions, will be accepted if the larger countries can be easily outvoted by coalitions of tiny countries.

An alternative to the one-country-one-vote approach is associated with the World Bank and the IMF, which weigh votes by financial contributions to the respective institution. This rule of "one-dollar-one-vote" grants a structural majority to industrialized countries, and has therefore been objected to by developing countries for decades, even though emerging economies have managed to increase their votes in recent years. China now holds more votes than Germany, and India more than Italy. In total, the structural majority of industrialized countries in World Bank decision making has shrunk to 52.81 percent (World Bank 2010). Yet overall, because the one-country-one-vote and one-dollar-one-vote approaches give a dominant majority to one or other side of the long-standing North-South cleavage, both lack universal acceptance and legitimacy.

Another alternative is the novel system first developed in the Montreal Protocol on Substances that Deplete the Ozone Layer. This system evolved in two stages. The first approach was similar to the one used by the international financial institutions: participating governments decided to weigh votes by the countries' relative consumption of ozone-depleting substances. Decisions of the meeting of the parties on the scope, amount, and timing of further adjustments and reductions required the support of two-thirds of the parties, which had to represent fifty percent of the total consumption of controlled substances of the parties (Montreal Protocol 1987, article 2.9.c). For the protocol to enter into force, instruments of ratification had to represent two-thirds of global consumption in 1986 (Montreal Protocol 1987, article 16). This approach gave a structural majority to industrialized countries, the main producers of ozone-depleting substances at that time. Most developing countries refused to accept these rules or to join the agreement. Industrialized countries therefore agreed to drop consumption-based majority voting and to accept a novel collective veto right for developing and industrialized countries. Article 2.9.c of the protocol as amended in 1990 now provides that decisions require a two-thirds majority of the parties, which must include a simple majority of both developing countries and industrialized countries. In essence, this system did away with the veto power of single countries in North and South by granting collective veto rights to both groups of countries.

Similar decision-making procedures have been agreed to for the governance of the ozone fund that reimburses the full incremental costs of developing countries in implementing the treaty. Unlike other multilateral funding institutions, the executive committee of the fund consists of an equal number of industrialized and developing countries, and takes decisions by a two-thirds majority vote that must include a majority of both industrialized and developing countries (Biermann 1997). Similar procedures were agreed to in 1994 for the Global Environment Facility (GEF): half of the thirty-two seats in the GEF council are held by developing countries, fourteen by donor countries, and two by countries with economies in transition. If no consensus can be reached, decisions are taken by an affirmative vote that must include a 60 percent majority of the total number of participating states, which favors the South, and a 60 percent majority of the total contributions, which favors the North (GEF 1994, articles 16 and 25.c.i). This institutional framework offers significant leverage to developing countries compared to their weak status in the World Bank group—for which they had demanded comparable voting rights in the 1970s (Ferguson 1988).

Could this approach of "double-weighted" majority rule also be a model for earth system governance in general?

One problem with such group-based decision-making procedures is agreeing on which country belongs to which group. Singapore, for example, is still seen as a developing country under the climate convention even though its national per capita income is higher than that of many industrialized countries. The Montreal Protocol grouped countries using an issue-based classification scheme that draws a line between developing countries that consume less than 300 grams of chlorofluorocarbons per person per year and all other countries, thus treating Kuwait, for example, as an industrialized country. The climate convention, for its part, has not adopted any issue-based classification but simply divided countries, and their commitments, using traditional political categories of industrialized and developing countries, which are, especially regarding the classification of a developing country, to a large extent based on self-definition. The issue-based classification of the Montreal protocol cannot be applied for earth system governance more generally. However, issue-based classification could well underpin double-weighted majority voting in specific institutions. Such voting could also include veto rights for multiple groups. In climate governance, for example, specific groups such as low-lying island states have been institutionalized in addition to traditional groupings such as industrialized and developing countries. Another option could be regional veto rights that draw on the support of the majority of countries in a region. Regional veto rights, however, are also problematic. They are relatively easy to conceptualize for some regions, such as Africa or Europe, but more difficult for others such as Asia.

Another alternative could be to depart entirely from the one-country-one-vote tradition and to weigh votes. Any powerful international institution requires a decision-making system that reflects the political realities of its time and the broader context within which specific issues are being addressed. Most UN organs follow the practice of intergovernmental diplomacy of the nineteenth century, granting each sovereign state the same vote. In the UN General Assembly or the Economic and Social Council, the seven countries that make up half of the world's population hold merely 3.6 percent of the votes. Likewise, the five countries that account for half of the world's GDP hold 2.6 percent of the vote. It is difficult to expect large countries such as China, or major OECD countries, to grant such institutions a powerful influence over their economic development or environmental policy.

Some institutions and organizations have weighted voting systems; yet these also appear outdated. The Bretton Woods organizations weigh their votes based on financial contributions and are, as laid out above, still biased in favor of industrialized countries, despite recent adjustments. The UN Security Council grants a veto right to five permanent members in a system that is widely seen as outdated and no longer legitimate. In the International Maritime Organization (IMO), the ten countries with the largest interest in providing international shipping services and the ten countries with the largest interest in international seaborne trade have guaranteed seats in the organization's executive body, along with twenty other countries. Yet such a system might be difficult to transfer to the more complex and interlinked issues in earth system governance. For sustainable development, some observers have recently called for a stronger role for the Group of 20 major economies, which some see as a more effective governance mechanism than the UN system. Yet the exclusion of the remaining 150 countries is a major problem for the legitimacy of such a role for this group.

Considerations of equity, specifically equality of the human person, might require that weighted voting in international negotiations will eventually have to be related to population size, granting each person the same right to be represented in global environmental decision making. In the current international system, however, voting rights of countries on a per capita basis would give a theoretical majority to the seven most populous countries: China, India, the United States, Indonesia, Brazil, Pakistan, and Nigeria. This is hardly acceptable for the other countries. In a BBC survey in 2007, for example, 51.2 percent of all polled US citizens objected to the idea of a global parliament that would have a mandate to take binding decisions while being based on country population sizes. However, more positive responses were reported for other industrialized countries, such as Germany and France. The most positive reaction came from India, where 63.8 percent of all surveyed citizens viewed a global parliament based on country population sizes as positive, with 36.3 percent even stating that this body would be "very likely" and "a good idea" (Bummel 2010, 24).

Various compromise proposals exist that combine population size with other indicators, such as economic weight. One influential proposal is Schwartzberg's (2004, 2009, and 2012) method for weighted voting in a reformed United Nations that calculates the vote of countries based on the average of three factors: population, expressed as a percentage of the world total; contributions to the UN budget, expressed as a percentage of the whole; and membership, expressed as a percentage of the whole (which is a constant, today 1/193 or 0.52 percent), reflecting the equality of countries. This system would at present give the largest vote to the United States with 10.1 percent, reflecting the combination of its share in world population (4.6 percent) and in UN contributions (as share of GDP, with 24.7 percent). The United States would be followed, in this model, by China with 9.8 percent of the votes, then India (6.9 percent), Japan (3.5 percent), and Germany (2.7 percent) (see, for this and various other models, Schwartzberg 2012). The higher voting power of the larger countries due to their population and financial contributions could be complemented by equally strong regional votes of blocks of countries. In all of these reform models for weighted voting, however, special care must be taken to provide viable safeguards so that smaller countries and those with particular interests are not overrun by the dictates of the majority. Domestic federal systems that combine majority voting with representation of subnational units, such as states or provinces, can provide models for how to combine fair representation of every global citizen with safeguards for smaller and less populated countries. More research and debate in this area are essential and would be timely.

As a proxy for increased representation of larger countries in the shorter term, governments could grant the members of the Group of 20 a primary seat in international decision making, for example in the UN Sustainable Development Council proposed earlier (drawing on Biermann 2012a; Biermann, Abbott, et al. 2012; Kanie et al. 2012). This is not meant to be a long-term solution, given that the membership of the Group of 20 is not based on clear and universally agreed criteria but rather on a mix of wealth and a general perception of political importance and geographic representation (Vestergaard 2011). Notably, some highly populated countries such as Bangladesh, Nigeria, and Pakistan—all of which are among the ten most populous countries—are not members of the current Group of 20, while some smaller economies, such as Argentina, are included. Integrating the Group of 20 into United Nations decision making, for example by granting its members a fixed share of the votes in a decision-making body, would thus require more transparency in the selection of the twenty countries. An alternative could be to loosely follow the IMO system of recognizing two categories of especially important countries, for instance granting 25 percent of the seats in the UN Sustainable Development Council to the ten countries with the largest population, 25 percent to the ten countries with the largest GDP, and the other 50 percent of the seats to twenty representatives of the remaining countries (adjusting for those countries that belong at the same time to the ten most populous and the ten richest countries, like the United States and China). Overall it seems a viable option, as a first departure from the one-country-one-vote system, to combine the advantages of a group of twenty larger countries—however eventually defined—with the broader legitimacy of the United Nations, in a novel decision-making system that could underpin all three main UN bodies proposed here: the World Environment Organization, the UN Sustainable Development Council, and the UN Trusteeship Council for Areas beyond National Jurisdiction. In these three bodies, countries could grant a special role and primary membership to the twenty largest countries, as the countries that are indispensable to any solution being implemented and supported.

For instance, fifty percent of the seats in a governing body could be allocated to the twenty largest countries (the status of which should be reassessed on a regular basis). In order to ensure the broad legitimacy of the decisions, especially in regions with many smaller and/or poorer countries, the other fifty percent of the seats could be allocated to the roughly 170 smaller countries (or 150 countries if the European Union is represented by one seat). This decision-making procedure would reintegrate the current Group of 20 meetings back into the United Nations, yet also include representation of the many smaller countries, thus increasing legitimacy and representativeness of decision making in the overall architecture of earth system governance.

Reassessing State Sovereignty

Finally, the issue of governance integration leads to a fundamental question regarding the architecture of earth system governance: If institutional fragmentation decreases the performance of earth system governance, what are the consequences when full consensus of all countries is not attainable? If international institutions provide more often for qualified majority voting, what is then the position of a minority of countries that do not seek to comply with standards of earth system governance that a majority of countries see as fundamentally required? In essence, this is the question of state sovereignty in the Anthropocene.

Theoretically, the principles of earth system governance outlined in chapter 2 suggest that such governance goes not only beyond but partially also above the state. It must include limitations to the autonomy of individual state behavior and some elements of a post-sovereign governance architecture that expresses the interests of the international community. As succinctly stated by Dieter Heinrich (2010, 14), "[t]he idea of unfettered national sovereignty, with every state a law unto itself, may have been tolerable in the days of the steamship, the telegraph and the cavalry."

This is not shorthand for world government. Instead, it describes existing state behavior in nonenvironmental policy fields, observable for example in the increasing subjugation of foreign economic policy to juridical decisions by the World Trade Organization. Such elements of subjugation of states to "governance above the state" are observable wherever governments accept limitations to their sovereign decision making. Regarding norm development in earth system governance, for example, governments have accepted in the Montreal ozone protocol binding majority decisions on the adjustment of the timetable for the phase-out of regulated substances (Montreal Protocol 1987, article 2.9). Likewise, the harmonization of trade policy under the World Trade Organization has limited the room for national policymaking, also on environmental issues. Regarding adjudication, the world has experienced a shift from voluntary adjudication such as through the International Court of Justice or ad hoc tribunals to compulsory adjudication, notably through the International Tribunal on the Law of the Sea, the International Criminal Court, and the WTO dispute settlement system.

But how can one then conceptualize state sovereignty in earth system governance? It appears questionable that national sovereignty can stand against the most essential standards of earth system governance, which rather ought to be seen as universally binding. One example is the prohibition of production of chlorofluorocarbons that destroy the stratospheric ozone layer. Within earth system governance, it is thus important to differentiate between classes of international legal standards; namely, those that are so essential that no abrogation may be permitted, and those that countries can freely choose whether to adhere to.

There are a variety of avenues of reasoning that can help distinguish such a class of special, universal norms that are binding upon all countries:

First, core standards of earth system governance that are based on widely accepted but not universal international agreements can be seen as an operationalization of the rule of international customary law that a country may not use its territory in such a way as to cause (serious) harm to another country. This general prohibition of transboundary pollution, which dates back to the Trail Smelter Arbitration (1938/1941), was incorporated as principle 21 in the Stockholm Declaration (1972) on the human environment, which reconfirms that all states must ensure that activities within their jurisdiction or control do not damage the environment of other states or areas beyond the limits of national jurisdiction. Today, this general responsibility of states is widely accepted as part of international customary law (for example Wolfrum 1990, 308–330; Brunnée 1989, 795). This obligation not to cause harm to other states is not to be determined by the result—the actual ending of any harmful transboundary impacts—but by certain standards of conduct, which may include those laid down in relevant treaty provisions or in acts of international organizations such as technical annexes, as long as a representative majority of states has ratified or accepted them.

Second, multilateral treaties can directly become customary law, thus binding all states (ICJ 1969; article 38 of the Vienna Convention on the Law of Treaties). In traditional international law, however, a treaty rule can only be seen as customary international law if there is established evidence of its being a general and consistent practice accepted as law. Consistent state practice normally requires near-universal adherence as well as a certain duration of practice regarding this rule, although there are instances in which custom was created in relatively short periods, for example in areas of rapid technological advances or the development of new means of warfare (Scharf 2013). In light of the nature of the challenges of earth system transformation, it can be assumed that customary law can evolve more rapidly in this domain as well, without the need to wait until a near-universal majority of states has consistently practiced mitigation measures. This absence of long-standing state practice is a problem, however, in the determination of the exact content of specific rules. Guiding indicators could be resolutions of international organizations and institutions that have been adopted by large majorities, or agreements that have been adopted at multilateral conferences with almost universal attendance (ICJ 1969, paragraph 73).

One indication of a special status for some core norms of earth system governance could be seen in the declaration of the UN General Assembly in 1988 of climate change as "a common concern of mankind, since climate is an essential condition which sustains life on earth" (UNGA 1989). Governments repeated this notion of a common concern of humankind in the 1992 preambles of the climate convention and the biodiversity convention. This approach was not entirely new. Previous legal documents have identified other issues, such as Antarctica, whaling, or the protection of the seabed from military installations, as involving a common "interest" of humankind, implying the necessity of international governance on those issues. The terminology of "common concern" indicates a higher status than "common interest," inasmuch as it emphasizes the potential dangers involved in issues such as global warming and biodiversity depletion. This could signify that international governance in these cases is not only necessary or desired but also essential for the survival of humankind (Brunnée 1989).

What does this imply for countries that do not want to be bound by core norms of earth system governance? Traditional international law has long held that states that persistently objected to an evolving rule becoming international customary law would not be bound by that rule (ICJ 1950 and 1951a). This "persistent objector" doctrine derives from the principle of state sovereignty and of noninterference in the internal affairs of states, the cornerstone of traditional notions of international law. However, new earth system challenges, such as climate change, may constitute matters that are no longer within the domestic jurisdiction of states. In particular, earth system transformation might require a reconsideration and concretization of two established legal concepts that place special limitations on state sovereignty: norms *erga omnes* ("toward all") and *jus cogens* ("peremptory law").

First, the notion of obligations *erga omnes*—which applies in particular to the legal standing of states in respect of other states having allegedly violated their duties—was developed by the International Court of Justice in 1970. The court stated that "[a]n essential distinction should be drawn between the obligations of a State towards the international community as a whole, and those arising vis-à-vis another State in the field of diplomatic protection. By their very nature the former are the concern of all States. In view of the importance of the rights involved, all States can be held to have a legal interest in their protection; they are obligations *erga omnes*" (ICJ 1970). As regards the material content of obligations that are the "concern of all States," the court listed examples such as legal norms that derive "from the outlawing of acts of aggression, and of genocide, as also from the principles and rules concerning the basic rights of the human person, including protection from slavery and racial discrimination" (ICJ 1970, para. 34). Importantly, the court seemed to be willing to accord *erga omnes* status to obligations "conferred by international instruments of a universal or quasi-universal character." The court added that obligations *erga omnes* are in particular those that are "by their very nature the concern of all States." This should include, I argue, some fundamental rules of earth system governance. At least as regards these norms, governments seeking to enforce general international environmental law, for instance by international litigation, would not have to prove any specific legal interest other than the protection of the interests of the international community as a whole.

Secondly, core norms of earth system governance can be *jus cogens*, that is, peremptory norms of international law. The concept of *jus cogens* restricts the sovereignty of states regarding the creation of international law (Verdross 1966). Article 53 of the Convention on the Law of Treaties (1969) states that any treaty is void if it conflicts with a "peremptory norm of general international law." Those are norms that are "accepted and recognized by the international community of States as a whole as a norm from which no derogation is permitted and which can be modified only by a subsequent norm of general international law having the same character" (Convention on the Law of Treaties 1969, article 53). Some core norms of earth system governance could fall under this category. One could object that most environmental treaties allow for the withdrawal of parties, which would contradict the intention of governments to create a legal norm of *jus cogens*. Yet even the 1948 Convention on the Prevention and Punishment of the Crime of Genocide provides in article XIV for the right of governments to renounce the treaty, although it is now widely accepted that the prohibition of genocide constitutes a peremptory norm of international law (ICJ 1951b). The mere inclusion of a withdrawal clause in a treaty thus does not per se impede the treaty norms from becoming *jus cogens*.

For example, given the vital importance of the stratospheric ozone layer for human survival and the universal support for the Montreal Protocol on the ozone layer (which has become the first treaty in the history of the UN to achieve universal ratification), it is a fair conclusion that its provisions today are *jus cogens*, that is, that no government may leave the protocol and contradict its provisions (also Brunnée 1989; Biermann 1996; Uhlmann 1998). Other norms of earth system governance are more complex, however. For example, in 2011 Canada announced its intention to withdraw from the 1997 Kyoto Protocol to the climate convention in order to prevent its being found in breach of its provisions at the end of the emission reduction commitment period; and it did this without facing much resistance from other governments. Hence, it is difficult, at present, to see the concrete commitments of the Kyoto Protocol as part of international *jus cogens*, despite the fundamental importance of mitigating anthropogenic climate change.

Also, the practical effect of endowing core norms of earth system governance with the superior status of *jus cogens* is difficult to assess. Hypothetically, certain treaties—for example, on the wrongful exchange of chlorofluorocarbon-related technologies—may be considered as contradicting *jus cogens* and hence void. But this is an unlikely scenario—what would be the more practical consequences? I see at least two areas where such legal distinctions could matter.

One is international litigation. Since neither the International Court of Justice nor arbitration tribunals have injunctive powers, litigation between states depends on the willingness of states to accept the court's decision. It is thus no easy route for affected countries. One option, for example, is for low-lying island states to submit a complaint to the International Court of Justice against states that are high emitters of greenhouse gases. Yet it is unlikely that major polluting countries will agree to have this issue tabled before the International Court of Justice. More promising is a request for an advisory opinion by the court. This request can be tabled by a number of international agencies in accordance with article 96 of the UN Charter, for instance by the World Meteorological Organization, the UN General Assembly, the UN Economic and Social Council, or even the Security Council. (UNEP is not authorized to do so.) A precedent has been set by the World Health Organization, which asked the court in 1993 for an advisory opinion on whether the use of nuclear weapons by a state in war or other armed conflict would be a breach of its obligations under international law in view of the health effects. When the court eventually rejected this request because it saw the WHO as acting outside its mandate, the UN General Assembly followed up, in 1994, with a similar request for an advisory opinion, which the court then delivered (ICJ 1996). A similar course of action is also conceivable for global environmental issues, for example— as proposed by Palau, Grenada, and others—regarding climate change (Yale Center for Environmental Law and Policy 2012). It is unlikely that the court would quantify countries' obligations to reduce their emissions or to compensate their "victims." However, an advisory opinion by the International Court of Justice would help put political pressure on polluting states by declaring their activities wrongful under international law. It could provide international organizations and civil society with the legal language to qualify certain state behavior as violating international norms, even if such violation cannot easily be addressed in a court of law.

Second, concepts of norms "toward all" and peremptory norms may help determine the degree of lawful measures that the international community may take against countries that do not accept, or do not comply with, widely accepted international environmental standards. One practical example is the Montreal Protocol, which requires its parties to restrict their trade with countries that do not accept the protocol by banning the import of goods produced with ozone-depleting substances in such third countries, even if the traded goods no longer contain such substances (Clapp 1997, 259–273). Such environmentally motivated trade restrictions generally contradict several obligations under GATT, such as the most favored nation principle, the principle that imported goods must be treated similarly to like domestic goods under article III, and the prohibition of quantitative trade restrictions under article XI.I. Countries that restrict trade for environmental reasons, however, can justify their actions by invoking certain exemptions to such principles. In particular, trade restrictions called for by multilateral environmental agreements could be justified under a general exception clause under article XX. This is not the place to review in detail the complexities surrounding the legality of trade restrictions under world trade law (see my arguments in Biermann 2001b in more detail; also the book-length treatments of Zelli 2010; van Asselt 2014). It is nonetheless important to emphasize that legal notions of customary law or even *jus cogens* can open up argumentative space for governments to justify restrictions on trade, including through border tax adjustments, special subsidies, and other means, in order to ensure global compliance with core norms of earth system governance.

Conclusion

This chapter has analyzed the institutional architecture of earth system governance. I have argued that institutional fragmentation in this domain is strong, and that this tends to decrease the effectiveness of earth system governance. While there are a number of positive consequences of institutional fragmentation, overall it hinders progress in negotiating stringent targets and actions, tends to privilege the more powerful countries, limits incentives of subnational actors to take urgently needed action, and reduces the overall credibility, stability, and coherence of the entire architecture of earth system governance.

To overcome this fragmentation, I have outlined a number of reforms to the global institutional architecture of earth system governance. First, there is an urgent need for innovative strategies to actively manage institutional interactions in order to minimize possible negative impacts of institutional fragmentation. In addition, I have argued that a World Environment Organization is needed as a new powerful agent in earth system governance (as discussed in chapter 3) and as a means to integrate the fragmented institutional architecture of earth system governance. Thirdly, a high-level UN Sustainable Development Council could help to integrate the broader institutional architecture for sustainable development, and in particular to integrate economic with environmental policies. Fourthly, a UN Trusteeship Council for Areas beyond National Jurisdiction could advance the integrated governance of those areas that are beyond the jurisdiction of any state. Across all institutional architectures, I have further argued that decision-making procedures in intergovernmental negotiations need urgent reform. Existing procedures are no longer fit for the particular challenges of earth system governance. The consensus principle, still widely applied, slows down intergovernmental rule making and caters to the wishes of the least interested actor. The one-country-one-vote rule creates imbalances in decision making that put Monaco and Liechtenstein on a par with China and Brazil—a system that is not likely to be accepted by such large countries for majority decisions that have significant political and economic consequences. Overall, weighted-majority decision making as proposed here would help to overcome the shortcomings of current systems that no longer reflect the political realities of the twenty-first century. Eventually, this will require a fundamental reconceptualization of the notion of state sovereignty. In particular, I have suggested that certain core norms of earth system governance should be seen as peremptory norms of international law, that is, as norms from which no derogation is permitted.

Frühe rundet Regen blau
Runde das Grün
Schlafe maies Land
Grüne Tropfen tropfenweise
Leise Tropfen tropfen leise
Runde schlaf Land
Schlafe grüne Tropfenwiese
Grüne Tropfen sanften Lied
Grünen Grüne grün.

Kurt Schwitters, 1919

Earliness Rounds Rain Blue
Round the green
Sleep, May-time land
Green drops drop by drop
Quiet drops drip quietly
Round sleep land
Sleep, green dripping-meadow
Green drops gentle song
Green Greens green.

5

Accountability and Legitimacy

Earth system governance is not only a question of institutional performance and effectiveness; the accountability and legitimacy of decision making is equally important. This relates to all levels of governance, from the local to the global. It involves the accountability and legitimacy of public regulation, but also of novel types of private governance arrangements within and beyond the state. In the twentieth century, legitimacy and accountability were mainly concerns of national governments and their decisions. In the twenty-first century, with its emerging trends of governance beyond the state, we must consider the challenge of securing accountability and legitimacy in a very different context. In this chapter I explore how and why securing more accountable and legitimate governance is important in its own right, particularly in light of debates over more democratic forms of earth system governance; but also whether and how it might contribute to institutional effectiveness.

The chapter is directly linked to the two preceding. One driving force in the search for more accountable and legitimate forms of governance is the increased institutionalization of earth system governance. While international environmental negotiations were fringe issues on the global agenda fifty years ago, today more than 1,100 international environmental treaties are in force, along with over 1,500 bilateral agreements (Mitchell 2013), ensuring an ever denser web of globally negotiated rules and restrictions on state behavior that require a reconsideration of the legitimacy and accountability of such arrangements (see chapter 4, on "Architecture"). The complexities of earth system governance also generated a stronger political role for actors beyond the state, from multinational corporations and transnational advocacy groups to science networks and global coalitions of municipalities. Where governments fail to agree on effective international rules, nonstate actors are now taking the lead in developing global norms and standards, such as the private

Forest Stewardship Council or the Marine Stewardship Council (see chapter 3, on "Agency"). This involvement of nonstate actors poses new challenges to securing accountability and legitimacy in global rule making, not least since traditional means of doing so in a national context, such as electoral accountability and constitutional representation, cannot be applied to global rule making and nonstate governance.

Identifying sources and mechanisms for enhancing accountability and legitimacy in earth system governance thus becomes all-important, extending both to state actors and intergovernmental governance and to new and emerging systems of governance in which state actors may play only a marginal role (Kingsbury 2007; Mason 2008a). This is the focus of this chapter, which draws on earlier work with Aarti Gupta (Biermann and Gupta 2011a and 2011b; also Biermann 2007 and 2008).

Let me first explain how I understand accountability and legitimacy in earth system governance. Both concepts are often ill defined, and there is little agreement on what they entail. Both terms are also often used interchangeably in academic research and policy debates, adding to conceptual confusion.

Accountability refers in laypersons' terminology to the willingness to accept responsibility or to account for one's actions. Accountability is thus related to notions of responsibility; often the terms are used interchangeably, as for instance in a special issue on this topic in *Global Environmental Politics* in 2008. In essence, accountability has four elements: (1) a *normative element*, that is, a standard of behavior defined with sufficient precision; (2) a *relational element* linking those who are held accountable to those who have the right to hold them to account; (3) a *decision element*, that is, a judgment of those actors who may hold other actors accountable about whether the expected standard of behavior has been met; and (4) a *behavioral element* that allows the governing actor to punish deviant behavior of those held accountable. All elements need to be present in sufficient degree to make any accountability relationship meaningful.

An important question thus becomes the consent of those who are held accountable to this accountability relationship and to the standards of expected behavior. For example, the staff of an intergovernmental bureaucracy can generally be assumed to consent to the standards of appropriate behavior expected in their particular function, as well as to the right of member states to request policy changes if so desired. Yet will they also consent to be held accountable to those affected by their action and decisions? This is related to an important distinction between what Keohane (2003) calls internal and external accountability, in the former of which the principal and agent are institutionally linked to each other, while in the latter those whose lives are impacted, and hence who would desire to hold to account, are not directly linked to the one to be held to account.

Accountability relationships are also of central concern with regard to private rule making in earth system governance, which has received much attention in academic writing in recent years (see chapter 3). Transnational labeling schemes, for instance, establish standards for the "sustainable" use of natural resources or other goods, which form the normative basis for an accountability relationship between firms that orient their behavior according to these standards and customers who expect compliance by firms, and who may opt to punish deviant firms by boycotting their products. The Roundtable on Sustainable Palm Oil is an interesting example of the complex accountability relationships that may arise from such novel governance mechanisms, including the role of inclusion and exclusion in establishing who accepts accountability claims by whom (Schouten and Glasbergen 2011; Schouten 2013). For example, some producers—in many cases in poor developing countries—may not have been sufficiently or effectively included in private rule-setting processes, or may not have consented to the private governance arrangement in the first place. Such problems of inclusion and exclusion—or, plainly put, of who is a stakeholder in earth system governance—becomes then a key question.

Another important element of accountability relationships—and an oft-assumed precondition for more accountable and legitimate governance—is the transparency of governance processes and outcomes. Transparency is widely assumed to be critically important to the search for more accountable and legitimate earth system governance (Florini 2007; A. Gupta 2008; A. Gupta and Mason 2014; Mason 2008b). Yet the diverse normative rationales underpinning the growing calls for transparency in governance, and its uneven institutionalization in specific governance arrangements, reveal complex links between transparency on the one hand and greater accountability and legitimacy of governance arrangements on the other (for detailed analyses of these relationships, see A. Gupta 2008 and 2010; A. Gupta and Mason 2014; Mitchell 2011).

Finally, accountability is also a core element of deliberative democracy. Deliberative democracy requires, in the terminology used by Dryzek and

Stevenson (2011), that the empowered space of political decision making be held accountable to the public space of deliberation. Even here, in the broader quest for deliberative democracy in earth system governance, problems of inclusion and exclusion remain prominent, for instance in deciding who is included in the empowered space of decision making, and whose voices carry more weight in the public sphere of deliberation. These problems are particularly relevant when it comes to global decision making in earth system governance, given the world's vast discrepancies of wealth and power (for example, Spagnuolo 2011), as well as in the emerging domain of private and private-public rule making.

Legitimacy commonly describes the state or quality of being legitimate, that is, of being in accord with established legal forms and requirements, or of conforming to recognized principles or accepted rules and standards of behavior. Core dimensions of the notion of legitimacy are the acceptance and justification of authority. Acceptance relates to how, and the degree to which, rules or institutions are accepted by a community as being authoritative. Acceptability thus relates to the reasons that justify the authority of certain rules or institutions (Bernstein 2005; Bernstein and Cashore 2007; Bodansky 2007).

Until very recently, legitimacy was a standard that only states could be expected to establish, as these were the only actors that could exercise authority in national and international governance. Only states could expect other actors to comply with their standards and had the formal means to enforce this compliance. As I laid out in chapter 3, however, the role of nonstate actors has increased substantially, and nonstate institutions and governance processes have become more common. Even though transnational public policy networks may be less effective in contributing to earth system governance than hoped for, it is evident that some nonstate institutions and mechanisms do impact upon political processes. The World Commission on Dams, for example, is a formally nongovernmental norm-developing body that has become rather influential in its issue area, even though its decisions are not legally binding. For this reason alone, the accountability and legitimacy of nonstate institutions becomes important, and the legitimacy of political institutions and policies beyond the state has received much interest among scholars and policymakers alike. Klaus Dingwerth (2007), for example, in his book-length treatment has distinguished three dimensions of democratic legitimacy beyond the state, which he describes as participation and inclusiveness, democratic control, and discursive quality. The core standard underlying participation is the extent to which those who are subject to a decision have been included in decision making. The standard of democratic control requires that those who are governed should be able to control those who govern them. The third standard, that of the discursive quality of decision making, requires that no groups be excluded from decisions and deliberations. Deliberations should not be limited to elite negotiations and should provide room for inclusion of critical opinions (Dingwerth 2007, 27–29). These standards of participation, democratic control, and deliberation are not the only ones possible, but are examples of how legitimacy in earth system governance can be analyzed.

In doing so, two distinctions seem especially important. The first is between input and output legitimacy, originally developed by Scharpf (1997) for the assessment of the legitimacy of European decision making. Input legitimacy refers to the procedural characteristics of rule setting, and output legitimacy to the acceptance of rules because of their (perceived) ability to solve problems. Output legitimacy is hence related to governance effectiveness, yet with the fundamental difference that legitimacy in this sense hinges on *perceived* effectiveness among stakeholders, which is not necessarily the same as actual resolution of underlying problems. The Roundtable on Sustainable Palm Oil, for instance, seems to be supported by some of its participants, who see it as legitimate because of its perceived achievements, while stakeholders that remain outside the organization continue to criticize its legitimacy (Schouten and Glasbergen 2011). The Clean Development Mechanism under the climate convention has seemingly high degrees of output legitimacy, which may compensate for a more limited input legitimacy (Lederer 2011). On the other hand, the legitimacy of the Global Environment Facility might be hampered by the fact that the focus of its activities misses key concerns of poorer developing countries (Rosendal and Andresen 2011).

A second important distinction is between internal and external legitimacy (similar to the discussion of internal and external accountability above). Internal legitimacy refers to the acceptance of norms by participants in an institution, for instance the members of an organization or the supporters of a rule-making mechanism. External legitimacy refers to the acceptance of a rule by nonmembers or nonparticipants. In empirical situations, distinctions between internal and external legitimacy can be complex, however. In the case of the Roundtable on Sustainable Palm Oil, for example, one can distinguish acceptance of norms by representatives of industries that participate in the roundtable; by representatives of industries that do not participate; and by other actors outside this production process who are affected by the decisions (Schouten and Glasbergen 2011; Schouten 2013).

Assessment

The quest for improved accountability and legitimacy of governance is not a new one. However, the emerging transformation of planetary systems, along with the resulting challenge of developing effective earth system governance, pose new challenges for securing the accountability and legitimacy of governance systems. I elaborate on these challenges in this section, drawing on the five core elements of the problem structure of earth system governance, as developed in chapter 2 above.

The accountability and legitimacy of earth system governance are affected, first, by high degrees of analytic and normative uncertainty. Key parameters of the earth system are insufficiently understood, which gives ample room for divergent interpretations in political discourse, generally requiring a broader degree of participation beyond the traditional government representatives. As laid out in chapter 3, for example, analytic uncertainty resulted in the emergence of novel types of global scientific organizations, such as the IPCC, whose own legitimacy has later become a matter for heated debate. Conflicts within the IPCC have arisen for instance around the low representation of experts from developing countries; the extent to which non-English and nontraditional publications are to be included in the panel's assessments; the inclusion of experts from advocacy organizations; and the assumptions underpinning scenario building. While many procedural changes to the functioning of the IPCC have increased its legitimacy in some constituencies (such as among developing countries, who have benefitted from a quota policy to increase Southern participation), they have also decreased its legitimacy in other communities, including in parts of the mainstream scientific community in some industrialized countries (see chapter 3).

Normative uncertainty is another problem for the legitimacy of global decision making in earth system governance. While in some cases, such as in addressing stratospheric ozone depletion, the appropriate standard of behavior at global and national levels was quickly and widely agreed, in other areas uncertainty and contestation still prevail concerning appropriate norms and behavioral standards. In climate governance, for instance, the relative emissions of countries can be interpreted according to different parameters, such as population or economic parameters, and the interpretation can include or exclude historical emissions, all of which affects the assessment of the relative responsibility of countries such as the United States or China in mitigating the problem. Any proposed global limit—say 350 or 450 parts per million for atmospheric carbon dioxide concentration—also depends on assumptions about relative risk aversion. Thus, while a limit of 350 parts per million represents the most risk-averse reduction goal for emissions, it is also the one with highest political and economic costs (see chapter 6, on "Allocation"). Such conflicts, and associated scientifically and normatively contested tradeoffs, fundamentally complicate the quest to enhance the overall legitimacy and accountability of global environmental decision making. Again, this might require broadening of participation in global politics beyond the traditional multilateral diplomatic processes.

Temporal interdependence is a second problem for the accountability and legitimacy of earth system governance. This includes the accountability challenge relating to future generations, that is, that decisions taken today have implications for future generations who are not involved in these decisions and who may not benefit from current policies. The prime example is global warming, most of the impacts of which are expected to fully manifest themselves only decades from now. This raises the complex question of accountability relationships between present and future generations, which calls for potentially unprecedented governance innovations. At present, multilateral institutions are centered around government representatives who are subject to election cycles of merely 4–5 years. This makes the representation of long-term interests and concerns notoriously difficult. A stronger role for civil society organizations or scientists in such institutions could help them to serve as institutionalized "watchdogs" that protect future interests.

Temporal interdependence also relates to accountability relations between past and present generations. In climate governance, advocates and governments from the less or later industrialized countries in Africa, Asia, and Latin America have submitted claims about the historical responsibility of European and North American societies, which in the past have emitted greenhouse gases to an extent that may now force limitations in growth upon some developing countries also. Can present Northern societies be held accountable for their societies' past emissions? The question can be posed for different time scales. One could consider more recent historical accountability, for instance since 1988, when the United Nations General Assembly declared the protection of the global climate a common concern of humankind. One could extend historical accountability back to the last two centuries, even though the global warming problem was not, or not sufficiently, known before 1988. Long-term historical responsibility of countries is not unknown to international law. For example, national debt or war reparations are often assumed to remain the legal responsibility of a country even if most inhabitants were not born when these responsibilities were incurred. Profound decisions on the accountability of past generations for future climate change, again, require broad participation of views and interests in global debates that will need to go beyond traditional diplomatic negotiations.

Earth system governance is further marked by functional interdependence across diverse sectors of global production and consumption. The sustainable production and consumption of palm oil is a prime example. The production and consumption of palm oil relates to various industrial products and production chains, from margarine to cosmetics, detergents, and fuel. Numerous environmental goods are affected, including the protection of biodiversity, the preservation of forests, and the mitigation of climate change. Socially, palm oil links various groups of consumers with producers, retailers, and affected communities in the producing countries, such as forest-dwelling indigenous people.

Functional interdependencies thus make any assessment of the accountability and legitimacy of rule making dependent on the boundaries of the group of stakeholders included. Should an evaluation of legitimacy include legitimacy among consumers, producers, retailers, biodiversity activists, climate campaigners, unemployed local poor, forest-dwelling tribes, or only some of these; and how can one resolve possible tradeoffs between accountability and legitimacy claims of different groups of potential stakeholders? One example is the controversies on how to design new climate governance arrangements that focus on the preservation of forests, in the form of reduced emissions from deforestation and forest degradation (REDD) initiatives (J. Gupta, van der Grijp, and Kuik 2013; A. Gupta, Lövbrand, et al. 2012). The protection of forests may require one set of policies and measures if the forests are considered only as carbon sinks, and another set if biodiversity protection is also considered a policy goal. The first would merely require increasing timber stocks (this could be achieved through plantations); the second would require qualitative measures to maintain the ecological integrity of a forest (plantations might be destructive to this goal). Furthermore, the beneficiaries of REDD initiatives would vary substantially under these two scenarios, ensuring that analyses of the legitimacy and accountability (and effectiveness) of evolving REDD governance arrangements will turn on whether and which functional interdependencies are acknowledged in their design and execution (A. Gupta, Lövbrand, et al. 2012; Rosendal and Andresen 2011; Lederer 2011). Functional interdependence in earth system governance ensures that complex questions of internal and external accountability and legitimacy come persistently to the fore and require innovative governance solutions.

Earth system transformation also creates new types and degrees of spatial interdependence. This interdependence is at times systemic (when noncompliance of a few countries can nullify the actions of all others, as in the case of stratospheric ozone depletion) and at times cumulative (when the accumulation of local harm creates problems of global impact, as in the case of desertification). In both cases, spatial interdependence poses particular accountability and legitimacy challenges.

The accountability of governance is particularly affected by the geographic distance between principals and agents, between those who seek to hold others accountable and those who are held accountable. Traditional systems of electoral accountability and legitimacy are limited to areas of national jurisdiction, while the effects of environmentally harmful behavior reach beyond national borders. However, those who are affected by transnational pollution have hardly any rights to hold polluters accountable (also Mason 2008a). International law might provide some means of redress, yet the political relevance of legal norms, such as the responsibility of states to ensure that activities within their jurisdiction or control do not cause damage to the environment of other states, is in all likelihood low. In the case of climate change, for example, it is difficult for countries that emit small amounts of greenhouse gases in proportion to their population to hold countries with much higher per capita emissions accountable for the excessive pollution of the atmosphere. Given the elements of accountability outlined above—normative, relational, and behavioral—one could posit that current earth system governance does not allow for establishing accountability relationships between countries with respect to global pollution, since neither agreement on the appropriate standard of behavior nor effective sanctioning mechanisms are discernible (see also the previous discussion in chapter 4).

Spatial interdependence also affects accountability relationships in transnational nonstate governance systems (Newell 2008). Here, the citizen as final instance of decision-making power in national political systems is being replaced by the social construct of the stakeholder. Transnational labeling schemes that prescribe behavioral standards for firms are meant to be accountable to stakeholders in this policy area, who can sanction noncompliance through consumer boycotts and general reputational damage to noncomplying companies. However, the stakeholder is difficult to define and subject to power conflicts among affected communities. Systems of inclusion and exclusion become vital in constructing the stakeholders within a governance system that may have the right to hold actors accountable to agreed standards of behavior. Actors that are not seen as stakeholders do not have the right to participate in decision making or to hold others accountable. If legitimacy comes from the consent of the governed, who then is the governed here?

This question is also of central relevance in analyzing deliberative democratic decision making in a global context (Dryzek and Stevenson 2011). Spatial interdependence becomes particularly crucial in the relations between North and South, whereby actors in the North might explicitly (in transnational organizations) or implicitly (by consumer decisions) assume a governing role over actors from the South who are less, or not directly, represented in decision making. Also the development of global administrative law—hailed as progress by many actors in the North—can be seen as problematic from the perspective of developing countries, which might be negatively affected by the globalization of legal standards that have been developed in, and benefit mainly, the richer countries in the North (Spagnuolo 2011).

However, questions of who represents whose interests transcend the dichotomous North-South relationship that has long been a mainstay of international environmental politics. Instead, earth system governance is also marked by conflicts of interest between developing countries themselves, between those that experience high growth rates and rapid industrialization and those still plagued by persistent poverty and lack of economic growth. One consequence of this is the need to accept increasing global diversity in perspectives and interests, and hence the need for innovative, novel governance systems that can legitimately manage and integrate such diversity in global norm-setting and deliberative processes (Spagnuolo 2011; Baber and Bartlett 2009).

Earth system governance has to contend also with the tremendous consequences that governance failure might bring. In particular the current stalemate in international climate negotiations has given rise to an increasingly alarmist discourse about the need to prepare for a global warming that exceeds 2 degrees Celsius above preindustrial levels (see chapter 7, on "Adaptiveness"). Part of this discourse is a renaissance of authoritarian claims, implicit in emerging concepts of global emergency governance along the lines more often evident in national decision making in times of war, civil unrest, or natural disasters. The potentially extreme effects of earth system transformation bring numerous crucial yet unexplored governance dilemmas. These include dilemmas that pit the adaptability of institutions to quickly emerging crises against long-term institutional stability and credibility, and tradeoffs between effectiveness and legitimacy and between governance effectiveness and fairness (see chapter 7). Resolving these dilemmas may require new and strengthened institutions at the global level. Ensuring the legitimacy and accountability of these institutions is then one of the most fundamental challenges.

Finally, higher degrees of accountability and legitimacy in earth system governance might enhance not only the democratic potential but also the actual performance of earth system governance. A general assumption in the literature is that governance can be expected to be more effective when its rules and representatives are seen as accountable and legitimate. Many governance mechanisms and arrangements—including in the realm of private and public-private cooperation—have thus sought to establish accountability systems and thereby to enhance legitimacy of governance rules and institutions in a variety of ways. In so doing, one key concern has been to understand potential tradeoffs between requirements of (environmental) effectiveness and high standards of accountability and legitimacy (Kalfagianni and Pattberg 2013c).

For example, numerous governance arrangements have attempted to include different stakeholders from civil society, ranging from direct, network-oriented collaboration, as in the transnational partnerships that are registered under the United Nations Commission on Sustainable Development; to the formalized decision-making system under other transnational governance arrangements (see chapter 3).

An important insight from the study of such governance mechanisms is the importance of inclusiveness in securing accountability and legitimacy. Inclusion of actors in decision making and norm setting can increase, for example, their sense of ownership of the outcomes, and hence compliance. The quality of the rules might increase since more voices have been included in decision making. Inclusiveness also gives the involved actors more information about the processes, hence increasing transparency (Mitchell 2011). However, there is also a large variation in the extent to which different stakeholder groups are included (see chapter 3). Many partnerships that seek to provide safe and sufficient water to communities, for example, often merely reproduce the traditionally dominant role of international organizations, governments, and multinational corporations in global rule making, with little involvement of traditionally underrepresented communities, contrary to claims made by proponents of such partnerships (Dellas 2011).

Overall, one of the key challenges for accountability and legitimacy in earth system governance is the need to ensure and possibly increase the representation and inclusion of citizens and local perspectives in global decision making. At present, multilateral decision making is driven by the central bureaucracies of states. In traditional intergovernmental rule making, legitimacy is based indirectly on the accountability of these government representatives to voters. While heads of government, diplomats, and ministerial bureaucrats thus generally remain accountable to their domestic constituencies within their national political systems, the influence of minority positions within their countries is often weak. In particular, environmentalist views, the interests of future generations, and the interests of less powerful countries are often marginalized in such processes. Such long lines of accountability have therefore been questioned in a series of studies (for example, Archibugi and Held 1995; Archibugi, Held, and Köhler 1998; Bodansky 1999 and 2007; Commission on Global Governance 1995; Dingwerth 2005; Dryzek 1999; Held 1995, 1997, and 1999; Scholte 2002; South Centre 1996). Jan Aart Scholte, for example, argues that

a notional accountability chain does connect voters via national parliaments and national governments to global governance organizations, but the links have in practice been very weak. National political parties have rarely addressed global governance issues with any prominence in election manifestos and debates. A few exceptions aside, national parliaments have exercised only occasional and mild if any oversight over most suprastate regulatory bodies. (Scholte 2004, 211)

Although civil society organizations can observe, and sometimes issue statements at, international negotiations, the most important political processes still normally exclude nonstate representatives. And as shown above, transnational governance systems outside traditional intergovernmental politics also lack legitimacy with certain constituencies. In particular, they might overrepresent Northern interests and disempower actors from the South (Spagnuolo 2011). This lack of involvement of civil society, potential imbalances in the discursive power of different perspectives from North and South, and the disproportionate influence of national bureaucracies in global rule setting are problematic. I will address this issue in the next section.

Toward Reform

As I have argued, earth system transformation poses particular challenges for the accountability and legitimacy of governance, especially regarding traditional multilateral decision making. Effective earth system governance requires that its rules and procedures be accountable and legitimate to a large variety of actors from the local to the global. Globally, accountability and legitimacy are particularly problematic with a view to the North-South divide. Both North and South, rich and poor, must accept the rules and norms of earth system governance as legitimate and see their representatives as accountable. What kinds of systems can generate such a balance of interests and perspectives to ensure a high degree of global legitimacy?

One way to secure the accountability and legitimacy of global earth system governance is to give primacy to multilateral decision making over alternative approaches, such as reliance on unilateral policymaking by a few powerful countries or decisions by the Group of 20 major economies that exclude the other 150 countries. For multilateralism to be effective, however, modes of decision making in international negotiations need to be fundamentally reformed and must allow for decisions by qualified majority that also account for countries' differences in population size or economic relevance. I have elaborated on this strategy in chapter 4 above.

Such qualified majority voting in international institutions, as outlined in chapter 4, benefits mainly governments, even though in the end the underpinning rationale is increasing the representation of the citizens of the (much) larger countries, which are structurally underrepresented in the traditional one-country-one-vote system.

It is equally important, however, to devise governance reforms that directly give a stronger role to citizens and civil society organizations in global governance. One approach is to more effectively include civil society representatives in national delegations to multilateral institutions and conferences. This increases the input of civil society in forming policy within negotiation teams and domestic foreign policy networks, although it might also lead to the cooptation of civil society in certain cases. In any case, governments remain in control of the overall position of their country in global decision making, and it is up to governments to decide which civil society representatives they will involve (Schroeder, Boykoff, and Spiers 2012).

An alternative approach is the establishment, and empowerment, of separate decision-making or consultative organs in international institutions and organizations, such as civil society chambers, parliamentary assemblies, or deliberative assemblies. Each of these three approaches has found a large number of supporters in recent years, who are largely affiliated with theories of liberal institutionalism, cosmopolitanism, or deliberative democracy.

Civil Society Assemblies

One option to increase the participation of citizens is the stronger representation of civil society organizations in multilateral institutions and intergovernmental organizations.

A long-standing example of such formalized empowerment of civil society organizations is the unique representation of labor unions and employers' associations in the International Labor Organization (ILO). One could see this as a first option for achieving a balance in the participation of private actors from North and South in order to make earth system governance more accountable and legitimate (also Charnovitz 2005). In the ILO, each state is represented with four votes, two of which are assigned to governments and one each to business associations and labor unions. The ILO procedure, if adopted for intergovernmental environmental institutions, would attend to the basic problem of civil society participation in global environmental governance—namely that environmental groups cannot adequately compete with the financial power of business associations, and developing country organizations often cannot compete with the financially well-endowed organizations of industrialized countries. An ILO-type structure would grant business interests and environmental interests equal rights, and would guarantee that Southern nongovernmental organizations would have a stronger influence. However, a straightforward adoption of the ILO formula for earth system governance may be difficult, given the higher degree of complexity of earth system governance compared to the ILO's more clear-cut "business versus labor" conflicts. Also, the ILO follows the traditional one-country-one-vote approach. Union and employer representatives from Monaco or the Maldives have thus formally the same voting power as their colleagues from the United States or India.

An alternative is separate decision-making bodies for civil society representatives in international institutions. One concrete proposal has been advanced by the Commission on Global Governance, which argued for an international Forum of Civil Society within the United Nations. This forum would comprise 300–600 "organs of global civil society," to be self-selected from civil society. The Forum could convene annually before the meeting of the UN General Assembly and try to develop consensus statements on key items of the Assembly's agenda (Commission on Global Governance 1995, 258).

A regional experience is the European Economic and Social Committee, which is a consultative body of the European Union established in 1957. This committee has 353 members, drawn from three major constituencies: employers, employees, and other interest groups (including environmental groups), selected from all European Union member states roughly according to population size. The European Economic and Social Committee must be consulted for a variety of EU legislative processes, including environmental policy, and can also voice its opinion on its own initiative. Even though the actual influence of the committee is open to debate, it allows for more civil society input than traditional governance systems at the global level and could even be seen as a form of "deliberative democracy via a functional assembly" (Smismans 2000).

Separate chambers for civil society representatives could also be established in international institutions for earth system governance, especially for any new bodies, as proposed in chapters 3 and 4 above: the World Environment Organization, the high-level UN Sustainable Development Council, and the UN Trusteeship Council for Areas beyond National Jurisdiction. The governing bodies of these new institutions could provide for a special chamber for representatives of civil society, which could have clearly defined consultative rights. The representatives in these special chambers would be chosen by special caucuses of a wide array of organizations, taking into account, importantly, regional balance and geographic representativeness.

Regional balance is highly important, given that representation of civil society organizations from developing countries in UN settings still remains lower than that of their richer and better-organized counterparts from industrialized countries (see also Kaasa 2007, 115–116). For this reason, networks of civil society organizations often seek to balance views and interests through self-regulation, and also by including financial support for representatives from developing countries. In some organizations, civil society has been formally divided into "Northern" and "Southern" constituencies, loosely following the traditional country groupings of the UN system. North-South quotas are common, for instance, in meetings and alliances of nonstate activists affiliated with the UN Commission on Sustainable Development. Also the IPCC, as a form of governance by nonstate actors, is an example of increased participation of developing countries and nonstate actors from the South (Biermann 2002b; see also chapter 3). North-South quotas are also part of the decision making of the Forest Stewardship Council (Pattberg 2005a and 2006; Gulbrandsen 2010), although conspicuously missing in other initiatives, for example the Roundtable on Sustainable Palm Oil (Schouten and Glasbergen 2011). Simple North-South quotas, however, are only proxies for a more balanced representation of the world's citizens, given that the vast majority of people lives in the South. Such North-South quotas, therefore, in effect institutionalize affirmative action for citizens of the North, who gain a larger influence than they would have if other indicators, such as population sizes, were used as a basis for balancing. The European Economic and Social Committee is an example of a consultative forum of civil society organizations that goes beyond the one-country-one-vote system and beyond simple quotas for country groupings, by loosely linking the selection of representatives to the population size of European countries. The representatives thus selected do not represent their countries but rather a societal interest, from farming to industry, labor, or environment. At the global level, this would imply that more representatives of civil society would be selected from countries such as Brazil, India, Indonesia, or the United States.

As for the interests to be represented by civil society organizations, these could include, for example, a revised form of the nine current "major groups" in UN sustainable development politics. These groupings have emerged since the 1992 UN Conference on Environment and Development in Rio de Janeiro, when traditional concepts such as "nongovernmental organizations" became less relevant in presenting common positions of civil society, and when traditional UN approaches—such as different categories of nongovernmental organizations based on their scope of interest—proved increasingly irrelevant. Nine "major groups" have been named in Agenda 21 as core elements of civil society and include women, children and youth, indigenous people, nongovernmental organizations, local authorities, workers and trade unions, business and industry, scientific and technological communities, and farmers. The "major group" concept has been criticized regarding both its rather spontaneous origin around 1992 and its current interpretation (Mert 2009 and 2014). While farmers are represented, for instance, fishers are not; while indigenous people are included, urban poor are not; while youth are represented, the elderly are not; and so on. Comparable mechanisms have emerged under multilateral environmental agreements, for example in the form of different "constituencies" of civil society recognized under the climate convention (Schroeder and Lovell 2012).

Many private governance mechanisms have meanwhile invented other ways of further defining interest representation in earth system governance, ways that can also serve as models for civil society representation in international institutions. In the Forest Stewardship Council and the Marine Stewardship Council, for example, stakeholders such as business or environmentalist groups have been organized into separate voting chambers (Kalfagianni and Pattberg 2013b). The Forest Stewardship Council has three chambers, for environmental, social, and economic interests, further subdivided in Northern and Southern chambers (Pattberg 2006; Dingwerth 2008; Gulbrandsen 2010). The Roundtable on Sustainable Palm Oil recognizes seven constituencies in its decision making: oil palm growers; palm oil processors or traders; consumer goods manufacturers; retailers; banks and investors; environmental advocacy organizations; and social and development advocacy organizations (Schouten and Glasbergen 2011). In health governance, the representation of civil society is also becoming more common. Public-private partnerships in the area of health give various rights to nongovernmental groups in their boards, including the right to vote (Abbott and Gartner 2011). The Joint UN Programme on HIV and AIDS (UNAIDS) is the first UN-related initiative that allows for formal civil society representation, by including delegates of five nongovernmental organizations in its program coordinating board and with the added requirement that delegations should include people living with HIV. However, these civil society representatives have only nonvoting status.

Despite the general attractiveness of the idea of special chambers for civil society representatives in multilateral institutions, there remain numerous problems with this proposal. To start with, the accountability of civil society representatives is in itself problematic. As Jan Aart Scholte concludes with regard to accountability,

most civil society groups have operated very limited and unimaginative accountability mechanisms in relation to their own activities. At best, the organizations have tended to have no more than loose oversight by a board (often composed largely of friends, who are in some cases paid), periodic elections of officers (with low rates of participation and sometimes dubious procedures), ... minimalist reports of activities (that few people read) and summary financial records (which often conceal as much as they reveal). ... [I]n civil society just as much as in governance and market circles ... formal accountability may fall well short of effective accountability. Worse still, some civil society players in global politics have not met even minimal standards of accountability. (Scholte 2004, 230–231)

What are needed, in this situation, are clear standards that vouchsafe effective minimal accountability mechanisms and prevent a flood of loud but dubious MONGOs (My Own NGOs), BRINGOs (Briefcase NGOs), and "come-and-gos." Despite such negative examples, however, it is still conceivable to construct improved accountability mechanisms for civil society organizations at the global level. Several civil society networks, such as the stewardship councils on forests and oceans, can serve as examples of relatively strong accountability mechanisms.

The legitimacy of civil society organizations is also problematic. In the domestic context, civil society organizations may derive legitimacy from their members or donors—even though members and donors often have no formal means to decide the policies of the organization. They can also gain legitimacy from effectively protecting environmental goods. In the Philippines, for example, nongovernmental groups have successfully claimed in court to derive legitimacy and *locus standi* by representing the interests of future generations. In the international context, however, with its high disparities in wealth and power, ensuring the legitimacy of private actors and their governance arrangements is more complicated. Most larger civil society organizations are headquartered in industrialized countries, and most funds donated to civil society causes stem from the North, both public and private. For example, given the size of its donations, even the Netherlands has been granted a permanent seat in the governing body of the World Wildlife Fund, together with a number of other major donor countries (Dombrowski 2013). It is possible that this imbalance indirectly influences the agenda of these groups, such that they are more accountable to Northern audiences (Dombrowski 2013; South Centre 1996). Yet as outlined above, there are a variety of institutional mechanisms available—such as regional quotas or a stronger selection of representatives from the more populous countries—that could correct some effects of these imbalances.

In sum, the parallel development of increasing reliance on global decision making and decreasing legitimacy of such global institutions creates a need to explore options for better civil society representation within them. This leads to the practical challenge of designing institutions that guarantee participation of civil society in earth system governance through mechanisms that ensure a balance of opinions and perspectives. Clear principles and decision-making rules that draw on fair geographical representation are thus crucial to ensure the legitimacy of civil society inclusion.

At present, almost all countries—with the possible exception of those in Europe—are unlikely to accept voting rights for nonstate actors (regardless of the precedent of the ILO, where unions and employer organizations can vote). It would be possible, however, to restrict the voting rights of civil society organizations, for instance by reserving agenda items of highest importance—including agreement on new legally binding rules—for a vote of governmental representatives only. For civil society, formal participation in deliberations as well as the stronger right to be heard and to table contending opinions, within the framework of a special chamber in bodies such as a UN Sustainable Development Council or the assembly of a World Environment Organization, would already be an important gain that could increase the legitimacy and accountability of intergovernmental decision making. Such reforms would help bring global decision making more in line with the political realities of the twenty-first century.

International Parliamentary Assemblies

A radically different approach is to create a United Nations parliamentary assembly of representatives of national parliaments, convening on a regular basis at the seat of the United Nations, possibly in the form of a second chamber of the United Nations to complement the chamber of government representatives (Commission on Global Governance 1995, 257; Falk and Strauss 2001; Bummel 2010; Heinrich 2010; see also the Campaign for a United Nations Parliamentary Assembly, http://en.unpacampaign.org). Such proposals are usually affiliated with theories of liberal institutionalism, cosmopolitanism, or, in their more radical versions, world federalism.

A parliamentary assembly would be elected most likely through the national parliaments, either from within their own ranks or from outside. Direct elections to a world parliamentary assembly, along the lines of elections to the European Parliament, are hardly conceivable at present. A parliamentary assembly would not need to have decision-making power but could be restricted to a consultative role. Even then, the double identity of the parliamentarians—for example as members of their national parliaments and of the world parliament—could guarantee some feedback across scales of negotiations and decision making.

Given the basic idea of formal representation of domestic interests at the global level, issues of the selection of representatives, their voting rights, and their rights of cross-national affiliation become important questions to be resolved in operationalizing such proposals. As for voting rights, a departure from the one-country-one-vote system toward a stronger recognition of larger, more populous countries is inevitable. The most radical version would assign seats by population, granting a large share of the seats to members of the parliaments of India, United States, Brazil, and Indonesia, along with representatives of the National People's Congress in China. Such equal representation of citizens might not, however, be acceptable to smaller countries, requiring adjustments that protect the interests of less populous countries (see on various models Bummel 2010; Schwartzberg 2012; and my discussion in chapter 4 on qualified majority voting). Parliamentary chambers could be included also in specialized institutions of earth system governance, for example potential new bodies such as a World Environment Organization (also Heinrich 2010, 30), a UN Sustainable Development Council, and a Trusteeship Council for Areas beyond National Jurisdiction (as proposed in chapters 3 and 4 above).

The support for a world parliamentary assembly is growing. It includes, as of October 2013, positive motions by the Canadian House of Commons Foreign Affairs Committee, the Pan-African Parliament, the Latin American Parliament, the Senate of Argentina, the Parliamentary Assembly of the Council of Europe, the European Parliament, the Parliament of Mercosur, and the East African Legislative Assembly, along with support by 372 nongovernmental organizations from 70 countries and the individual support of 862 members of parliament from 105 countries and hundreds of other individuals from science, journalism, and civil society (see list of endorsements at http://en.unpacampaign.org).

However, resistance from many countries is still strong. Many countries are likely to be veto players, including the United States and China, who might see parliamentary assemblies as a slippery slope towards a more federal global system. Granting only consultative rights to such an assembly might address some of these concerns. Most countries today are at least formally organized as parliamentary democracies, and a stronger consultative voice for national parliamentarians in global governance might eventually gain support from many national parliaments.

Deliberative Global Citizens' Assemblies
A third, again radically different approach to a strengthened involvement of citizens in global institutions of earth system governance is the

establishment of deliberative global citizens' assemblies. As in the other proposals, this could take the form of one separate assembly within the United Nations system or numerous specialized assemblies under distinct institutions, for example under an environmental treaty. There have been numerous experiences with deliberative assemblies, citizen juries, and participatory processes at the national level, from OECD countries to China (Dryzek 2006; Dryzek, Bächtiger, and Milewicz 2011). A global deliberative assembly would not include representatives of particular countries or interests, and would not be based on election. Instead, members of the assembly would be chosen by random selection, hence merely representing their own ideas in a process of deliberation among fellow citizens. In one proposal, an assembly would bring together 1,000 citizens, equaling about one citizen for every six million people. In this model, 200 citizens would come from China (Dryzek, Bächtiger, and Milewicz 2011, 36–37). Random selection of citizens would ensure that members of the traditional elites of political parties, major environmental organizations, or governments would be largely excluded. According to proponents of deliberative democracy, differentials in education, experiences, age, or language would not be a problem but rather would increase the authenticity of the deliberation—by bringing together, say, Indian farmers, Brazilian migrant workers, and Canadian suburbanites in one global citizens' assembly (with the support of facilitators and translators). Such assemblies could focus on questions of particular saliency and complexity in the intergovernmental policy process. Dryzek, Bächtiger, and Milewicz (2011, 35) suggest climate change as a particularly prominent issue to be tackled by a deliberative global citizens' assembly.

A related idea—advanced by Baber and Bartlett (2009 and 2013)—is to create not an assembly but a global deliberative process that would generate global norms for earth system governance based on deliberations of numerous citizen juries all over the world. If implemented properly, such a series of citizen juries could well help ascertain globally acceptable norms in contested areas of earth system governance. To become effective international law, these norms would eventually need to be affirmed and implemented by governments and other governance institutions. Even if the global network of citizen juries did not result in binding law, its normative force, if grounded in sufficient numbers of professionally run citizen juries, could be substantial (see Baber and Bartlett 2009 and 2013). Here too, fair representation of different interests across the globe remains a problem. For example, so far most citizen juries of this kind have been organized in industrialized countries, thus overrepresenting the views of Northern citizens. Yet even here, different normative views among Northern countries have been identified, for example different views of a proposed right to food by citizens in the United States and in Italy.

One further radical alternative would be a stronger reliance on the Internet and social media, enabling millions of people to participate in a global deliberative process. However, the potential for global e-democracy is severely hampered by the digital divide between rich and poor. In 2013, 61 percent of all people did not use the Internet, including 84 percent of Africans and 68 percent of people in the Asia/Pacific region. In comparison, only 25 percent of Europeans had no Internet access in 2013 (ITU 2013). While this strong divide in Internet accessibility among regions could technically be corrected in global surveys through stronger weights given to voices from less accessible regions, a global deliberation through social media is still likely to be fraught by strong biases in favor of the better-connected global middle class in both North and South.

Conclusion

Taken together, developing systems to ensure the accountability, legitimacy, and democratic quality of earth system governance remains one of the central political challenges and reform tasks of our time. The Anthropocene poses particular challenges for the accountability and legitimacy of decision making, requiring unique and innovative analytical approaches and political strategies. There is also substantial variation in existing governance arrangements and innovations in terms of their legitimacy, accountability relationships, and democratic quality. The analytical problem of understanding earth system governance in terms of accountability and legitimacy thus needs to be accompanied by research on concrete options for political reform.

In this chapter, I have thus outlined ways in which earth system governance could be made more legitimate and accountable through a more institutionalized involvement of citizens in intergovernmental decision making. I have sketched essentially three avenues for greater citizens' participation in international decision making: through special chambers of civil society, through a parliamentary assembly, or through a global deliberative citizens' assembly.

All three proposals can serve as a blueprint for either a general high-level body within the UN system, such as a second (consultative) chamber in addition to the UN General Assembly, or issue-specific special assemblies within distinct institutions and agencies of earth system governance. A parliamentary assembly, for example, could be part of the governance structure of a World Environment Organization or could be a subsidiary body of the conference of the parties to a multilateral environmental agreement, such as the climate convention, potentially helping to break deadlocks in intergovernmental negotiations. At present, any new assembly is likely to be restricted to a consultative role, possibly linked with the right to expect a particular treatment or recognition of the advice within intergovernmental decision making.

All three proposals raise the important consideration of political feasibility, especially when it comes to getting the support of larger countries. The Chinese government, for example, might feel less threatened by a deliberative citizens' assembly than by a global parliamentary assembly of elected representatives, while countries with strong national parliaments might feel more attracted by a consultative parliamentary chamber or assembly, for example under the climate convention. The strongest political support, so far, seems to be for the campaign to establish a United Nations Parliamentary Assembly, which has received the endorsement of numerous politicians and national and intergovernmental organizations, as well as over 300 academics including Richard Falk, Peter Haas, David Held, Thomas Pogge, Saskia Sassen, and Michael Zürn (see http://en.unpacampaign.org). However, as pointed out by critics, support among the mainstream US political community is largely absent, with 51.2 percent of US citizens polled in a 2007 BBC survey clearly objecting to the idea of a global parliament that would be based on country population sizes and have a mandate to take binding decisions (Bummel 2010, 24).

In sum, the political feasibility of such proposals remains an open question, and the proposals themselves are still insufficiently concrete. A key conclusion is hence that the study of the accountability, legitimacy, and democratic quality of earth system governance is still in its infancy, despite all efforts to date. More academic and policy-oriented research is urgently needed. For this reason, the field of earth system governance, with its highly complex and politically divisive issues, could well serve as an important testing ground for further experimentation with institutionalized citizens' involvement in global decision making. Experiences with potentially innovative consultative bodies might not only drive forward key policy processes in earth system governance, but more broadly advance the democratic quality of global governance.

Demetrius

Es ist die große Sache aller Staaten

Und Thronen, daß gescheh, was Rechtens
ist,

Und jedem auf der Welt das Seine werde.

Denn da, wo die Gerechtigkeit regiert,

Da freut sich jeder sicher seines Erbs,

Und über jedem Hause, jedem Thron

Schwebt der Vertrag wie eine
Cherubswache.

Doch wo – – – – – – –

Sich straflos festsetzt in dem fremden Erbe,

Da wankt der Staaten fester Felsengrund.

– – – – – – – Gerechtigkeit

Heißt der kunstreiche Bau des
Weltgewölbes,

Wo alles eines, eines alles hält,

Wo mit dem Einen alles stürzt und fällt.

Demetrius

'Tis the most dear concern of every state

And throne, that right should everywhere
prevail,

And all men in the world possess their
own.

For there, where justice holds uncumbered
sway,

There each enjoys his heritage secure,

And over every house and every throne

The contract keeps its angel watch.

But where – – – – – – –

With impunity the heritage is taken

There shakes the ground of all the states.

– – – – – – – Justice

Is the ingenious keystone of the world's
wide arch,

The one sustaining and sustained by all,

Which, if it fail, brings all in ruin down.

Friedrich Schiller, *Demetrius*, 329–341 (unfinished fragment)

6

Allocation

When astronauts first photographed the earth from the moon and created the powerful imaginary of our "blue planet," their picture suggested a common destiny of the human race with a common interest and purpose. Yet the human species, as main driving force of the Anthropocene, is in itself profoundly divided in wealth, health, living standards, education, and most other indicators that define well-being.

According to the World Bank (2008, 4), the richest 20 percent of humanity accounts for 76.6 percent of world private consumption (purchasing power parity, in US$). The poorest 20 percent, for their part, account for just 1.5 percent. Almost half of humanity—roughly three billion people—lives on less than US$2.5 per day (Chen and Ravallion 2008, 41). The world's 946 richest people—the billionaires—are worth as a group US$3.5 trillion (Kroll and Fass 2007). This alone equals around 5 percent of global wealth and is more than the gross domestic product of India or of the entire African continent. The life of the poorest humans is harsh. 842 million people lack sufficient food. The poorest 25 percent of humanity—including 706 million South Asians and 547 million Africans—still have no access to electricity (UNDP 2007). Earth system governance is concerned about future generations, yet many of today's children do not fare well: about a third of all children in developing countries are underweight. Every day, 29,000 children under the age of five die from largely preventable diseases, amounting to 10.6 million deaths each year. The lives of over one billion children are blighted by poverty (UNICEF 2004, 9–10). Today, one billion people lack sufficient access to water, and 2.6 billion have no basic sanitation (UNDP 2006). To provide water and sanitation for all people would cost about US$9 billion. This is about what people in the United States spend each year on cosmetics. Each year Europeans invest US$11 billion on ice cream, US$50 billion on cigarettes, and US$105 billion on alcoholic drinks (UNDP 1998, 37).

This global inequality has increased even further in the last decades. While in 1960 the richest 20 percent of humanity were thirty times wealthier than the poorest 20 percent, this ratio has increased to 74 times by 1997. If the world were a country, a social revolution would not be surprising. Inequalities have increased within most countries, too. In the United States—admittedly an unusual example among richer countries—80 percent of the total income increase in 1980–2005 went to the top 1 percent of the population (Freeland 2011), who today take home 22 percent of the national income (Stiglitz 2013).

Earth system governance has to operate in this global situation of large inequalities in resources and entitlements. Politics is about the authoritative allocation of resources and values, and earth system governance is no different. Whatever architectures of earth system governance are created or strengthened (see chapter 4), they must take account of the extreme inequality as well as the particular needs of the poorest. The analysis of agency in earth system governance—that is, of those actors who have the authority to set and enforce rules and norms—requires an understanding of the vast social divisions on our planet (see chapter 3). The accountability and legitimacy of earth system governance also needs to be seen in light of global inequalities and persisting widespread poverty (see chapter 5). Finally, given the potentially disastrous consequences of earth system transformation, questions of fairness in adaptation arise as well, including concerns about compensation and support by the global community of the most affected and most vulnerable regions, such as small island states (see chapter 7).

Questions of allocation are, in short, central to the challenges of earth system governance (see also, e.g., Adger, Brown, and Hulme 2005; Biermann, Abbott, et al. 2012; J. Gupta 2005; Newell 2005; Vieira 2012). Modes and mechanisms of allocation are needed that actors in North and South perceive as fair and will support over the long term. What such modes of allocation might be, and the normative rationales underpinning them, stand at the center of this chapter.

The question of fair allocation is an old one in political philosophy, and there are multiple ways of studying the distributive outcomes of earth system governance. To start with, the outcomes of earth system governance can be assessed according to the distribution of costs across different actors—such as countries, municipalities, or individuals—in complying with the obligations of an environmental institution. Earth system governance can also result in different gains for some actors, for example extra profits through efficiency gains or through certain mitigation schemes, such as trading in ecosystem services. Even ineffective governance that does not resolve the underlying environmental problem has allocative effects by harming some actors more than others. The same allocation scheme can involve both costs for some and benefits for others. For example, when local actors decide to regulate river pollution, this decision may allocate environmental or financial costs to the upstream or the downstream country. Moreover, earth system governance can affect the distribution of power and authority and access to natural resources. While allocation in earth system governance hence covers a broad set of issues, my analysis in this chapter focuses on the allocation of the *costs of environmental action through international governance*. Without denying the continued relevance of domestic allocation challenges—including the problem of environmental equity within countries—I focus here on *global* allocation questions, which in this form are unprecedented in world politics and are highly contested.

The allocation of the costs of earth system governance can be studied from both an analytical and a normative perspective. Analytically, distributive outcomes can be conceptualized as the dependent or independent variable. Taking distribution as a dependent variable, one can analyze the distributive outcomes that any particular mechanism of earth system governance might have, and assess how different governance mechanisms have distributive effects among social groups or countries. When distributive outcomes are studied as the independent variable, the focus can be on variant impacts of distributive outcomes on governance effectiveness. For instance, financial and technological support to poorer countries through international transfer mechanisms can improve the overall performance of a multilateral agreement.

From a normative perspective, an analysis of distributive outcomes can be linked instrumentally to broader policy goals. For example, policy prescriptions can suggest certain modes of allocation that promise to increase the environmental effectiveness of a governance system. A normative analysis can also investigate whether certain distributive outcomes can be seen as "fair" under certain normative predispositions and theories of justice.

In this chapter, I focus on this second option in analyzing distributive outcomes. Specifically, I study different types of distributive mechanisms in earth system governance with a view to the fairness of their outcomes, assessed according to competing perspectives in political philosophy. I do so for two reasons.

First, I believe it is of utmost importance to more explicitly relate current academic discourses in earth system governance to normative assumptions and theories of justice. As I laid out in chapter 2, earth system governance is plagued by high degrees of normative uncertainty, given the inherent newness and lack of a shared normative perspective on the core problems of the Anthropocene. For example, what are the appropriate normative principles for determining the required mitigation action of a country, or of an individual? What norms underpin the obligations of countries to assist other countries that are suffering from negative impacts of earth system disruptions? Myriad similar normative questions arise in the context of earth system governance, which are often fundamentally different from questions in other policy domains. While some scholars have begun to explore the normative implications especially of climate change, these issues are still discussed at the margins of academic discourse.

Secondly, negotiating the normative basis of diverse action pathways is of fundamental importance for political practice. For example, the current climate negotiations are to a large extent about the political obligations of countries to reduce their emissions or to transfer funds. While theories of justice will not directly guide political decisions by governments, better-grounded normative theories can help explicate the positions of countries, and possibly foster compromise once shared normative visions emerge.

In this chapter, I seek to contribute to a normative theory of earth system governance by applying two theories of justice to three specific modes of allocation. The theories of justice that I analyze are extremes, with much middle ground possible between them. Yet by focusing on extreme positions in normative theory, I seek to explicate their implications, and possibly to forge common ground.

The first normative perspective favors modes of allocation that preserve entitlements. It views existing wealth distribution as legitimate as long as such wealth has been gained by lawful activities. Redistributions of wealth through governmental action are, from such a perspective, unjust. The function of government needs to be restricted to the protection of life, liberty, and property and to the enforcement of contracts. This perspective has been most forcefully laid out by Robert Nozick (1974), who developed a libertarian theory of justice in response to the work of John Rawls, drawing on earlier philosophers such as John Locke and Friedrich Hayek. In Nozick's view, it is not the outcome per se that matters—for example, whether individuals receive goods in accordance with a certain principle such as need—but rather the process. If the process of acquiring wealth has been lawful and just, then the final distribution of wealth is also just and merits protection by the state.

Redistribution of wealth is hence only possible with the consent of the wealthy (as opposed to forceful redistribution by means of taxation or social levies), since "the state may not use its coercive apparatus for the purpose of getting some citizens to aid others" (Nozick 1974, ix).

In the following, I refer to these propositions as the *libertarian perspective*. I rely here on the modern American use of the term "libertarian," which is often further qualified as right-libertarian or market-libertarian, in contrast to other countries and languages, where such ideas would be labeled "liberal." In the libertarian view, a minimal protection of the environment is still part of a restricted set of state functions, yet this environmental protection must not lead to a redistribution of wealth that has been acquired by lawful means. This holds even more for international environmental policies. To put it drastically, the claims to wealth of the 20 percent of humanity who account today for 76.6 percent of total private consumption (World Bank 2008, 4) should not be negatively affected, to the extent that this wealth has been acquired in accordance with rightful procedures, such as the workings of the international market economy. Or, as famously argued by US President George H. W. Bush in 1992 at the first Rio conference, "The American way of life is not up for negotiation. Period."

A radically competing tradition in political philosophy is egalitarian cosmopolitanism. Its basic tenet is that theories of justice must not stop at historically contingent national borders but must take the entirety of humankind into consideration (for instance, Beitz 1979; Caney 2001 and 2006). Such a perspective argues that Rawlsian principles of justice are applicable also at the global level, and that they should not be restricted to domestic situations. This differs from the position of John Rawls himself, who had maintained that his ideas should be differentially applied in domestic and global contexts (Rawls 1999). In *The Law of Peoples*, Rawls (1999) described a global society of peoples, each individually defined by a common system of government, common sympathies, and a moral nature. In this global society, obligations among peoples would be substantially lower than those among the citizens of a country. Essentially, countries would be expected to support other countries with less favorable conditions only insofar as not doing so prevents them from having a just and decent political and social regime.

Cosmopolitan thinkers such as Beitz (1979) and Caney (2006), however, contest this differentiation between domestic and international justice, and seek to apply Rawlsian principles to the global level as well, notably the principle that social and economic inequalities are to be arranged so that they are both to the greatest benefit of the least-advantaged members of society (difference principle, see Rawls 1971, 83). In the words of Beitz (1975), "it seems that there is a threshold of interdependence above which distributive requirements such as a global difference principle are valid." In cosmopolitan political theorizing, current modes of (unequal) allocation can thus be open to revision, with the aim of promoting improvement in the living conditions of the poor. In particular, international mechanisms would need to advance the economic interests of the poorest 20 percent of humanity who account for merely 1.5 percent of global private consumption and who lack sufficient access to water, basic sanitation, and education. In what follows, I characterize this perspective as *egalitarian*.

Assessment

I next assess three modes of allocation in earth system governance from these conflicting perspectives: direct allocation through international agreement, notably through international funds; allocation through markets created under international agreements, such as emissions trading; and allocation through environmentally motivated restrictions of global trade and investment. These modes of allocation are the three central mechanisms that are at present used within earth system governance.

Direct Allocation through International Agreement

The principal approach to managing transboundary environmental problems has been the negotiation of an intergovernmental agreement. Such agreements do not necessarily imply any international allocation of costs. In the most traditional approach, all countries bear their own costs in complying with international environmental norms. This is typical for most early environmental agreements, for instance in the areas of marine pollution or species protection.

Since the early 1970s, however, governments have agreed on the establishment of modest international funds to support the implementation of environmental policies in poorer developing countries. These public funds are governed by the community of states. For instance, developing countries are supported by a small fund under the World Heritage Convention for their implementation of this agreement. This World Heritage Fund is financed through compulsory contributions by countries and additional voluntary contributions. Other sources of income include profits derived from sales of World Heritage publications, or trust funds that countries donate for specific purposes. UNEP manages several similar funds that draw on voluntary, often earmarked contributions by governments for specific purposes (Bauer 2009b). However, most of these funds are rather small and contingent on the goodwill of donor countries. The World Heritage Fund, for example, has a mere US$4 million per year to support developing countries in implementing the agreement.

This situation is now changing quite fundamentally. One path-breaking new institution in the 1990s was the Multilateral Fund for the Implementation of the Montreal Protocol on Substances that Deplete the Ozone Layer. This fund was established to compensate "all agreed incremental costs" that developing countries incur in phasing out the production and consumption of ozone-depleting substances. Eligible projects include the conversion of fire-extinguisher plants or cooling installations in developing countries. In such projects, industrialized countries pay the extra conversion costs that have no direct benefit to developing countries but only benefit the global environment. Industrialized countries must contribute to the fund according to the UN scale of contributions (Biermann 1997; Zhao 2005). Between 1991 and July 2013, 45 donor countries contributed US$3.1 billion to this fund (updates at www .multilateralfund.org). This has financed about 7,000 projects and activities in 145 developing countries. Overall, 450,524 tons of ozone-depleting substances have been phased out in the South in the last twenty years.

A similar funding mechanism is the Global Environment Facility (GEF). The GEF was set up in 1991, much inspired by the multilateral ozone fund, and under the joint management of the World Bank, the UN Environment Programme, and the UN Development Programme (Andler 2009). The Facility serves to compensate developing countries for the costs they incur in implementing the international agreements on climate, biodiversity, and the oceans, and in addressing land degradation and emissions of persistent organic pollutants. The climate convention, for example, obligates Western industrialized countries to provide "new and additional financial resources to meet the agreed full costs incurred by developing countries in complying with their obligations" (UNFCCC 1992, article 4.3). This duty to provide new and additional funding has also been included in the Stockholm Convention on Persistent Organic Pollutants (2001; see article 13.2) and the Convention on Biological Diversity (1992; see article 20.2). In total, the GEF has allocated US$9.2 billion, along with over US$40 billion in cofinancing, for more than

2,700 projects in over 165 developing countries and countries with economies in transition (www.thegef.org). The focus of the GEF is on global environmental problems, and thus excludes environmental policies with mainly local benefit. Also, both environmentalists and Southern governmental representatives regularly complain that the financial support through Northern governments remains insufficient. On the other hand, industrialized countries have transferred, over a period of twenty years, about US$12 billion through the GEF and the ozone fund to developing countries to help them implement international environmental policies.

Institutionally, both the GEF and the ozone fund are based on international legal agreement and guarantee developing countries a degree of control over the conditions of funding and modes of execution. Funding decisions are taken by double-weighted majority, that is, the majority of industrialized countries and the majority of developing countries have to agree. This rather equal decision-making approach is unprecedented for the governance of a North-South funding institution. Developing countries had requested such voting systems in the 1970s for the World Bank and the IMF, with no success (Biermann 1998). In earth system governance, they could successfully press through their demand for a balanced voting mechanism that requires full consent of both donors and recipients about the distribution of the funds. This might indicate the increased bargaining power of developing countries in this policy domain, because action by both North and South is essential to address global environmental problems.

Public control and intergovernmental agreement are guiding principles also for a few additional international transfer mechanisms that are now emerging. For example, there are several funds under the climate regime to assist developing countries implement their climate policies. First, an Adaptation Fund under the 1997 Kyoto Protocol is financed through a 2 percent levy on transactions under the protocol's Clean Development Mechanism to assist developing countries that are particularly vulnerable to the adverse effects of climate change in meeting the costs of adaptation. So far, the fund has dedicated US$190 million to projects in 28 developing countries to increase climate resilience. Second, a Special Climate Change Fund, set up in 2001, finances projects to strengthen a developing country's adaptive capacity, with US$200 million spent so far by the GEF. Third, a Least Developed Countries Fund assists the poorest countries in preparing National Adaptation Programs of Actions. By July 2013, pledges to this fund equaled US$775 million, of which US$627 million had actually been received. Seventy percent of the funding goes to sub-Saharan Africa. Both the Special Climate Change Fund and the Least Developed Countries Fund fall under the climate convention and are largely financed by the governments of industrialized countries (see generally Bouwer and Aerts 2006; Adger et al. 2006).

In 2010, governments decided to set up a new entity, the Green Climate Fund, which was formally launched in 2011 by the conference of the parties to the climate convention (UNFCCC 2011a). The Green Climate Fund is governed by a board of twelve developing and twelve industrialized countries, and intends to make a significant contribution to the implementation of the climate convention in developing countries through promoting a paradigm shift toward low-emission and climate-resilient development pathways in such countries (see also Abbott and Gartner 2011). Funding aims to address both mitigation and adaptation. The Green Climate Fund is not yet fully operational, and its effectiveness, funding levels, and relationship to other public funding mechanisms in this domain remain to be seen (Schalatek 2013).

All these funds share core similarities. All are governed by intergovernmental agreement through committees and boards that consist mainly or exclusively of representatives of states and intergovernmental organizations (for a critical perspective on these funds, see Abbott and Gartner 2011). All are affiliated with intergovernmental organizations, largely from the United Nations system. Almost all financial transfers are from public sources, and most funds are disbursed through the governments of host countries, or at least with their consent. Yet there is also substantial institutional innovation in this mode of international transfers: voting rights have been changed over time, notably through the increase of voting rights for governments from developing countries; sources of funding include levies on certain activities, such as environmental projects; and the role of private actors has grown. The distributive effect of these funding arrangements depends on the amount of funding available in relation to the real costs that are incurred by poorer countries. In some cases, notably the ozone regime, the additional costs incurred by developing countries in participating in earth system governance efforts have been largely reimbursed by the North (Biermann 1997).

Normative assessment: A libertarian perspective would view these funding mechanisms rather critically. First, by their very nature, international funds are set up and managed by governments and international bureaucrats, who decide on the distribution of funds. International funds such as the GEF increase the role of government in earth system governance. Second, all funds are largely replenished through tax income from governments, with most funds coming from the wealthy countries. As such, the funding mechanisms place a disproportionate claim on the lawfully acquired wealth of people in richer countries by transferring this wealth to government-run programs in developing countries. Such funding mechanisms thus run against the core tenets of libertarian philosophy. To the extent that funds are necessary and inevitable—for example because some actors simply have no means to purchase much-needed technologies—libertarians would argue that funding mechanisms should be small, focused on the poorest and most needy countries, and remain under the control of donors.

Egalitarians, conversely, support such funding mechanisms to the extent that they help further the interests of the poorest. The protection of the earth system, as a global collective good, requires a solution that is largely funded by those who are most able to contribute. The funds can also be seen as a compensation for prior injustice, that is, the over-consumption of the natural resources of the planet by a few rich countries. Given the historical responsibility of rich countries and the existing vast inequalities, the principle of the compensation of the "full agreed incremental costs" of developing countries seems legitimate from an egalitarian perspective.

Market-Based Mechanisms under Public Control

Costs of mitigation and adaptation can instead be allocated through market-based mechanisms that are under public control and based on international agreement. In recent years, a number of public regional markets have been developed, including the EU emissions trading scheme (Skjærseth and Wettestad 2008 and 2009; Clò 2009) and regional markets in North America, Australia, and New Zealand (Tuerk et al. 2009; Haites and Mehling 2009; Sterk and Kruger 2009; Jotzo and Betz 2009). A private trading system has evolved around various offsetting schemes that rely on commitments of private or semipublic actors, largely in industrialized countries (Stripple and Lövbrand 2010).

Yet there are only a few examples of public markets that allocate environmental mitigation costs across national borders (except for the special case of Europe). Apart from an early form of joint implementation of commitments among industrialized countries in the ozone regime, only one intergovernmental system at present trades mitigation obligations—the flexible mechanisms under the Kyoto Protocol to the climate convention. The protocol provides for three mechanisms: joint implementation between industrialized countries, emissions trading between industrialized countries, and some modified version of joint implementation in the form of the Clean Development Mechanism (CDM).

The CDM is part of the implementation system for the Kyoto Protocol (Greiner 2009; Lövbrand, Rindefjäll, and Nordqvist 2009). Industrialized countries that have ratified the protocol may include certain emission reductions that have been achieved in developing countries in their own national emissions accounting. Industrialized countries can either initiate environmental projects that reduce emissions in developing countries themselves, or buy CDM credits from projects undertaken by others (Stripple 2010). The rationale behind the CDM is that emission reductions in developing countries are cheaper. Thus, the CDM may help reduce the overall compliance costs of industrialized countries under the protocol. At the same time, developing countries may hope for the transfer of environmental technology, new investments, and various environmental and economic side benefits from CDM projects. Formally, CDM projects must support the sustainable development of their host countries in the South. How this works in practice is to be determined by the host country.

Some evidence seems to indicate that the sustainable development benefits in developing countries are less relevant than the pure economic profits to be reaped from CDM projects (Rindefjäll, Lund, and Stripple 2011). The global distribution of CDM projects is also highly biased in favor of a few, highly active and (financially) attractive countries such as China or India. Sub-Saharan Africa gains less from the CDM (Lederer 2011; Winkler, Davidson, and Mwakasonda 2005, 208–209). Overall, however, it is evident that the CDM has generated a sizeable transfer of funds from North to South to enable developing countries to reduce their greenhouse gas emissions. By 2012, the CDM will have offset about 2.6 gigatons of carbon dioxide, which is three times the emissions of a country like Germany. CDM credits in 2009 were worth US$2.7 billion (Lederer 2011). The overall financial impact of the CDM is hence higher than North-South financial transfers through the Global Environment Facility, which also finances climate protection programs in developing countries.

A similar mechanism to implement the climate convention is known as "reduced emissions from deforestation and forest degradation"

(REDD). REDD is meant to initiate substantial transfers from industrialized countries to tropical forest countries in exchange for strengthened protection of their forests (Corbera and Schroeder 2011; A. Gupta, Lövbrand, et al. 2012). The protection of forests is a major element in a global strategy to limit global warming. The destruction or degradation of forests may account for about 15–20 percent of the greenhouse gas emissions from human activities (IPCC 2007), and past efforts in halting deforestation have been largely unsuccessful. In addition, the protection of tropical forests is an important factor in the global efforts to preserve biological diversity and reduce the current mass extinction of species. Hence, REDD is likely to become a key mechanism in earth system governance. The expectation is that REDD-related transfers will create stronger economic incentives in developing countries to preserve tropical forests instead of clearing them. Tropical forests—at present with limited economic value for many developing countries—would then turn into a much more valuable resource that generates substantial international transfer payments for their protection. The North-South transfers under REDD will be linked to stringent monitoring and verification procedures. Similar to the CDM, REDD projects are also expected to further sustainable development and create incentives for sustainable forest management (for an insightful comparison of the CDM and REDD, see Lederer 2011). Overall, one can expect REDD payments to be substantial. One influential estimate puts the costs of halving deforestation by 2030 through the REDD mechanism at US$17–33 billion per year (Eliasch 2008), which would dwarf existing mechanisms such as the GEF or the CDM. Both the CDM and the REDD mechanisms could at some point become part of a global emissions trading scheme under the climate convention, even though REDD negotiations at present seem to veer more toward a fund-based approach (ENB 2013b).

Public international markets for mitigation costs need not be limited to climate governance. John Whalley and Ben Zissimos, for example, have proposed setting up an international agency that would create global markets for all kinds of environmental goods that could be traded. This agency would provide the organizational, legal, and financial arrangements needed for deals between states and other actors that have an interest in the environmental behavior of others, on the one hand, and those who would receive financial offers in exchange for adopting certain policies. This new international agency would function like a stock exchange, trading offers from developing countries not to use portions of their natural resources with offers of industrialized countries to compensate them for this. This would be akin to emissions trading without the focus on emissions (Whalley and Zissimos 2001).

Normative assessment: How are such mechanisms to be judged based on different normative perspectives? A libertarian perspective would view such market-based mechanisms favorably. The unfettered working of market forces leaves a higher degree of freedom to participants, and reduces the power of governments to allocate scarce resources. However, most egalitarians too would have few concerns with such market mechanisms per se, given that they promise to increase the efficiency of earth system governance and allow, if appropriately designed, for governmental intervention to protect the most vulnerable. The Clean Development Mechanism, as mentioned, requires all projects not only to protect environmental goods but also to advance the sustainable development of the host countries, which is generally understood also as advancing the interest of the poor (on implementation of this requirement see Rindefjäll, Lund, and Stripple 2011).

In the end, however, the distributive effect of intergovernmental market-based mechanisms depends on the initial allocation of mitigation obligations. It is on this crucial element that libertarian and egalitarian perspectives are likely to differ. At present, many international environmental agreements provide for a differentiation of obligations between countries. In the climate regime, for instance, such obligations are based on broader political criteria, such as the exemption of the Group of 77 and China from quantified reduction commitments and the norm differentiation among industrialized countries based on economic costs, bargaining power, and negotiation skills. When the climate regime was established in the 1990s, this procedure was inevitable in order to find sufficient support in the international community for negotiating the climate regime in the first place. Yet it is doubtful whether this willingness-to-pay approach can continue. At some point, generally agreed a priori criteria for the definition of a country's emissions reduction obligation will be required. The question of burden sharing in future climate governance has hence produced a significant amount of academic literature, as well as a number of proposals from governments (see reviews in Biermann, Pattberg, and Zelli 2010). Governments now need to agree in tedious negotiations on new sets of targets and commitments for different countries.

A libertarian view on these negotiations would support two allocation principles: either agreement on commitments that are based on equal relative emissions reductions, so that all countries have to engage in similar efforts, or allocation in relation to the actual consumption and hence wealth of a country, which ensures that an environmental policy does not result in distortions of wealth distribution. Both principles would ensure that all actors have to make roughly similar efforts and shoulder similar burdens with respect to existing wealth and distribution.

Such equal allocation of mitigation commitments has in fact been the traditional approach in environmental policy. It was the original allocation principle in the European regime on long-range transboundary air pollution, in which all countries had to reduce their emissions by 30 percent. In the international ozone regime, all countries were initially meant to have to reduce their emissions by an equal percentage. This approach results in "grandfathering," that is, permitting countries that have higher emissions and thus a higher share in the causation of the collective problem to preserve their higher consumption levels. This approach is libertarian in protecting lawfully acquired wealth and the resulting higher levels of consumption.

In current earth system governance, however, there is vast agreement that some differentiation of obligations is essential. Back in 1992, the climate convention requested industrialized countries "to take the lead" in combating climate change, and most governments accept that poorer developing countries cannot be expected to reduce their already low emissions in the same way as industrialized countries do. Yet what the exact contribution of each country should be remains open to debate.

Assuming this basic need for some form of norm differentiation, it would be important from a libertarian perspective to design the allocation system in a way that prevents a general redistribution of wealth and, through this, an increasing expropriation of lawfully acquired wealth and related legitimate levels of resource consumption. Thus, libertarians would seek to link future emissions reductions commitments, for example in climate governance, to (a combination of) key principles, such as the principle of equal allocation of emissions rights per unit of gross national product (which links environmental policy efforts proportionally to wealth), the principle of protection of "acquired" past emission rights (grandfathering), and the principle of equal energy efficiency (carbon intensity targets). Such interlinked principles would result, if operationalized, in comparably smaller obligations for richer industrialized countries. The sum of these principles could also be seen as the principle of equal cost of environmental policy, since each country will have to reduce emissions in proportion to its overall economic activity.

Egalitarians instead would take as their point of departure the individual person and assume her identical claims to planetary resources, even if this would result in a reallocation of global wealth. In global emission control regimes, such as those that address climate change or stratospheric ozone depletion, this would entail an allocation of emissions rights according to the consumption of harmful substances on a per capita basis. A principle of equal entitlement of all human beings to equal emissions would suggest the allocation of emission rights to countries based on their current population. Further, a principle of historical responsibility would suggest the allocation of current emission rights in negative correlation to the quantity of past emissions, which would favor developing countries. Third, a principle of basic or survival emissions, deriving from egalitarian principles that focus on supporting the least advantaged, would relieve countries from emission reduction obligations below a certain flat-rate basic emission level. Fourth, a principle of economic acceptability within the context of poverty reduction would relieve countries from emission reduction commitments if their economic development was below a certain minimum. While these principles are derived from different overarching claims for justice and fairness, they are related and would, if operationalized, impose lesser obligations on developing countries in proportion to economic development and wealth. If the principle of equal per capita emissions is implemented within a global emissions trading system, it would result in a transnational wealth transfer from industrialized to (some) developing countries.

Underlying this conflict between different principles is the overall conceptualization of the global warming problem, especially whether it is being framed as a global resource (to be allocated) or as an environmental problem (to be resolved). The egalitarian conception comes down to the view that the earth's greenhouse gas absorption capacity constitutes a global resource that is to be allocated based on need (that is, in favor of the poorest) or on the basis of equal per capita entitlements (essentially a human rights claim). This approach has also been taken by the South regarding the allotment of deep seabed mining resources, Antarctica, the geostationary orbit (here linked to quasi-territorial claims), or even "the moon and other celestial bodies" (in the 1979 Agreement Governing the Activities of States on the Moon and Other Celestial Bodies). Underusing one's own quota of resources would then justify a transnational wealth transfer from those who wish to exceed their share.

The libertarian conceptualization, on its part, views the global warming problem instead as a burden to be fairly shared by all countries in a way that allows all countries, rich and poor, to suffer to comparable degrees and as little as possible. Transnational wealth transfer is in such a view unjustified. Böhringer and Helm (2008) for instance argue that developing countries should be fully compensated for their emission abatement efforts, but should not receive any further transfers. Existing entitlements to wealth are to be protected and preserved.

Environmentally Motivated Restrictions on International Trade and Investment

A third mode of allocation in earth system governance works through environmentally motivated restrictions on international trade that force producers and investors in some countries to change their process and production methods according to the environmental standards of their trading partners. In other words, environmentally motivated trade restrictions either reduce the market share of exporting countries or force them to adjust their product designs and production processes. Such consequences are powerful allocating mechanisms within earth system governance. They force smaller countries—that are generally standard takers—to adapt to the rules and standards developed and enforced by larger consumer countries.

Trade restrictions can be either binding, through incorporation into the law of the importing country, or voluntary, for example through labeling programs that allow consumers in importing countries to decide whether they would like to buy a specific imported product (de Boer and Kuik 2004). Binding restrictions on trade must be in accordance with the agreements under the World Trade Organization (WTO), notably the General Agreement on Tariffs and Trade (GATT). This conflict between trade and environment has led to much contestation in the last two decades, with interstate trade disputes on issues as diverse as tuna, shrimps, automobiles, furs, asbestos, or meat of cattle treated with growth hormones. In these and many other cases, some states wanted to ban importation on environmental grounds, while exporting states invoked their right of nondiscrimination in trade granted under the GATT and other WTO agreements. A key area of conflict here is the legitimacy and legality of unilateral action and national decision making as opposed to multilateral decision making, with governments of the large developed (importing) markets in the North, with their strong environmentalist movements, often arrayed against the developing world. This is not the place to review twenty years of intense debate and research on the nexus of trade and environment (see with further references Eckersley 2004a; Charnovitz 2007; Gehring 2011). Instead, I discuss two cases in order to exemplify how the use of environmentally motivated trade restrictions can be analyzed from diverse perspectives of global justice and fairness.

The first example relates to trade restrictions that are based on (environmentally harmful) process and production methods in the exporting country (that is, that have no discernible influence on the quality of the traded product). A landmark decision in this area was the *United States— Import Prohibition of Certain Shrimps and Shrimp Products* adjudication of the WTO Appellate Body of 1998 (WTO Appellate Body 1998; Cone 1999; Howse 1998; Mavroidis 2000). In this case, India, Malaysia, Pakistan, and Thailand complained that the United States had banned import of shrimps caught by their fishers using methods not corresponding to US environmental standards. The United States argued that too many sea turtles were killed by these fishing practices (as accidental catches, since the fishing nets being used hindered sea turtles from escaping). The US trade restrictions did not discriminate between Asian and North American shrimps but only between fishing practices. In other words, the United States banned the import only of those shrimps that had been produced with methods not consistent with US environmental standards. With this, however, the United States targeted environmental assets *beyond its territory*, hence unilaterally assuming a stewardship for global environmental goods. The case thus had wider implications. In its decision, the WTO Appellate Body justified trade restrictions concerning foreign process and production methods and approved trade restrictions that seek to protect exhaustible natural resources outside the jurisdiction of the importing state. The body did not fully endorse the extraterritorial application of the exception clause of GATT, but recognized that in the case in question there was sufficient connection between the United States and the Asian sea turtles, because the species of migrating turtles in question lived in both Asian and US waters and in the high seas (WTO Appellate Body 1998, para. 133). In the end, however, the United States lost the case on the basis of procedural flaws in its legislation (Biermann 2001b; DeSombre and Barkin 2002).

Prima facie, the case relates only to shrimps. Yet if the ruling found wider application, it could well justify unilateral trade restrictions of richer countries regarding the global climate and other core issues of earth system governance. Exporting countries would then be forced to produce their goods in accordance with the environmental production standards of importing countries, even if different process and production methods leave no trace in the product and if the environmental harm does not directly affect the importing country. Production standards would be set unilaterally by importing countries without the exporting countries having a right or opportunity to participate in the elaboration of these standards. Smaller trading nations in the developing world would have to adopt the environmental preferences and standards of larger economies in order to safeguard their export markets, without compensation through the GEF, the Green Climate Fund, or other global funds. In the end, this inflicts additional costs on developing countries.

A second example of the instrumentalization of global commercial relations for allocating costs and benefits in earth system governance concerns conditionalities attached to export credit schemes or development aid, both bilaterally and multilaterally, for instance as World Bank conditionalities. For instance, many industrialized countries subsidize their exports and investments in developing countries by special guarantees. Until the 1990s, these guarantees were largely granted based on an assessment of economic viability. However, in the last two decades environmentalist organizations have begun to pressure governments in industrialized countries to subject these subsidies and guarantees to an assessment of their environmental and social benefits. Projects financed under such conditions are then likely to have to meet higher standards in terms of environmental protection than required by the host government in the South.

A key issue here is who sets the environmental standards. As for development assistance or export credit conditionalities, the applicable standards are in the end decided by governmental agencies in industrialized countries, such as export credit agencies, public investment banks, or overseas development ministries. Nongovernmental organizations often have an influence on these decisions and are consulted. In most cases, however, this includes predominantly civil society representatives from industrialized countries. In some cases, actors from affected developing countries are invited to voice their views, but the selection of these Southern groups, and the weight given to their insights and interests, rests eventually with policymakers in the North. The same holds, at a different level, for most multilateral development banks, such as the World Bank. Decisions are taken by governments, and in most cases governments from industrialized countries hold the majority of votes and shape policy outcomes.

Normative assessment: Unilateral restrictions on trade based on the process and production methods and unilateral conditionalities in export credit schemes follow the same logic: one country develops policy criteria to protect environmental goods, and uses trade and economic exchange relations to press other countries to adopt these standards. Such unilateral policies can help improve earth system governance inasmuch as the environmental standards that are enforced unilaterally are usually higher than the ones that the affected countries would implement otherwise. On the other hand, decisions about the appropriate standard rest with the importing country (in the case of trade) or with the country that grants export finance and development aid.

From a libertarian perspective, this would be a just outcome. Trade restrictions lead to the global adoption of higher environmental standards without the wealth-redistributive effects of either large international funds or a trading system that builds on equal per capita allocation of entitlements. Libertarians would also support the full freedom of choice of the consumer, which she might express either individually (through buying products that are certified for a specific environmental quality) or collectively (through governments that restrict the import of certain products that are produced by methods that are seen as environmentally harmful, as in the shrimp-turtle case). An expansion of such mechanisms would allow rich consumer markets to globalize their own environmental preferences and production methods and to define and shape production standards in poorer countries. There would be no reimbursement of incremental costs for environmental policies in developing countries, and no right of codecision by representatives of developing countries—both of which are viewed negatively by libertarians anyway.

Egalitarians would instead criticize the potential disempowerment of the poor in developing countries, and the disproportionate role for rich consumers in shaping environmental policies across the globe. Allocation through environmental restrictions on global trade in goods or investments also places additional costs on poorer exporting countries. Egalitarians would question as well the legitimacy of unilateral action (see chapter 5), since the standards that are enforced on developing countries through the market do not result from domestic decision making in these countries. The long-standing discussion about conditionalities on World Bank funding for large dams in India and other countries in the South is an example. Despite the critique from industrialized countries and local NGOs, the decision by Indian authorities to dam the river Narmada and other rivers for the generation of electricity and irrigation purposes has been taken in accordance with democratic decision-making procedures at state and union level. One might disagree with this decision, yet it results from a democratic process in line with the country's constitution.

Some suggest, as a solution to such legitimacy concerns, that unilateral trade restrictions would merely serve to implement international agreements. This, too, is problematic, not least because many international environmental standards differentiate between countries according to their economic development. For example, the climate regime does not require developing countries to accept quantitative emission reduction targets. For highly controversial areas, such as large hydropower dams, global agreements are unlikely, or at least extremely difficult. The standards developed by the World Commission on Dams, for example, do not garner unequivocal support from all countries (Dingwerth 2005).

Those who do support them argue that stronger environmental standards are in the interest of taxpayers in countries granting development assistance, export credits, and other types of support. This argument is an example of the libertarian discourse in earth system governance, that is, that consumers are allowed to influence global political processes through their decisions. In the end, this gives pride of place in decision making to rich countries of the North. From an egalitarian perspective, however, unilateral trade restrictions or unilateral conditionalities in export credit schemes, development assistance, and other types of economic exchange between industrialized and developing countries are less preferable than multilateral negotiations and norm setting (see chapter 4).

Toward Reform

Modes of allocation are key to the stability, credibility, and inclusiveness of earth system governance. Ultimately, earth system governance needs to be seen as fair and equitable in order to be effective. As discussed so far, the three main allocation modes in earth system governance represent different allocation logics that are more or less aligned either with libertarian or with egalitarian normative principles.

First, international funding mechanisms—such as the Multilateral Fund for the Implementation of the Montreal Protocol, the Global Environment Facility, or the Green Climate Fund—build on state-based, multilateral decision making. They come closest to domestic modes of allocation: on the revenue side, the contribution to the funds is largely based on the relative wealth of countries; this could be seen as coming close to taxation. Regarding disbursements, the funds are governed by state representatives in a way that grants both developing and developed countries a de facto veto right. The disbursement of the funds largely follows egalitarian principles: the funds often reimburse the full incremental costs of countries incurred in their efforts to reduce environmentally harmful activities or to adapt to the adverse effects of earth system transformation.

Second, public markets for mitigation obligations—or to put it differently, for emission entitlements—also build on state-based, multilateral decision making inasmuch as governments decide on the allocation of mitigation obligations. The market structure is assumed to guarantee an efficient allocation of mitigation costs and may induce technological innovation. The eventual distributive effects of such systems depend on the initial allocation of mitigation obligations and can hence differ from the allocative effects of international funds. In the case of climate governance, for example, the initial allocation of emission entitlements would favor many developing countries if per capita allocation is the agreed norm. Some developing countries might then gain more than the incremental costs of their environmental action. Global emissions markets, however, might also benefit richer countries if allocation follows existing emissions or greenhouse gas intensity. In this case, some developing countries might not get reimbursed for all incremental costs and might fare worse than under alternative allocation principles.

As a third mode of allocation, environmentally motivated restrictions on international trade and investment force producers in exporting countries to adjust their process and production methods according to the environmental standards of importers. This allows governments in richer consumer markets to unilaterally globalize their preferences through trade restrictions, investment standards, or labeling and certification schemes without the consultation and consent of governments and people in exporting countries. Since the power of unilateral standard setting is here directly based on the wealth and consumption potential of importing countries, environmentally motivated restrictions on trade and investment broadly follow a libertarian logic.

Which normative perspective is preferable? This is not the place to engage in a metadebate on the respective merits of libertarian and egalitarian political philosophies and theories of justice. The essential arguments have been exchanged in the fundamental works in this literature, such as Rawls (1971 and 1999), Nozick (1974), or Beitz (1979). My more limited ambition in this section is to understand the relative value of libertarian and egalitarian perspectives in light of the principles of earth system governance developed in chapter 2 and the empirical findings and discussions in chapters 3–5, and to turn this into policy-relevant conclusions.

Primacy of Multilateralism

To start with, one core argument of my analysis of earth system governance is the primacy of multilateralism over unilateral approaches (see chapter 4). This holds for the allocation of costs and benefits of earth system governance as well. When earth system challenges require major adjustments of national policies in multiple sectors, only multilateral agreement will ensure long-term stability, legitimacy, and effectiveness of earth system governance. Stability is required to deal with questions of normative and analytical uncertainty and the risks of unpredictable extreme events. Consequently, an earth system governance architecture needs to be based on widely accepted constitutional principles and norms. This is in line with scholarly writings in international relations that emphasize that the political behavior of states is not merely guided by calculations of material interest and power but by international norms that prescribe and prohibit types of behavior and hence help to create an international society that "socializes" states (Finnemore 1993; Barnett and Finnemore 1999; Keck and Sikkink 1998).

Unilateral restrictions on trade or investment—identified here as a third mode of allocation in earth system governance—are thus less preferable. As governments agreed in their 1992 Rio Declaration twenty years ago, "[u]nilateral actions to deal with environmental challenges outside the jurisdiction of the importing country should be avoided. Environmental measures addressing transboundary or global environmental problems should, as far as possible, be based on an international consensus" (Rio Declaration 1992, principle 12).

This does not imply that trade restrictions concerning process and production methods with extraterritorial application have no place at all in earth system governance. In some cases, trade restrictions are important for governance effectiveness in areas where the problem stems largely from such trade, for example trade in endangered species or hazardous waste. Yet even such trade restrictions must be under the auspices of multilateral agreements that guarantee and protect the rights and interests of smaller, standard-taking countries. Such objectives can best be furthered by multilateral environmental agreements that muster broad acceptance even when they require trade restrictions based on foreign process and production methods (Biermann 2001b). Many such multilateral agreements that restrict trade on environmental grounds are in place. For example, the 1973 Convention on International Trade in Endangered Species of Wild Fauna and Flora bans trade in protected species with third parties unless they comply with treaty provisions. The 1989 Basel Convention on the Control of Transboundary Movements of Hazardous Wastes and Their Disposal bans the import or export of wastes from states that are not party to the treaty. The 1987 Montreal Protocol on Substances that Deplete the Ozone Layer restricts trade with nonparties by requiring governments to ban the import of goods that have been produced with ozone-depleting substances in nonparties, even if those goods no longer contain such substances. Similar examples are the 1998 Rotterdam Convention on the Prior Informed Consent Procedure for Certain Hazardous Chemicals and Pesticides in International Trade and the 2000 Cartagena Protocol on Biosafety to the 1992 Convention on Biological Diversity.

As I have argued in chapter 4, multilateral agreement does not have to be based on the actual consent of all countries. Instead, norm-setting processes can, and should, rely more strongly on majority decisions and innovative mechanisms of weighted voting. The final decision might not meet the approval of all countries if based on majority decisions, yet this mode of decision making is still preferable to unilateral decision making through trade and investment restrictions. Multilateral agreements can work through global funds, such as the Global Environment Facility or the Green Climate Fund, or through the establishment of global markets under public control, which might increase overall efficiency of earth system governance if properly implemented.

In sum, from a policy perspective, one of the core requirements of effective earth system governance is the primacy of multilateralism also in decisions on the (international) allocation of costs of actions. This is not synonymous with a consensus-based approach, however. Instead, multilateralism can effectively be combined with, and in fact strengthened by, a stronger reliance on systems of qualified majority voting.

Equal Rights for Every Person
What then should be the appropriate norms guiding the concrete allocation under multilateral agreements? To begin with, for global norms of earth system governance to be effective they must be relatively simple, cross-culturally appealing, and sufficiently clear and unambiguous. For instance, the success of the world trade regime in liberalizing trade and reducing customs duties worldwide within half a century is partially attributed to the simplicity and general acceptability of its basic principles, notably reciprocity and the most favored nation clause.

It is here that certain propositions of egalitarian philosophy might have an inherent appeal due to their link to the basic individual rights of people in South and North. As Kant postulated two hundred years ago, there is a shared right of common ownership of the Earth's surface ("Recht des gemeinschaftlichen Besitzes der Oberfläche der Erde"; Kant 1795, 214 [BA 41/42]). This would imply that in the allocation of the burdens to protect global environmental goods—such as the atmosphere—an equal right for all people to similar emissions levels should be used as the basic norm. In the case of climate governance, for instance, this would entail that emissions reduction obligations of countries should be allocated, within an overall global limit, according to the countries' emissions per person. This would place the burden of environmental policy on countries that pollute the atmosphere more on a per-person level. Only such a clear principle is likely to generate, in the long term, the normative power to grant earth system governance the institutional stability that is needed.

Such a norm of equal obligations for each person would also help to move away from the traditional dichotomy of developing and developed countries, which has lost its relevance owing to the rapid economic growth in many countries in Asia, Latin America, and Africa. For example, when determining which developing countries receive financial assistance in the ozone regime, governments agreed on allocation in line with per capita consumption of harmful substances. The threshold was a consumption per person per year of less than 300 grams of controlled substances. This threshold was so high that only Kuwait, Lebanon, Slovenia, United Arab Emirates, and Cyprus crossed it in the beginning. With this per-capita-based allocation of environmental obligations of countries, the ozone regime might serve as a model also in more complex domains of earth system governance, such as climate change.

This is supported also by strategic considerations. Politically it seems unlikely that major developing countries will sign up to demanding regimes in earth system governance that do not, at least broadly, follow international principles of justice as proposed by egalitarian theory. These include, in particular, the principle of equal per capita allocation. In the unequivocal words of a former Indian prime minister, it does not seem that "the ethos of democracy can support any norm other than equal per capita rights to global environmental resources" (Vajpayee 2002).

The precedent of the North-South politics around stratospheric ozone depletion is particularly informative. In the 1980s, neither the Vienna Convention on the Protection of the Ozone Layer (1985) nor its original

Montreal Protocol (1987) had strong provisions in terms of financing environmental policies in developing countries. Both agreements originally followed a libertarian approach that expected all countries, rich and poor, to finance their own contributions to protect the stratospheric ozone layer. Yet this proved not to be persuasive for poorer developing countries (see, for example, India 1989a and 1989b). Consequently, two years after adoption of the protocol, only ten developing countries had ratified the treaty, despite a grace period that allowed developing countries a ten-year delay in reducing the production and consumption of ozone-depleting substances (Benedick 1998, 148–162). Of the thirteen developing countries whose chlorofluorocarbon consumption appeared to rise in 1987 most sharply, only Mexico, Nigeria, and Venezuela had ratified (Kohler, Haaga, and Camm 1987). Because ozone-depleting technologies were widely available, it was expected at that time that more advanced developing countries were on the verge of large-scale production of chlorofluorocarbon-based refrigerators and air-cooling systems. This would have jeopardized the chlorofluorocarbon reduction efforts of industrialized countries. In August 1989, a UN working group hence warned that "for the Protocol to be fully effective in its purpose of controlling the emissions of chlorofluorocarbons and halons, all countries must become Parties" (Informal Working Group of Experts 1989, para. 8). Both China and India agreed to ratify the treaty only after substantial changes to its basic structure had been made toward a more egalitarian approach. Industrialized countries agreed in 1990 to revise the treaty and to create a novel financial mechanism by which they would provide additional resources to finance all agreed incremental costs of developing countries to enable their compliance with the protocol (Montreal Protocol 1990, article 10). Put differently, all costs of the policies on ozone depletion in the South that have no economic benefit for the country (such as efficiency gains through improved technology) are to be reimbursed. In sum, while the original Montreal Protocol of 1987 followed a libertarian logic, in 1990 the regime was adjusted, after extended conflicts between North and South, to follow rather an egalitarian approach to earth system governance.

This result is striking also because negotiators at that time were aware that they might set a precedent for future issues such as climate change. As US chief negotiator Richard E. Benedick noted (Benedick 1998, 152f.), "creation of a financial mechanism and the related question of modalities for transfer of technology proved to be the most difficult issue in the entire treaty revision process. ... No other subject required so many meetings and consultations or generated so much documentation." Yet similar allocation norms were later also accepted for the conventions on climate and biodiversity. Article 4.3 of the climate convention obliges the North to provide new and additional financial resources to meet the agreed full incremental costs of measures agreed between developing countries and the Global Environment Facility. Article 4.7 stipulates that the extent to which developing countries will effectively implement their commitments under the convention will depend on the effective implementation by industrialized countries of their commitments related to financial resources and transfer of technology. These agreements indicate the strong bargaining power of developing countries in earth system governance, which may result in outcomes that libertarians would perceive as paradoxical. For instance, during an economic recession in which Chinese state funds were investing heavily in the economies of the United States and Europe, these industrialized countries agreed in 2011 to transfer US$265 million to China to allow this country to reduce its consumption and production of hydrochlorofluorocarbons (a powerful gas that harms both the ozone layer and the climate) by 2015.

Many arguments have been brought forward against egalitarian norms, notably the norm of equal per capita entitlements. For example, some have claimed that equal per capita entitlements will create perverse incentives for population growth (Smith, Swisher, and Ahuja 1993, 72). This overestimates, however, the likely market value of emission rights and underestimates the serious policy problems that come with population growth. Others claim that per capita entitlements might create incentives for Southern countries to push in international negotiations for ever more stringent global emission caps (because this would increase the market value of their excess emission rights). This incentive could be reduced through the introduction of double-weighted majority voting, as under the Montreal Protocol or the Global Environment Facility, or of other forms of qualified majority voting (see chapter 4). Alternative critiques suggest that extra income from emissions trading based on per capita entitlements will not be used for environmental policies but for other purposes—but so it is with any marketable resource. Likewise, different developing countries will benefit differently from equal per capita entitlements—richer countries such as South Africa will benefit significantly less if at all—yet this also seems justified.

Equal per capita entitlements, if linked to emissions trading, will create potentially significant financial transfers from North to South. This will be a major incentive for developing countries to join a multilateral environmental agreement but will also be a key disincentive for the North to accept it. For a transition period, therefore, political pragmatism could call for compromises by combining elements from libertarian and egalitarian perspectives. Substantial debate has centered on such compromises in recent years. Hybrid modes of allocation may generate acceptable compromises for the coming years, for example through emission entitlements based on weighted indicators for population and wealth. Such compromise formulas could also be linked to certain minimum thresholds, such as the relief from commitments of developing countries with per capita emissions below the global average (which would serve as a safety valve for developing countries to enter global agreements). Hybrid formulas could also be combined with a transition trajectory that results only later in equal per capita entitlements as final allocation norm (so-called "contract and converge"). Finally, hybrid allocation norms could be accompanied by transaction fees for emissions trading that could be used to pay for environmental projects in the South. This would direct some of the transferred financial resources to global mitigation efforts and still benefit Southern interests.

A World Environment Fund

In addition to the primacy of multilateralism and the strong appeal of the principle of equal rights for every person, a third policy-related question concerns the most effective organizational setting for financial transfers and support mechanisms in earth system governance. At present, the organizational arrangements for financial transfers suffer from ad hocism and fragmentation that do not fully meet the requirements of transparency, efficiency, and participation of all parties involved. Many industrialized countries strive for a strengthening of the World Bank and the affiliated GEF, to which they wish to assign most financial transfers. Yet many developing countries continue to perceive the World Bank as a Northern-dominated institution ruled by decision procedures based on financial contributions, giving disproportionate power to donor countries. Though the GEF was substantially reformed in 1994 and is governed not only by the World Bank but also by UNEP and the UNDP, it still faces criticism from the South. Institutional fragmentation has also increased through the establishment of a number of new funding mechanisms, notably under the climate convention, to cater to the particular needs of certain groups of countries.

Such fragmentation is likely to increase transaction costs and reduce effectiveness of transfer mechanisms in earth system governance.

Further reforms to increase coherence in the system of funding mechanisms seem thus important. One possibility is to consolidate within one body the tasks of overseeing capacity building and financial and technological assistance for earth system governance. This body would need to reflect the distinct character of North-South relations in earth system governance and be able to link the political and technical aspects of financial and technological assistance. It would also have to be strong enough to overcome the fragmentation of the current multitude of funds.

A World Environment Fund could fulfill such functions, possibly under the purview of the World Environment Organization proposed in chapters 3 (regarding its agency function) and 4 (regarding its architecture function). A World Environment Fund could be empowered to coordinate various financial mechanisms and administer funds linked to specific environmental issues and sectoral regimes in trust. In addition, a World Environment Fund could host the CDM and the clearinghouse for any future emissions trading scheme, which would reduce bureaucratic overlap, increase efficiency, and assist in preventing conflicts with other environmental problems. Such trading schemes could contribute through user fees to the financing of a World Environment Fund. Finally, the Fund could be used to implement innovative future arrangements— such as global user fees on air and maritime transport—or to coordinate private funding mechanisms, such as those of foundations or public-private partnerships.

There is no need to set up large new financial bureaucracies. Instead, a World Environment Fund could make use of the expertise of the World Bank or the UNDP, including their national representatives in developing countries. By designating a World Environment Fund as a central coordinating body for the various existing financial mechanisms and funds, however, control of developing countries over implementation could be strengthened, without ceding existing organizations' advantages of technical expertise and knowledge. The norm-setting functions of the GEF, for example regarding the criteria for financial disbursement, could be transferred to the governing body of the World Environment Fund. The World Environment Fund would thus have its own governing bodies, which would set general guidelines and administer various trust funds earmarked for particular conventions and agreements. These governance bodies, for their part, would fall under the authority of the World Environment Organization and its highest decision-making assembly.

Conclusion

The allocation of costs and benefits of earth system governance is certain to become one of the most fundamental political questions in the twenty-first century. Despite their vast differences in wealth, health, and living standards, earth system governance requires societies to collaborate, and hence to address, and possibly to reduce, the tremendous differentials between the haves and the have-nots on our planet. This is not only a moral proposition informed by cosmopolitan political philosophy; it is a political necessity. Given weak current global governance structures, poorer countries are hardly willing or able to fully participate in earth system governance if richer countries do not address their high consumption levels that place the highest burden on planetary systems.

As for the modes of allocation that are currently part of earth system governance, it is fundamentally important that all mechanisms be based on multilateral agreement, as laid out above. In the long run, unilateral action, through restrictions in trade or investment based on environmental standards that lack approval of the community of countries, is not likely to advance the institutional stability and credibility that would guarantee the effectiveness of earth system governance. International funds, such as a World Environment Fund, would be one way to ensure a fair allocation of the costs of earth system governance. Another option is international markets of environmental obligations that increase efficiency and flexibility in governance and could at the same time—depending on the underlying allocation principles—advance the interests of the poor.

Overall, the analysis has also shown that research in this field is still sketchy compared to the other core concerns of earth system governance. As Adger, Brown, and Hulme (2005) wrote almost a decade ago in their editorial for *Global Environmental Change*, a "more explicit concern with equity and justice will be important in furthering the study of global environmental change." Few research efforts have yet been directed at understanding the causal pathways that lead to specific allocation mechanisms. Little systematic analysis has also been devoted to studying allocation as an independent variable and to analyzing allocation mechanisms in relation to variant effectiveness of the core institutions of earth system governance. In sum, given the growing relevance of earth system governance in the twenty-first century in terms of mitigation and adaptation costs, allocation is certain to become a major concern for researchers and practitioners alike.

Faust:

Wie das Geklirr der Spaten mich ergetzt!

Es ist die Menge, die mir frönet,

Die Erde mit sich selbst versöhnet,

Den Wellen ihre Grenze setzt.

Das Meer mit strengem Band umzieht.

Mephistopheles:

Du bist doch nur für uns bemüht

Mit deinen Dämmen, deinen Buhnen;

Denn du bereitest schon Neptunen,

Dem Wasserteufel, großen Schmaus.

In jeder Art seid ihr verloren;—

Die Elemente sind mit uns verschworen,

Und auf Vernichtung läuft's hinaus.

Faust:

How the clattering of shovels cheers me!

It's the crews still labouring on,

Till earth is reconciled to man,

The waves accept their boundaries,

And ocean's bound with iron bands.

Mephistopheles:

And yet with all your walls and dams

You're merely dancing to our tune:

Since you prepare for our Neptune,

The Water-demon, one vast feast.

You'll be lost in every way—

The elements are ours, today,

And ruin comes on running feet.

Johann Wolfgang von Goethe, *Faust: Der Tragödie zweiter Teil*, 5. Akt, Großer Vorhof des Palastes, 11539–11550

7

Adaptiveness

Four hundred, five hundred, or even higher—such data for atmospheric carbon dioxide concentrations, expressed in parts per million, might well define the future of our societies in the second half of this century. The widely cited paper by Johan Rockström and colleagues (2009) suggested as a safe level for atmospheric carbon dioxide a maximum concentration of 350 parts per million. Yet this limit was crossed some decades ago. Other earth system boundaries are also close to being violated, taking into account potential negative feedback loops in the system. Under such circumstances, what are the prospects that earth system governance can be effective?

The previous four chapters on agency, architecture, accountability, and allocation have outlined possible reforms to strengthen the overall governance system. Yet there is, possibly, not much room for optimism that political progress will be speedy enough. Current efforts might be too little and too late. Regarding climate change, the World Bank claims that if all current political commitments are fully implemented, the world would still be heading for a global warming of 3 degrees Celsius or even, with a 20 percent likelihood, of 4 degrees. If current commitments are not met, a warming of 4 degrees could occur as early as the 2060s, substantially undermining food security (World Bank 2012). Even a 1–2-degree increase could be enough for the Arctic summer sea ice to melt and for Greenland summer ice sheets to exceed critical tipping points (Lenton et al. 2008). In 2008, Robert Watson, chief scientific advisor to the UK Department for the Environment, Food and Rural Affairs, already warned in a widely cited article that because "we don't know in detail how to limit greenhouse gas emissions to realise a 2-degree target, we should be prepared to adapt to 4C" (Watson 2008). Given all uncertainties around the nonlinearity of earth system processes, Lenton et al. (2008, 1792) warned that our societies "may be lulled into a false sense of security by smooth projections of global change." Some voices are becoming even more radical, such as science journalist Mark Lynas with his award-winning *Six Degrees: Our Future on a Hotter Planet* (Lynas 2007).

Even as leading earth system analysts voice concern that it will be difficult, if not impossible, to limit global warming to safe levels, policymakers fail to address the consequences. How would drastic global change affect our societies? What adaptive governance mechanisms exist and are in need of reform, and what new institutions and mechanisms are urgently needed?

These questions about future global adaptation governance have remained at the fringes of the discourse in global environmental politics and international relations. Most scholarly concern has been on mitigation in the quest to turn course and prevent large-scale earth system transformations. This is important, no doubt. Yet at the same time, we need to start exploring the unknown and uncharted territories of governing a substantially warmer world. Rather than waiting for catastrophic events to occur, research must explore how governance systems can be better prepared and able to cope if large-scale earth system transformations should become a reality.

This is what this chapter is about. It first develops a framework of analysis on global adaptation governance that may be useful to guide future research in this area. I then apply this framework to the specific problem of climate migrants, that is, the large numbers of people who might be forced to leave their homes in the second half of the century due to climate change.

The focus in this chapter is on drastic earth system transformations, notably global warming that exceeds 2 degrees Celsius compared to preindustrial levels (see also Jordan et al. 2013). A substantial body of literature exists on local and national adaptation to climate change and on the resilience and adaptive capacity of (local) social-ecological systems to change and crisis (overviews in Adger, Arnell, and Tompkins 2005; Folke et al. 2005; Huitema et al. 2009; Lebel et al. 2006; Nelson, Adger, and Brown 2007). Yet hardly any literature addresses the consequences of drastic earth system transformations for international relations and the global architecture of international institutions and governance mechanisms. Regarding national and local governance, it has been argued for instance that resilient social-ecological systems can use a crisis as an opportunity to transform themselves into a more desired state (Folke et al. 2005). Yet the resilience of the global institutional system to drastic earth system transformations has been much less studied. My analysis therefore focuses on this *global* adaptation governance.

If appropriate measures are not taken, global adaptation governance could well need to address future situations of unprecedented, quickly evolving disasters and large-scale, possibly sudden and unpredictable harm to socioeconomic systems. Mechanisms of such "emergency governance" exist in most national political systems for situations of war and civil unrest, and also for natural disasters such as dike breakthroughs, earthquakes, or pandemic diseases. Yet there is no equivalent to such governance mechanisms at the global level, particularly for crucial challenges of earth system transformations.

One methodological problem in studying global adaptation governance is that the potential impacts of earth system transformations are unprecedented in scale and partially in type. For example, climate-induced migration as one consequence of such transformations might displace many more people than all categories of refugees recognized by the UN system today. Sea level rise might make small islands inhabitable and change the landscapes and means of production of many regions. Climate change might also cause the large-scale breakdown of ecosystems, with grave consequences for food production, especially in Asia and Africa (World Bank 2012). Flight, famine, and floods have been part of human history for as long as we can remember. Yet in modern times, in a highly interdependent global system with now seven billion people, the threats of large-scale migration, coastal devastation, drought, and resource depletion pose challenges that current systems of global governance—from the United Nations to regimes that govern commerce and cooperation—have not needed to address before. In short, scholars of global adaptation governance cannot rely solely on experience. They have to offer possible future solutions to possible future problems whose contours, nature, and scope remain unprecedented and partially unpredictable. Methodologically, this is no easy task, and students of global adaptation governance need to develop new methodologies and modes of scholarly validation, such as "futurefactuals"—methods to understand the effectiveness of current institutions of earth system governance against future events, the nature and impacts of which remain uncertain (thus similar to counterfactuals).

Many issues that are central to global adaptation governance are related to this question of future institutional effectiveness. How will current institutions perform if faced with the new multifaceted crises that may result from a substantially warmer world? To the extent that we may conclude that current institutions will not live up to the governance demands of a warmer world, what other institutional designs and institutional arrangements could we envision that might better cope with the worldwide impacts of drastic earth system transformations? And what research methods and designs can we use to evaluate potentially conflicting claims about the expected performance of different institutional designs and institutional arrangements that are being proposed? We can build here on the extensive literature on international environmental regime effectiveness (overviews in Young 2001; Mitchell 2003; Jordan 2008). Yet the transferability of these lines of research to global adaptation governance needs to be carefully assessed and validated.

Assessment

What are the most important issue areas requiring global adaptation governance? While a number of areas of world politics merit global adaptation governance (see Biermann and Boas 2010a for more detail), the type and degree of institutionalization and presence of effective support mechanisms vary greatly across them.

One issue is the likely migration pressure resulting from large-scale earth system transformations, with impacts such as sea level rise, water scarcity, increased storm surges, and drought. At present, no international institution explicitly addresses the plight of future climate migrants. I explore the governance challenges of this problem later in this chapter in more detail.

Global water governance also seems inadequate to address large-scale perturbations. As the IPCC has found, "in many regions, changing precipitation or melting snow and ice are altering hydrological systems, affecting water resources in terms of quantity and quality" (IPCC 2014a). Yet at present global water governance remains highly fragmented and weak (Conca 2006; Dellapenna and Gupta 2008 and 2009; Pahl-Wostl, Gupta, and Petry 2008, 425–428). Institutions in global water governance include the World Water Council, the UNDP (for example its Water Governance Facility), UNEP, UNESCO, the World Bank, as well as many regional organizations. Most of these focus on capacity building, dissemination of knowledge, and exchange of best practices, with little overall coordination.

In comparison, global food governance is better and more coherently institutionalized (J. Gupta 2004). Similar to the water domain, the overall architecture of food governance is highly complex, given that it relates to broader poverty, health, and economic issues. Yet even though various institutional arrangements exist, the FAO serves as organizational core. The World Bank is the major funding body, including its Global Food Crisis Response Programme and the Agriculture Finance Support Facility. The adaptive capacity of global food governance may thus be better compared to global water governance, given the presence of an organizational core and the existence of established financial support mechanisms. The institutionalization in global health governance is even stronger. The core agency here is the WHO, with additional activities by the World Bank, some other international agencies, and private foundations. With its relatively strong and coherent set of institutions, this policy domain is better prepared to address broader external shocks.

The adaptability of global economic governance is an open question and requires a more detailed assessment than is possible here. The issue area undoubtedly contains relatively strong institutions, including the World Bank and the IMF, along with many bilateral and regional institutional agreements. In recent years, the role of the IMF has been further strengthened following the financial crisis. However, it is questionable to what extent these institutions could also cope with the economic impacts of drastic earth system transformations. Economic institutions would be challenged by the need to provide quick and substantial financial assistance to countries that are affected by climate-related disasters such as drought or floods, including effects such as breakdowns in infrastructure, loss of property and means of production, and a declining investment climate. Also, the costs of large-scale internal and international migration would need to be addressed by international financial institutions. Yet the current funding available to international economic institutions is far less than what is predicted to be necessary for adapting to drastic earth system transformations.

Last but not least, earth system transformations could affect international security through conflicts over natural resources or streams of climate-induced migrants. At present, global security governance revolves around the United Nations Security Council and regional institutions, such as the North Atlantic Treaty Organization. These institutions lack legitimacy with many governments in the developing world, and the effectiveness of the Security Council is curtailed by the veto power of its five permanent members (China, France, Russian Federation, United Kingdom, and United States of America). The initiative of the United Kingdom to discuss climate change within the Security Council has met with fierce resistance from developing countries (UNSC 2007). It is doubtful whether the present international security regime under the United Nations Charter will be able to effectively resolve the security implications of drastic earth system transformations.

In sum, the degree of institutionalization, coherence, and funding differs across the areas of world politics that would be most heavily affected by drastic earth system transformations. All domains need to be better institutionalized, made more coherent, and better supported by strong funding mechanisms. This is no easy political task. In particular, creating more adaptive institutions and a stronger global adaptation governance architecture will almost certainly require tradeoffs and pose dilemmas in public decision making. For example, certain responses to drastic earth system changes could be highly effective but at the same time be perceived as less accountable, legitimate, or fair.

Such governance dilemmas are not new. Yet earth system transformations might pose very particular challenges for international governance, including many that come with difficult political and moral choices.

Core Dilemmas of Global Adaptation Governance

I turn here to three central dilemmas of global adaptation governance that seem to be most important: the adaptability versus stability of governance systems; the effectiveness versus accountability and legitimacy of governance systems; and the effectiveness versus fairness and equity of governance systems.

Adaptability versus stability: A first fundamental tension that will challenge global adaptation governance is the need to create institutions that can adapt to rapid changes and the need for predictable long-term stable expectations for actors. It is, in short, the tension between adaptability, stability, and credibility of governance (see chapter 2).

On the one hand, drastic earth system transformations create a highly uncertain environment characterized by various problems with high spatial and functional interdependence. Here it is essential that systems of governance provide a long-term stable institutional framework that survives changes to global, regional, and national political and economic systems. The credibility of reciprocity in multilateral agreements is crucial, and legally binding agreements based on clear and widely agreed principles are thus generally more promising to enlist long-term support of governments. Governments are likely to accept long-term costs of regulation only if they can expect that others—such as other governments—will do the same now and in the future. Earth system governance must also ensure effective financial and technical support with a coherent operational and implementing system that continues to function even in a time of crisis.

Yet this conflicts with the inherent uncertainty in the evolution of the earth system. Both global and regional impacts of drastic earth system transformations are still uncertain, particularly at the level of detail that is important for policymaking. Such impacts will fundamentally shape the interest constellations of countries as well as national and subnational policy processes, but remain largely unpredictable.

For this reason, earth system governance needs to be able to flexibly adapt to changing circumstances within the boundaries of an overall stable institutional framework. Governance must be reliable and predictable yet at the same time responsive to sudden or extreme and irreversible changes in the earth system, to new scientific findings, or to new social and economic circumstances. Global adaptation governance must thus allow for a sufficient degree of social learning and variety, and stimulate dynamic and innovative behavior (Folke et al. 2005; Pahl-Wostl et al. 2007).

This dilemma between adaptability and quick response mechanisms, on the one hand, and long-term stable expectations in governance outcomes, on the other, is not entirely new. Yet the combination of uncertainty, a dynamic knowledge base, a mixture of global, regional, national, and local socioeconomic forces, and potentially great harm makes the adaptability-versus-stability dilemma particularly challenging in the case of drastic earth system transformations.

The literature on international institutions suggests a number of institutional design elements that could help in addressing this challenge. One such mechanism is the institutionalized regular review of commitments and policies of countries, including both their adequacy in light of new scientific findings and the status of implementation by governments. Regular review mechanisms include institutionalized review committees, long-term review schedules, and the regular reporting of findings and trends to decision-making bodies. For example, the quick evolution of the 1987 Montreal Protocol on Substances that Deplete the Ozone Layer has been partly attributed to the existence of strong and regular review mechanisms (Oberthür 1996). Such mechanisms are also likely to be effective in systems of global adaptation governance. Flexible yet authoritative decision making in times of drastic earth system transformations will also require revisiting the current pattern of consensual decision making in international bodies. Consensus-based decisions take more time and are often less demanding. Innovative systems of qualified majority voting are becoming important, as laid out in chapters 4 and 5.

For less demanding decisions, tacit-acceptance procedures could also be used more often, as common for example in the decision making of the International Maritime Organization. While many international agreements—including the climate convention—stipulate that any amendment requires ratification by a certain number of countries, the tacit-acceptance procedure provides that an amendment will become binding at a given date unless a specified number of parties objects to the amendment before that date. In international maritime policymaking, this tacit-acceptance procedure has substantially speeded up the evolution and adaptation of treaties that abide by the procedure (overviews in Kirchner 2003). Finally, the wide ratification of new rules could be accelerated by specific reporting and review mechanisms on the state of ratification in all countries, including requiring countries to justify why they cannot assent to a new rule. Such procedures are relied upon, for instance, in the rule-setting mechanisms of the International Labor Organization, and might prove to be useful elements of other core areas of world politics, in particular if quick and flexible rule setting is required in times of drastic earth system transformations.

Effectiveness versus legitimacy: A second dilemma in global adaptation governance is that between effective international governance, on the one hand, and the perceived accountability and legitimacy of such governance on the other (see also chapter 5). If drastic earth system transformations require large-scale international adaptation measures, along with possibly stricter mitigation obligations, then this situation may come close to the global equivalent of emergency governance akin to the management of natural disasters or pandemics. Such governance in emergency mode is marked by the need to take quick decisions with high authoritative force. Effectiveness as a driving concern could conflict, however, with democratic principles of deliberation and inclusiveness, and adversely affect the perceived accountability and legitimacy of the decisions taken. For instance, effective adaptation governance under conditions of drastic earth system transformations could curtail procedural equity. While the interests of the most vulnerable groups are at stake in decision making on global adaptation governance, these groups may not be sufficiently represented in global forums, nor able to advance their interests in international decision making (Nelson, Adger, and Brown 2007, 410).

Authoritative decision making at the global level will be the pre-rogative of governments, which are the key actors driving decision making and implementation within their jurisdictions. Governments will also provide for the authoritative allocation of goods and resources in response to drastic earth system transformations. This central role of state-led global decision making, however, will further strengthen the role of the executive branches of government and of state bureau-cracies in international decision making, which poses demanding challenges of transparency, accountability, reflexiveness, and eventually acceptance of global adaptation governance. Smaller, less powerful countries might also lack influence and be subjected to stronger global regulation by major industrialized and emerging countries. Overall, this creates a tension between the effectiveness and the legitimacy of global adaptation governance.

For these reasons, more inclusive mechanisms are needed to ensure that global adaptation governance is legitimate and accountable and serves the interests of those in need of assistance. One approach, as laid out in chapter 3 of this book, has been the development of public policy networks and other new types of participatory governance arrangements. However, a stronger involvement of private actors in international gov-ernance creates legitimacy and accountability deficits as well. One way of addressing this challenge is the stronger involvement of civil society actors, parliaments, and citizens in global adaptation governance, for example through special advisory chambers for civil society representa-tives, parliamentary assemblies, or deliberative assemblies in interna-tional institutions, as laid out above (see chapter 5 in more detail).

Effectiveness versus fairness: A third dilemma is between the effectiveness of global adaptation governance in coping with drastic earth system transformations and the equity of the outcomes (see also chapter 6). Swift and effective action in response to drastic earth system transformations will require implicit or explicit choices about the distribution of costs and benefits of response programs. Drastic earth system transformations are likely to lead to an overall reduction in global welfare, but with highly uneven distribution of costs. International response mechanisms are unlikely to be able to redress all impacts to the same degree. To avoid substantial losses in the short and long term, stable, fair, and authorita-tive mechanisms are required that will ensure quick and just distribution of costs and benefits. Nevertheless, in the intergovernmental domain, such mechanisms are weak and often nonexistent.

The unequal distribution of vulnerabilities and potential harm is also problematic (Nelson, Adger, and Brown 2007, 410). Any choice for a particular adaptation strategy will disadvantage certain groups and privilege others. For instance, the Netherlands plans to create more space for rivers in order to cope with an expected increase in water levels because of climate change (Ministry of Transport, Public Works and Water Management et al. 2006). Although this policy advances the collective national interest, it may not serve the short-term needs and interests of those who may be forced to leave their homes as a result of this policy (Roth and Warner 2007). Such situations require effective decision making to ensure that measures are taken on time. At the same time, such decision making must take into account equity and ensure a fair distribution of vulnerabilities, costs, and benefits. It is difficult and challenging to reconcile these two goals. Developing countries in particular are likely to be faced with significant costs relating not only to emissions reduction but also to adaptation. Even poor developing countries with low per capita greenhouse gas emissions that will be exempt from the climate change mitigation regime need to take costly adaptation measures against sea level rise, drought, natural disasters, and other climate change impacts.

In sum, global adaptation governance is faced with a number of core dilemmas that are not unknown to other policy domains, but that are particularly prominent in this area. Some of these dilemmas are addressed in more detail in other parts of this book, for example the need to combine effective decisions within stable governance architectures, such as through qualified majority voting (chapter 4); the need to combine the effectiveness of governance with accountability and legitimacy (chapter 5); and the need to link effectiveness with fairness (chapter 6). The remainder of this chapter will further discuss some of these issues with special relevance to global adaptation governance.

The Case of Climate-Related Migration

Let me turn now to one specific area of global adaptation governance in order to explore how these dilemmas are being addressed in practice. I focus on climate-change-related migration (drawing on Biermann and Boas 2010b), that is, on the protection of people who have to leave their homes, immediately or in the near future, because of sudden or gradual alterations in their natural environment due to sea level rise, extreme weather events, and drought and water scarcity. Similar studies are needed for other areas outlined above, from water governance to health and food governance.

In the case of climate migration, many studies predict that millions of people might be forced over the course of this century to leave their villages and cities because of climate change, although the exact number of future climate migrants varies considerably from assessment to assessment, depending on underlying definitions, methods, scenarios, time frames, and assumptions. Despite the multiple methodological challenges inherent in migration projections, substantial migration movements over the course of this century are not to be ruled out. Some earlier estimates have suggested that the number of people at risk of becoming climate migrants by 2050 could well be around 200 million (Myers and Kent 1995; Myers 2002), though this might have been overly dramatic and more nuanced estimates now prevail (see in more detail Biermann and Boas 2010b; Boas 2013; IPCC 2014a). As the IPCC has argued, "there is low confidence in quantitative projections of changes in mobility, due to its complex, multi-causal nature" (IPCC 2014a, 20). The World Bank warns that a global warming of 4 degrees Celsius—which has a 20 percent likelihood even if all current political commitments are met— with its "projected impacts on water availability, ecosystems, agriculture and human health could lead to a large-scale displacement of populations" (World Bank 2012, xvii). A 2012 IPCC report found that "if disasters occur more frequently and/or with greater magnitude, some local areas will become increasingly marginal as places to live or in which to maintain livelihoods. In such cases, migration and displacement could become permanent and could introduce new pressures in areas of relocation. For locations such as atolls, in some cases it is possible that many residents will have to relocate" (IPCC 2012, 16; see also IPCC 2014a).

In the richer countries of the North, climate migration can be prevented through adaptation measures such as reinforced coastal protection or changes in agricultural production and water supply management. Many poorer countries, however, are unlikely to be able to initiate sufficient adaptation programs, and climate-induced migration might be the only option for many communities in the South (see in more detail Mayer 2011b, 371f.). It is thus people in developing countries who are most likely to be compelled to leave their homes, owing to low adaptive capacities, their often vulnerable location vis-à-vis climate change events, high population densities, already existing hunger and health problems, low GDP per capita, often weak governance structures, political instability, and other factors (Stern 2007; German Advisory Council on Global Change 2007, 119–120; IPCC 2014a). In these situations, climate migrants will need to rely on effective protection and support from the international community, regardless of whether such migration will be internal or transnational.

Protecting climate migrants, however, is challenging for a variety of reasons. For one, it is difficult to politically and legally define this group of people. Even the appropriate terminology is marked by confusion and contestation. In public discourse, the most widely used term is "climate refugees," drawing on the broader notion of environmental refugees that dates back thirty years to a study by UNEP (El-Hinnawi 1985). This UNEP report defined environmental refugees as "people who have been forced to leave their traditional habitat, temporarily or permanently, because of a marked environmental disruption (natural and/or triggered by people) that jeopardized their existence and/or seriously affected the quality of their life" (El-Hinnawi 1985, 4). The notion of environmental refugees generally includes climate refugees (see for example Myers and Kent 1995; Myers 2002, 611), although the category's breadth makes it impossible to specify or quantify climate-related migration. The term "environmental refugees" was also used by the World Commission on Environment and Development (1987, chapter 11) and in Agenda 21, the program of action agreed upon at the 1992 United Nations Conference on Environment and Development (UN 1992, chapter 12). The narrower notion of "climate refugees" has found acceptance in some national political debates. For example, Australia's Labor Party proposed an international coalition to accept climate refugees from the Pacific (Australian Labor Party 2006)—in response to the (then) Australian government's position that rejected the notion of climate refugees (Renaud et al. 2007). Australia's Greens party even tabled (unsuccessfully) a Migration (Climate Refugees) Amendment Bill in the Australian Parliament that would have provided for "a class of visas to be known as climate change refugee visas" for foreigners who have been "displaced as a result of a climate change induced environmental disaster" (Parliament of the Commonwealth of Australia 2007).

In the language of diplomats, international bureaucrats, and migration experts, however, the term "climate refugees" is largely avoided today. Some intergovernmental agencies—such as the International Organization for Migration and the UN High Commissioner for Refugees (UNHCR)—reject using the term climate "refugee" because of the legal rights that the intergovernmental system currently bestows upon "refugees." In their view, the term "refugee" should remain limited to transboundary flight, in line with the 1951 Geneva Convention Relating to the Status of Refugees that is restricted to persons who are persecuted in their home state because of their political views, religion, ethnicity, and so forth. As an alternative, some international agencies prefer the notion of "environmentally displaced persons" (Keane 2004; Zetter 2011) or, as is now becoming common in the expert literature, climate (-induced) migrants.

There are also strong political interests that discourage the notion of "climate refugees." Not least, refugees have clear legal titles to protection, which migrants lack. Especially for the powerful governments of industrialized countries, which are also the main donors of most funding agencies in this domain, it is politically more attractive and opportune to frame the issue as a problem of "migration" rather than as a "refugee crisis," which might require a legally and politically different, and more costly, response. As this debate suggests, the term "refugee" has strong moral connotations invoking societal protection in most world cultures and religions. If this term were used, the protection of these people would receive the legitimacy and urgency it actually deserves. There is no compelling reason to reserve the stronger term "refugee" for a limited category of political refugees who stood at the center of attention in 1951, when the Geneva Convention was agreed, and to invent less appropriate terms for new categories of people who are forced to leave their homes now, with similar grim consequences. Why should inhabitants of some atolls in Tuvalu who might require resettlement given the prospect of inundation by 2050 or 2080 receive less protection than those who fear political persecution? Maybe for these reasons, the term "climate refugees" remains the most popular, with about 1,180,000 hits in Google in November 2013, as opposed to merely 34,800 hits for "climate migrants" in the same period. Given the current discursive developments in the expert literature, however, I use the term "climate migrants" in this book, though more for the sake of convention than out of conviction (see Biermann and Boas 2010b in more detail on terminology).

I now turn to the question of what institutions of global governance are available to protect climate migrants. One regime dealing with people fleeing their own countries, as mentioned, is the 1951 Geneva Convention Relating to the Status of Refugees and its 1967 Protocol Relating to the Status of Refugees. This regime, however, is restricted to individual political refugees who flee their countries because of state-led persecution, and thus does not cover climate refugees (Mayer 2011a and 2011b). A broader definition of refugees has been adopted in two regional conventions, the Organization of African Unity Convention Governing the Specific Aspects of Refugee Problems in Africa (1969) and the Cartagena

Declaration on Refugees (1984) concerning refugees from Central America, Mexico, and Panama. Both regional conventions cover people fleeing events seriously disturbing public order, and the African convention applies not only to individuals but also to groups. Even though the extension of protection to people affected by a seriously disturbed public order and to groups may permit these two regional conventions—which happen to cover areas most likely to be severely affected by future climate change—to include climate refugees, both conventions were originally not intended to do so (Renaud et al. 2007, 12; Keane 2004, 216).

The main agency in the United Nations system for the protection of refugees is the UNHCR. Its primary focus is (political) refugees protected under the Geneva Convention and the Protocol of 1967. By 2012, about 10.4 million people were identified by the UNHCR as "refugees," of which roughly 6 million were actually being assisted by the organization (UNHCR 2013). Given the restrictive definition of political refugee under the Geneva convention, the executive committee of UNHCR and the UN General Assembly permitted the agency to extend its activities to other groups, such as former refugees who have returned to their homeland, internally displaced people, and people who are stateless or whose nationality is disputed, even though these people have a different legal status and are not formally referred to as refugees. By 2012, the UNHCR had dealt in total with 33.9 million affected people in 125 countries (UNHCR 2013).

In the current institutional context, climate migrants could be conceptualized as internally displaced persons (UN Secretary-General 2012). The UNHCR has a variety of programs for such people, even though the High Commissioner lacks a legal mandate in this area (UNHCR 2007; Mayer 2011b). Environmentally internally displaced persons also fall under the Guiding Principles on Internal Displacement of the Office of the High Commissioner for Human Rights (Office of the High Commissioner for Human Rights 1998, Introduction article 2). However, the concept of "environmentally internally displaced persons" serves only "as a descriptive term, not as a status that confers obligations on states" (Keane 2004, 217). All rules and regulations on internally displaced people place the primary duty to provide protection and humanitarian assistance with national authorities (see in more detail IASC 2006; UN Secretary-General 2012; Mayer 2011b).

In sum, current global governance on migration and refugees provides only limited protection, with no specific mandate, for climate migrants. The main responsibility to address this issue is placed with the home country, which contradicts the longstanding debate on global responsibility for the victims of climate change and the need for international cooperation and supporting institutions. As has been recognized in a number of recent expert meetings, there is currently "a significant normative gap with respect to climate-induced external displacement [and a need for] a guiding framework or instrument ... and ... a more coherent and consistent response to the protecting the needs of peoples displaced due to sudden-onset disasters" (Edwards, Kerber, and Wirsching 2013, 29 and 39; see also Oliver-Smith 2009, on the need for legally binding policies to address mass climate migration). I will address this situation in the following.

Toward Reform

As I have argued above, global adaptation governance requires adjustments and reforms in almost all domains of world politics, from health to energy, water, food, migration, and even security governance. I have identified some crosscutting reform needs in the previous chapters of this book. For example, as with effective architectures and accountability mechanisms for earth system governance, international decision-making procedures that combine speed with legitimacy are equally important for global adaptation governance. Qualified majority voting in international institutions might help increase the pace of decision making, while ensuring representation of key groups in international society (see chapter 4). The legitimacy of global adaptation governance could also be increased by more inclusive decision making through formal involvement of affected and vulnerable communities, for example through special consultative chambers of (affected) civil society organizations that could include, for instance, Southern farmers, fishers, indigenous people, and others (see chapter 5).

In addition to reforming decision-making procedures, I now focus on two other areas of political reform, one cutting across all areas of global adaptation governance (funding global adaptation), the other issue-specific (climate migration).

Funding Adaptation
One general conclusion from the current state of global adaptation governance is that effective policies are likely to require the strengthening of existing funding mechanisms and possibly the development of new funding avenues. These additional financial resources need to achieve a

double goal. First, they need to increase long-term adaptive capacity in vulnerable regions, for example as part of larger development cooperation programs. Second, they need to provide emergency funding as part of disaster relief.

One short-term solution is the integration of global adaptation governance into existing funding mechanisms of the World Bank or the UNDP. For example, the World Bank and partners established the Global Facility for Disaster Reduction and Recovery in 2006, a partnership of 41 countries and eight international organizations. This facility assists developing countries in reducing their vulnerability to natural hazards and adapting to climate change. Among other things, the facility seeks to mainstream climate change adaptation into country development strategies (www.gfdrr.org). The IMF has developed an Exogenous Shocks Facility to assist developing countries that experience exogenous shocks, which could include climate change impacts (IMF 2008). In addition, several specialized funds operate under the global climate regime, including an Adaptation Fund under the 1997 Kyoto Protocol to fund projects in developing countries; a Special Climate Change Fund to fund adaptation projects to strengthen adaptive capacities of developing countries; a Least Developed Countries Fund to help the least developed countries in preparing their National Adaptation Programs of Actions, and the more recent Green Climate Fund (see chapter 6).

These funding structures could play a role in coping with drastic earth system transformations. Nonetheless, funding is not enough even for current adaptation needs. The funds are neither sufficiently capitalized nor institutionally strong enough to deal with the future impacts of climate change, and therefore require further development.

This situation might require new mechanisms to ensure regular and predictable funding for global adaptation governance. Innovative proposals include the Climate Impact Relief Fund proposed by Müller (2002, 89–91) and the International Air Travel Adaptation Levy developed by Müller and Hepburn (2006) (with the potential to raise US$4–10 billion each year). Alternative mechanisms include climate change insurance schemes. For example, as early as 1991, the Alliance of Small Island States proposed an International Insurance Pool to assist small islands and low-lying coastal developing countries affected by sea level rise (Linnerooth-Bayer and Mechler 2006). In 2007, Caribbean island states formed the Caribbean Catastrophe Risk Insurance Facility as the world's first multicountry catastrophe insurance pool, with assistance from the World Bank and Japanese funding (see www.ccrif.org). The Munich Climate Insurance Initiative has been established as a network of nongovernmental organizations and policy analysts to develop and evaluate insurance options for climate change (Bals, Warner, and Butzengeiger 2006). Such novel institutions are important policy experiments; yet to assess their full potential over the course of the next decades, including their equity implications, more policy-related research is needed (see, for example, Stadelmann et al. 2014).

The legal dimensions of financing adaptation are also important to consider. As observed in the interbellum by the Permanent Court of International Justice, "it is a principle of international law, and even a general conception of law, that any breach of an engagement involves an obligation to make reparation" (PCIJ 1928). Some developing countries, particularly low-lying countries or small island countries, argue that industrialized countries are liable for past wrongful acts and have to provide compensation, for example for damage by sea level rise (Benoît 2011a and 2012b). Arguments along these lines have been brought forward by various representatives of the developing world. Notably, some small island states—Fiji, Kiribati, Nauru, Papua New Guinea, and Tuvalu—declared, upon signing the climate convention, that they would not renounce by this act any rights under international law concerning state responsibility for the adverse effects of climate change, and that no provisions in the convention can be interpreted as derogating from the principles of general international law.

In practice, however, legal concepts of state responsibility, international liability, reparation, or compensation are unlikely to be broadly accepted in international climate policy. It is more likely that such legal concepts form the implicit, if not explicit, basis for the creation of the many multilateral trust funds to assist developing countries in adapting to climate change impacts. Thus, liability and state responsibility may be seen as general legal principles underlying proposals that have been made since the 1980s for the establishment of various multilateral funding mechanisms or insurance mechanisms to assist climate change victims in the South (see also chapter 6).

A more recent way in which compensating poorer countries for harm suffered by climate change has entered climate governance is the debate on "loss and damage." The Bali action plan adopted by parties to the climate convention in 2007 noted the need to include, in the next climate change agreement, "means to address loss and damage associated with climate change impacts in developing countries that are particularly vulnerable to the adverse effects of climate change" (UNFCCC 2007, paragraph 1.c.i). Since this meeting, loss and damage have become more important in climate negotiations, with developing countries claiming their right to compensation for climate-change-related damages to their countries in the future, and arguing that compensation of "loss and damage" would be separate from adaptation support. In 2012, industrialized countries agreed to a decision of the conference of the parties "to establish, at its nineteenth session [in 2013], institutional arrangements, such as an international mechanism, including functions and modalities ... to address loss and damage associated with the impacts of climate change in developing countries that are particularly vulnerable to the adverse effects of climate change." The outcome of these negotiations is difficult to foresee, and the decision has been essentially postponed to future conferences of the parties (ENB 2013b). It seems unlikely that developing countries will agree on any further cooperation on the climate issue unless significant support in addressing their losses and damages through climate change is guaranteed (Center for Participatory Research and Development 2013).

In sum, global adaptation governance poses fundamental challenges to the multilateral systems. The potential financial needs to support poorer countries are substantial, yet at present richer countries are not yet prepared to provide this support. In the course of the next decades, financing global adaptation is thus likely to further grow into a major conflict area between richer and poorer countries. Important elements of earth system governance discussed in other chapters of this book—notably decision-making procedures (chapter 4), questions of accountability and legitimacy (chapter 5), and modes of allocation (chapter 6)—will hence have a major bearing also in this political domain.

Protecting Climate Migrants

One area where additional support is needed is in the area of climate migration. The 2012 decision of the conference of the parties explicitly referred to the issue of "[h]ow impacts of climate change are affecting patterns of migration, displacement and human mobility" (UNFCCC 2012; see also UNFCCC 2010). Even though the focus here is less on forceful action than on acknowledging the need to further build up expertise in this domain, climate migration has entered the agenda of climate negotiations and is likely to stay.

One theoretical reform option could be to extend the mandate of the 1951 Geneva Convention and of the UNHCR to cover "climate refugees." This has been proposed by the Republic of the Maldives but does not find much support in the literature (see discussion in Biermann and Boas 2008). The maximum number of persons the UNHCR can currently deal with is a small fraction of the additional number of climate migrants that many studies predict for 2050. Politically it is unlikely that donor countries would allow the current refugee regime with its well-delineated set of refugee rights to be extended to cover a much larger group of people.

Moreover, climate migrants require a different kind of protection. For one, most climate migrants will not leave their home countries, and in most cases their governments will strive to protect, not persecute them. Also, areas most likely to be affected—notably low-lying coasts and islands—can be predicted within limits. Climate-related migration can therefore be planned and organized with the support of governments and public agencies, in contrast to migration stemming from political or religious persecution. As such, the problem of climate migrants is at its core a problem of development policy. It requires institutions that take account of this special character.

For these reasons, what is needed is a sui generis regime for the recognition, protection, and resettlement of climate migrants. This regime must be tailored to the particular needs of climate migrants, and it must be appropriately financed and supported by the international community. This regime could become part of the institutional mechanisms currently being negotiated within the climate regime on adaptation and "loss and damage" (UNFCCC 2012).

Five principles would need to serve as a basis for the institutional development of the regime (the following section draws on Biermann and Boas 2010b). First, even though climate change impacts will eventually manifest themselves in unpredictable singular events—such as storms, floods, or droughts—the increase in magnitude and frequency of such events can be predicted, and the consequent need for local populations to leave regions that suffer from increased risk can be foreseen. The governance of climate migrants can thus be better organized and planned than can assistance to victims of political turmoil or war, and can be carried out in planned, voluntary relocation and development programs over several decades.

Second, over the long term, most climate migrants—especially victims of sea level rise—will not be able to return to their homes. Thus, the underlying assumption in current refugee governance that affected people may return to their homes once state-led persecution in their home countries has ended needs to be replaced by an institutional design that conceives of (most) climate migrants as permanent immigrants to the regions or countries that accept them. Third, while current refugee law is based on individual persecution, a climate migration regime would need to be tailored to address groups of people, such as the populations of certain villages, cities, regions, provinces, or—as in the case of small island states—of entire countries.

Fourth, climate migrants enjoy in principle the protection of their own countries, and in many cases serious climate change impacts will affect only parts of a country. Thus, an international regime for climate migrants will focus less on the protection of persons outside their countries than on supporting governments, local communities, and agencies in protecting people within their own territory. The governance challenge of protecting and resettling climate migrants is thus essentially about international assistance and funding for the domestic support and resettlement programs of affected countries that have requested such support.

Fifth, climate change is a global problem in causation and consequences, and the industrialized countries bear most of the moral responsibility for its victims. This suggests that institutional elements from existing agreements on climate or from similar areas apply also to the protection of climate migrants. These include the principle of common but differentiated responsibilities and respective capabilities (which suggests that richer countries have to bear higher costs for protecting climate migrants); the principle of reimbursement of full incremental costs of affected countries incurred through resettlement of climate migrants; and the equity principle underpinning decision-making procedures that gives both developing and industrialized countries equal clout in a new institution on climate migrants.

These principles need not be linked to a specific institutional form. Theoretically, an international legal framework could emerge from a resolution from the UN General Assembly outside the climate convention context, as proposed by Mayer (2011b); but this does not seem to be very likely given the existing climate regime. Governments could also agree on a new treaty on climate migrants, such as the "cross-sectoral multilateral convention" on climate migrants that was proposed by the German Advisory Council on Global Change (2007, 129, see also 205,

206–207). Such a new treaty, however, could require a lengthy negotiation process on core principles and would weaken the link with the climate negotiations and their existing agreements on equity, responsibility, and international cooperation. In the current context, a separate convention on climate migrants seems highly unlikely.

A more feasible solution would be to include the protection of climate migrants *within an institutional mechanism under the climate convention*. In 2008, Ingrid Boas and I proposed a special protocol on climate migrants under the UN Framework Convention on Climate Change (Biermann and Boas 2008 and 2010b). This still seems to be the right way forward. In 2010, governments for the first time agreed, at the conference of the parties to the climate convention in Cancún, to invite

all Parties to enhance action on adaptation under the Cancun Adaptation Framework, taking into account their common but differentiated responsibilities and respective capabilities, and specific national and regional development priorities, objectives and circumstances, by undertaking, inter alia, … [m]easures to enhance understanding, coordination and cooperation with regard to climate change induced displacement, migration and planned relocation, where appropriate, at the national, regional and international levels. (UNFCCC 2010, para. 14.f)

Such measures and related frameworks might be integrated within the more general institutional mechanisms on adaptation and loss and damage that are currently being negotiated.

A legal instrument or framework under the climate convention would support climate migrants by integrating their protection into the overall climate regime, including progress in climate science that defines risks for people in certain regions. For developing countries, such a legal instrument for climate migrants based on the principle of common but differentiated responsibilities and full incremental costs could become a major negotiation goal (integrated into the current adaptation and loss and damage debates), in light of the increasing pressure from the North to integrate advanced developing countries into a global mitigation regime of quantified emission reduction obligations.

Concerning procedural operationalization, the legal instrument or protocol on climate migrants could provide for an executive committee that would function under the authority of the conference of the parties to the climate convention. This executive committee could maintain a list of specified administrative areas (such as villages, islands, districts) under the jurisdiction of member states whose population is determined to be in need of, or threatened by, relocation due to climate change. Any state party to the agreement—and in fact only state parties—would be entitled to propose areas under their jurisdiction for inclusion in the list of affected areas. In line with the sovereignty principle, inclusion of affected areas, as well as the type of support measures to be chosen, would be determined only upon formal proposal from the government of the affected country. While the composition and procedures of such an executive committee will be likely to be contentious in negotiations, it would appear reasonable to agree on decision-making procedures that would allow both the affected developing countries and the donor countries to hold collective veto rights over the future evolution and implementation of the protection regime.

Inclusion in the list of populations in need of relocation due to climate change could trigger specific rights and support mechanisms, including financial support, voluntary resettlement programs over decades, together with the purchase of new land and, especially in the case of small island states, organized international migration. It would be reasonable to restrict such rights to inhabitants of developing countries as defined in the climate regime.

Within climate negotiations, some governments and think tanks have proposed a broader "adaptation protocol" to the climate convention (Okereke et al. 2007, 36–37; Ayers, Alam, and Huq 2010). While I cannot engage here in a detailed discussion of the disadvantages and advantages of such a broader legal instrument, it is important to note that the core elements proposed here for a legal instrument on climate migrants could theoretically also be incorporated into a broader adaptation protocol. Integration of the protection of climate migrants into a broader adaptation protocol could allow for more holistic adaptation planning in regions at risk, which will include in many cases a combination of adaptation and voluntary resettlement programs. However, such an integration of the climate migration problem into a larger adaptation context also places forced migrants in competition with other interests in affected areas. This might endanger the effective protection and financial support of the people—often the poorest—for whom adaptation is no option and who have to leave their homes and resettle elsewhere. These potential conflicts thus need to be prevented if a broader legal instrument on adaptation is being negotiated.

The protection and resettlement of possibly millions of climate migrants over the course of this century will require substantial funds. Since climate migrants will often (though not exclusively) live in poorer developing countries and generally seek refuge in their own or neighboring countries, the funds will largely have to come from the international community. One can envision here three types of financial mechanisms for climate migrants: general development funding agencies, environment-related funds, or a new funding agency to be created especially for climate migrants.

Regarding development agencies, the World Bank group and the UNDP are probably most relevant at present, though others will have to play a role too (for example the WHO or the FAO). These agencies are increasingly integrating climate change impacts into their work programs, along with a number of specialized environmental funds such as the Adaptation Fund and the Green Climate Fund.

Yet while the protection of climate migrants is likely to fall under the terms of these funds, it is questionable whether they are the most appropriate mechanisms for supporting climate migrants. For one, funding is not enough even for the current purposes of the funds (see chapter 6). Furthermore, it is doubtful whether climate migrants can be best protected through inclusion in these general funding mechanisms. Climate migration would then compete with other concerns, be they mitigation as in the case of the GEF or the Green Climate Fund or overall adaptation in the case of the adaptation funds, where adaptation measures that also protect powerful economic interests might be prioritized. Integrating climate migrants into general environmental funding schemes might blur the specific moral link between climate migrants and potential donor countries and hinder claims for compensation, liability, and responsibility from industrialized countries. Thus, as in my previous discussion of the institutional setting to govern the recognition, protection, and voluntary resettlement of climate migrants, the best funding option also appears to be the creation of a sui generis regime to finance the protection of climate migrants, such as a Climate Migrants Protection Facility, for example within the overall framework of the Green Climate Fund or the Adaptation Fund. While the operational aspects of this facility could be linked with other financial mechanisms to increase efficiency, its governance should be independent and remain under the authority of the meeting of the parties to the proposed legal instrument on recognition, protection, and resettlement of climate migrants.

A key question for such a new facility for climate migrants would be the amount of funding required from the international community and the funding principles. For mitigation programs under the climate convention, industrialized countries have committed in article 4.3 of the climate convention to reimburse developing countries the agreed full incremental costs. Similar provisions apply to adaptation. In addition, the climate convention obliges industrialized countries to assist the most vulnerable countries in meeting adaptation costs (article 4.4) and gives special rights to least developed countries (article 4.9). This suggests applying the principle of reimbursement of full incremental costs also to the protection and resettlement of climate migrants, at least in those situations where causality by climate change is undisputed, namely in the case of sea level rise. For other situations in which climate change is only one causal factor in environmental degradation—for example in the case of water scarcity—the principle of additional funding instead of full reimbursement may be more appropriate.

I thus suggest four principles to govern a potential Climate Migrants Protection Facility. First, all funds would be provided on a grant basis. To the extent that larger development projects financed through loans include the resettlement of climate migrants, the resettlement costs would be fully reimbursed as a grant. Second, all funds provided for by the Climate Migrants Protection Facility would be new and additional, to prevent competition with other sustainable development needs. Third, in the case of migration because of sea level rise, the fund would reimburse the full agreed incremental costs incurred by developing countries in protecting and relocating these migrants (no matter from which country they come), taking into account that a large part of the financial transfer will be channeled through international development agencies. In cases where climate change is only one cause of environmental degradation, the fund would pay a portion of the protection and relocation costs, the exact amount of which could be determined in intergovernmental negotiation.

This blueprint of a governance system would ensure, I argue, the sufficient and timely recognition, protection, and resettlement of climate migrants. Yet the question of political feasibility arises. To begin with, the proposals included here would need to overcome significant practical hurdles. How to deal, for example, with funding requests from countries with autocratic governments or with a record of human rights violations: should the executive committee grant all financial and administrative support to these governments? Or how to deal with rent-seeking behavior by countries that try to leverage support for climate migrants to gain increased overall foreign financing? Such problems are likely, yet are not different from those faced by existing mechanisms of international support, from World Bank loans to GEF projects. Such problems can be addressed through appropriate institutional designs, including a balanced decision-making system that grants both recipient and donor countries sufficient control over the evolution of the funding mechanism.

A more difficult challenge is that the system proposed here would place a significant financial burden on donor countries. The costs of resettling millions of people, for instance, from the low-lying coastal regions of Africa, Asia, and Oceania are likely to be substantial, even if such processes proceed over several decades. Are donor countries ready for it? At present, the indications are not promising. The protection of those who are especially vulnerable to climate change has long been a fringe issue in climate negotiations, despite the new adaptation funding mechanisms that have been set up in recent years. One step that is being taken is the Migration Emergency Funding Mechanism being set up by the International Organization for Migration (IOM 2011). Yet the focus of this mechanism is neither climate change nor the planned relocation of people affected by rising sea levels, but rather emergency relief in more traditional crisis situations.

And yet the limited current efforts cannot predict what governments will decide, should the scenario forecasts reviewed above hold. One important factor is the likely security and stability implications of large-scale climate change impacts (also Mayer 2011b, 377–378). It is perhaps not surprising that military and defense planners in the North are among those paying the most attention to climate-induced migration, for instance in a 2014 study by the US Center for Naval Analyses that identifies climate change as a severe risk to US security and as a catalyst for global political conflict (Davenport 2014). Early support for climate migrants might not only attenuate human suffering, it might also prevent violent conflict. Investment in the protection of climate migrants is also investment in global security in the twenty-first century. This rationale of self-interest may well change current Northern attitudes to the financial support of climate change adaptation programs in poorer countries of the South. It might also lead to renewed efforts and a sense of urgency to mitigate climate change.

Conclusion

The hope remains that governments will soon agree on far-reaching mitigation actions to combat climate change and limit global warming to less than 1.5 or 2 degrees Celsius. Maybe technological break-throughs or large-scale societal adjustments toward low-carbon life-styles will help fuel governmental action or compensate for governmental inaction.

Even as we remain hopeful, let us also prepare for the worst. If drastic earth system transformations cannot be prevented, the existing international institutions, governance mechanisms, and intergovern-mental political processes face a massive, unprecedented challenge. Food shortages, water scarcity, land degradation, natural disasters, mass migration, or disruption of international commerce and com-munications will require quick and effective responses from the inter-national community. For many people in developing countries, it will become increasingly difficult to ensure subsistence. Earth system trans-formations could therefore compel millions of people to flee their homes in order to escape the grim circumstances caused or aggravated by climate change.

This chapter argues that current systems of international gover-nance do not suffice to cope with this challenge. I have outlined three governance dilemmas that will inevitably come to the fore should drastic earth system transformations materialize (stability versus adapt-ability, effectiveness versus legitimacy, and effectiveness versus fair-ness), and I have sketched a number of institutional design options that could be further explored in preparing for effective global adapta-tion governance.

In this sense, the chapter is explorative and poses more questions than it answers. Appraising the adaptability of current global governance arrangements to drastic earth system transformations requires more in-depth analysis that better integrates climate modeling and governance research. In addition, the possible reform options require more detailed research, including on lessons to be drawn from other domains of inter-national relations and the transferability of institutional design elements. One example of possible adaptation governance reform is the specialized regime on the recognition, protection, and resettlement of climate migrants that I have outlined in this chapter.

The serious impacts of climate change are largely predicted only for the second half of this century, based on the current state of climate science. However, the regions where major climate change impacts, such as sea level rise, are likely to cause harm and dislocation are broadly known and allow for preparation and planning. We thus need to research global adaptation governance not in terms of emergency response and disaster relief, but as planned and organized global adaptation. In particular when it comes to sea level rise, there is no need to wait for extreme weather events to strike. This calls, however, for early action in terms of setting up effective and appropriate governance mechanisms. The planning for effective global adaptation governance cannot wait until 2050 or 2080, when it might be too late for orderly and organized responses. It must begin now.

Der Schneider von Ulm (Ulm 1592)

Bischof, ich kann fliegen
Sagte der Schneider zum Bischof.
Pass auf, wie ich's mach!
Und er stieg mit so 'nen Dingen
Die aussahn wie Schwingen
Auf das große, große Kirchendach.

Der Bischof ging weiter.
Das sind lauter so Lügen
Der Mensch ist kein Vogel
Es wird nie ein Mensch fliegen
Sagte der Bischof vom Schneider.

Der Schneider ist verschieden
Sagten die Leute dem Bischof.
Es war eine Hatz.
Seine Flügel sind zerspellet
Und er liegt zerschellet
Auf dem harten, harten Kirchenplatz.
Die Glocken sollen läuten
Es waren nichts als Lügen
Der Mensch ist kein Vogel
Es wird nie ein Mensch fliegen
Sagte der Bischof den Leuten.

Bertolt Brecht, 1934

The Tailor of Ulm (Ulm 1592)

Bishop, I can fly
Said the tailor to the bishop.
Just watch me try!
And with a couple of things
That looked like wings
To the big, big roof of the church he
climbed.

The bishop walked by.
It's nothing but a lie
A man is not a bird
No man will ever fly
Said the bishop of the tailor.

The tailor has passed away
Said the people to the bishop
A farcical affair.
Broken-winged he crashed
And now lies smashed
On the hard, hard city square.
Let the church bells ring
It was nothing but a lie
A man is not a bird
No man will ever fly
Said the bishop to the people.

8

Conclusion

"Bishop, I can fly," claims the Tailor in the poem that opens this chapter, "Just watch me try!" "A man is not a bird / No man will ever fly," responds the Bishop, adding that what the Tailor claims is "nothing but a lie." This exchange between the Bishop and the Tailor in the mediaeval city of Ulm evokes current discussions on the feasibility of effective earth system governance. Today, too, it seems that there are too many bishops and too few tailors. Too few people who believe that, yes indeed, with imagination and courage, we can take off—to better modes of governance and better pathways of human-nature coevolution.

Such new modes are undoubtedly needed. Despite twenty years of global negotiations and national policies, carbon dioxide emissions increased in 2010 by 5.9 percent—toward a new record high in atmospheric concentrations (Peters et al. 2012; IPCC 2014b). In the academic community, pleas for drastic change in global governance are becoming a frequent feature of scientific gatherings. For example, the 2011 Nobel Laureate Symposium on Global Sustainability called in its Stockholm Memorandum for "strengthening Earth System Governance" as one of eight priorities for coherent global action (Third Nobel Laureate Symposium on Global Sustainability 2011). One year later, the 2012 State of the Planet Declaration, supported by various global change research programs and international agencies, called for "[f]undamental reorientation and restructuring of national and international institutions." It is essential, the declaration continued, "to overcome barriers to progress and to move to effective Earth-system governance. Governments must take action to support institutions and mechanisms that will improve coherence, as well as bring about integrated policy and action across the social, economic and environmental pillars" (State of the Planet Declaration 2012, C1). A press release preceding this declaration, supported by the International Council for

Science and others, even requests governments to fundamentally "overhaul" the entire UN system (Planet under Pressure Conference 2012).

Whither Multilateralism and International Cooperation?

No man will ever fly, says the Bishop. From such a perspective, stronger global institutions are impossible and multilateralism is doomed. The near breakdown of negotiations at the 2009 climate conference in Copenhagen shows the difficulties inherent in multilateral intergovernmentalism and its prospects to stimulate much-needed reforms (Dimitrov 2010). A more recent example is the outcome of the 2012 United Nations Conference on Sustainable Development, also known as "Rio+20." Despite an unprecedented number of people in attendance—in total 44,000 participants, including 79 heads of state and government—the conference delivered much less than many hoped for. The official diplomatic achievement of the conference was a nonbinding document, entitled "The Future We Want." After ten days of intense negotiations, this document had shrunk to the least common denominator that all countries could support. Controversial paragraphs on trade and environment, for example, were deleted from the final document when no compromise was in sight. This strategy worked inasmuch as the conference document was accepted by consensus. A complete breakdown of negotiations, or a final declaration that did not find the support of all countries, was thus prevented. The price for this minimalistic approach, however, was that "The Future We Want" is largely an affirmation of the status quo (see Biermann 2013).

Many argue, therefore, for alternatives to multilateralism, such as incremental minilateralism through negotiations among only a few countries with particular interests and resources (see chapter 4). Others claim that the answer to effective sustainability governance does not lie with the United Nations system but with a stronger reliance on bottom-up approaches driven by the private sector and civil society, including through nongovernmental agreements, transnational movements, and multisectoral partnerships (see chapter 3). Dutch political scientist Maarten Hajer, for example, has argued forcefully for an "energetic society" that would bring about change that governments are no longer able to foster. Consequently, he advised participants at the 2012 Rio conference to focus not on the diplomatic negotiations but on the side events (Hajer 2011; see also van Vuuren et al. 2012). Similarly, Mark Halle of the International Institute for Sustainable Development, in his review of the 2012 Rio conference, claims that "the principal problem lies with national governments, and [in] particular the groupings in which they congregate to negotiate" (Halle 2012, 4) and that our last hope lies with cities, the private sector, and civil society. Some observers also contend that the time for megasummits is over and that their benefits are not worth their costs, in terms of both resources spent and carbon emissions (Haas 2012; Andresen and Underdal 2012; Halle 2012).

There is no doubt that engagement of cities, civil society, and the private sector is urgently needed. Earth system governance cannot be addressed by governments alone. It must include all societal actors and individual citizens. For one, technology change and effective policies at local and national levels need to become a driving force of progress (Cohen, Brown, and Vergragt 2013). For instance, simply cutting down the emissions of black carbon and methane—which is a precursor of locally harmful tropospheric ozone—could be a win-win solution by reducing global mean warming by around 0.5 degree Celsius by the middle of the twenty-first century (Shindell et al. 2012). Win-win solutions are easily identifiable at the local level. Many companies around the world are taking action to reduce the environmental impacts of their products and production processes (critically see Dauvergne and Lister 2013). Municipalities can become important agents of change. The Swedish city of Kristianstad, for instance, has essentially phased out the use of oil, natural gas, or coal to heat the homes and businesses of its 80,000 citizens even during the Nordic winter, replacing fossil fuels with a mix of biological waste such as potato peels, manure, and wood waste (Rosenthal 2010). Solar energy production is taking off in many parts of the world, providing for example 7 percent of Germany's electricity consumption; worldwide, the installed capacity for solar energy went up in the last 13 years from 1.4 to 130 gigawatts (Powers 2013). A mix of technological change and climate change policy has allowed European Union member countries to cut greenhouse gas emissions by 18 percent from 1990 while growing their economies at the same time by 48 percent (European Commission 2013; see Huitema et al. 2011; Jordan et al. 2012).

Transformation in social behavior is crucial as well, moving from a focus on mere efficiency to broader notions of "sufficiency" (Princen

2003 and 2005). Large-scale lifestyle changes are likely to be nonlinear and might depend on "social tipping points" (UNEP 2012a). There are many examples of such tipping points in perceptions of good and appropriate lifestyles, often motivated by religion, national renaissance (for example, Gandhism), or philosophy. In Roman times, stoic philosophy led even an emperor, Marcus Aurelius, to sleep on a stone bench in order to comply with notions of a simple, or simplified, life. Environment-related changes in public perceptions of good living include the general disapproval of cigarette smoking as inappropriate behavior for movie actors, politicians, and other perceived role models; the change in perception of whale meat consumption that is unaffected by a recovery in stocks of some whale species; and the rising social movement of vegetarianism.

Another example is the increasing acceptance of bicycles as the default mode of transportation in cities. In October 2013, seventy top managers of Dutch companies publicly left their chauffeur-driven cars behind to support a weeklong national "Low Car Diet" campaign, thus accepting a partial redefinition of the appropriate lifestyle in the most affluent segments of society (Takken 2013). The branding of bicycle transportation as the "new normality" is also rapidly taking off in parts of North America. New York City, for instance, has in recent years increased its net of bicycle lanes by 700 kilometers and currently counts 73,000 members in its bicycle-sharing program, with 35,000 rides per day. According to a Dutch bicycle exporter, buying bicycles for daily use has become "hip" in New York City (Kuin 2013). Such transitions in social perceptions of good and appropriate behavior are unlikely to be "manageable" by public intervention alone (even though the role of local and national authorities remains important). What are required are fundamental changes in world-views and perceptions of the "good life" (Hedlund-de Witt 2013), possibly supported by the ongoing transformation in global communication, with now 2.7 billion people online and thus able to access rapidly spreading information on changes in dominant lifestyles (Pfanner 2013).

And yet it would mean throwing out the baby with the bathwater if governments and multilateral institutions were discarded in favor of a reliance on nongovernmental organizations, technology initiatives, partnerships, and societal movements. In the end, governments will need to take the lead. Governmental policies stand behind much of the environmental successes of the past decade, such as the progress in solar energy production that is driven by special feed-in tariffs in several countries. Multilateral institutions will be an important vehicle through which governments can coordinate their actions at the global level. Multilateralism and strengthened international cooperation are not the only solution; yet they are vital components of a globally effective strategy of multilayered, polycentric earth system governance that achieves progress at various levels and in various sectors. The UN system and multilateral negotiations do not stand in antagonistic relationships with local action and nonstate movements. Each needs the other. Both are essential and complementing.

At the global level of earth system governance, there are hardly any promising alternatives to multilateral institutions and negotiations. "Minilateralism" is unlikely to achieve the much-needed legitimacy among countries that are not invited to participate. The long-term effectiveness of solutions agreed upon at Group of 8 or Group of 20 meetings is open to debate, especially when it comes to broad questions of sustainability governance. More than 150 countries are not represented in the Group of 20 (see chapter 4). Transnational partnerships of private actors are important but cannot be more than a partial solution (see chapter 3). In any case, multilateralism is not dead despite recent setbacks, as evidenced by the more than 1,100 multilateral environmental agreements now in force (Mitchell 2013).

And yet: the current structure of international negotiations does not reflect the realities and exigencies of the twenty-first century. *New forms of multilateralism* are thus needed. This is the main conclusion of this book.

Toward Effective Earth System Governance

To sum up, the blueprint for a transformation of global institutions that I suggest in this book is not the only answer to the challenge of earth system transformations. Other reforms at national, local, and individual levels are equally important. Yet in a world with over 190 sovereign states, there is no way around strong and effective international institutions. Effective international cooperation must be a basis for earth system governance in the twenty-first century. Rather than a dismissal of the international institutional architecture as ineffective, a concerted effort is needed to bring these institutions into line with the exigencies of the changed political context of earth system transformation in the Anthropocene.

In chapters 3–7, I have outlined a set of fundamental reforms of the multilateral system that would advance, I argue, global decision making toward more effective earth system governance. To strengthen the clout of environmental concerns in the international system, I have proposed to upgrade the UN Environment Programme to a full-fledged World Environment Organization, on par with existing specialized agencies such as the World Health Organization and the International Labor Organization. I have also discussed different ways of strengthening the effectiveness of public-public partnerships and the science-policy interface for environmental governance in the UN system. For the latter, I have highlighted the need for a Global Environmental Assessment Commission as a statuary body within the United Nations, serving as an institutionalized early-warning voice of the global change research community for the intergovernmental political system (see chapter 3).

Regarding the overall institutional architecture of earth system governance, I have discussed in chapter 4 the lack of integration of international environmental policies; the lack of integration of environmental governance with other policy domains, notably global economic governance; and the lack of high-level regulatory competence and oversight regarding areas beyond national jurisdiction. These problems can be addressed, I have argued, by an appropriate adjustment of the current international institutional architecture. A World Environment Organization could help to coordinate the fragmented landscape of international environmental regimes and to reinforce decentralized efforts in institutional interplay management. A high-level UN Sustainable Development Council could ensure that economic and environmental policies are streamlined and earth system concerns are taken into account. A UN Trusteeship Council for Areas beyond National Jurisdiction would help strengthen the current governance systems on Antarctica, the high seas, and outer space.

In all multilateral institutions, one major obstacle to more effective governance is the outdated mode of decision making that is either based on consensus or, if votes are taken, grants each country the same vote regardless of size or relevance. As laid out in chapter 4, stronger reliance on majority voting would overcome the core problem of consensus-based decision making in most of current environmental multilateralism, that is, that the least interested country shapes the outcome of the negotiations. It is impossible to expect larger countries to accept binding decisions by a gathering where Monaco and Liechtenstein have the same voting rights as China and India. One way forward is to acknowledge the vast differences in population size among countries and explore novel systems of *qualified majority voting* in international negotiations. Qualified majority voting would allow international negotiations to advance more quickly and adopt more demanding decisions that were supported by the larger countries.

Such a transformation of global institutions would have to be accompanied by parallel reforms to ensure their accountability, legitimacy, and equity. A World Environment Fund, as outlined in chapter 6, would provide additional support to poorer countries for their efforts in contributing to earth system governance. Special legal agreements on adaptation and climate migrants, as explored in chapter 7, would make sure that the most vulnerable people were protected by the international community from those impacts of earth system transformation that could no longer be mitigated. A stronger involvement of citizens in global institutions could ensure that increased international cooperation would not become detached from the views and interests of the citizens (see chapter 5). Today, civil society organizations in the UN system have the right to be informed and voice their opinion, but there is no institutional mechanism in place for civil society organizations to influence decisions. With 44,000 participants and 3,500 official and unofficial events, the Rio+20 conference in 2012 exceeded the size of past landmarks such as the "Woodstockholm" in 1972 or the 1992 Rio Earth Summit. Brazilian President Dilma Rousseff hailed the 2012 Rio Conference as the most participatory conference in history and a "global expression of democracy" (ENB 2012, 1). And yet political decision making was left to the realm of governmental bureaucrats, without any formal input from civil society. One way forward, as proposed in chapter 5, would be to strengthen the involvement of citizens in intergovernmental institutions by setting up chambers of representatives of civil society organizations, global parliamentary assemblies, or deliberative assemblies.

International summits in themselves are also likely to remain an important part of international norm development (Seyfang and Jordan 2002; Pattberg and Mert 2013). A complete assessment of the 2012 conference in Rio de Janeiro, for example, includes the many preparatory conferences and dialogues at which governments, nongovernmental organizations, the science community, the business communities, and others worked toward agreement on key issues. There is now new consensus on the state of the planet and on the core issues to be negotiated by governments. This is a vital step in furthering a reform agenda for global sustainability. The question remains, however, whether such discursive developments cannot be achieved by other means. An alternative could be more focused conferences on an issue not covered by any existing negotiation. Examples could be global summits on sustainability education or on the future provision of food for nine billion people. Such specialized summits could ensure a more concrete, and hence more sustainable, outcome. A second option is to grant sustainability more prominence in the UN General Assembly, which marshals the attendance and attention of most heads of state and government. Sustainability summits could be integrated into the procedures of the General Assembly, generating momentum for new discursive developments without the high political, financial, and environmental costs incurred with megaevents such as Rio+20.

The institutional blueprint suggested in this book would be the largest transformation of the United Nations system since 1945. It would be the constitutional moment that many actors in recent years have called for, and would bring the UN system in line with the urgent needs of planetary stewardship and earth system governance. The new or reformed bodies in this institutional blueprint could form an "Earth Alliance" consisting of a World Environment Organization, as the chief global intergovernmental body for environmental protection; a high-level UN Sustainable Development Council for the integration of global environmental with economic governance; a new UN Trusteeship Council for Areas beyond National Jurisdiction to provide vital oversight over those areas that do not belong to any state; a UN Global Environmental Assessment Commission to feed authoritative insights on the state of the environment into intergovernmental decision making, drawing on the vast experience and findings of numerous larger assessment institutions, such as IPCC; and a World Environment Fund, to support the poorest countries in their efforts.

The establishment of such bodies would build on existing institutions that are at present weak and not influential enough: The new high-level political forum on sustainable development, which will replace the former UN CSD, could be upgraded to a UN Sustainable Development Council as a main organ of the United Nations, with a revised decision-making structure that would give a stronger role to the largest countries and allow the council to exert meaningful influence over the Bretton

Woods institutions (see chapter 4). The UN Environment Programme would be upgraded to a World Environment Organization. And the defunct UN Trusteeship Council would be reformed as a strengthened mechanism for stable, long-term governance and oversight by the entire international community over areas that lie outside the jurisdiction of individual states.

A complete implementation of these proposals would need a revision of the UN Charter (UN 1945). This would require, according to article 108 of the Charter, the support of two-thirds of United Nations member states, including the five permanent members of the Security Council. So far, the UN Charter has not been amended except for a few revisions that increased the number of countries represented in the UN Security Council (1965) and ECOSOC (1965 and 1973), reflecting the almost fourfold increase in the number of independent countries since 1945. Yet despite this reform-resistant trajectory of the UN Charter—which is also related to lack of consensus on some of its core elements, such as the UN Security Council—there is no reason to rule out the possibility of a charter amendment in the future. In fact, article 109 of the UN Charter explicitly foresees the need for further revisions and amendments of the Charter, which were originally—in 1945—planned for a revision conference in 1955. In the latter year UN General Assembly established a committee to report on options for UN reform, terminating this effort in 1967 in the midst of the cold war. New efforts to revisit the Charter, however, are not outside the realm of possibility.

Moreover, many core elements of the reforms outlined in this book do not require amendment of the UN Charter. The UN Sustainable Development Council can be instituted through a decision of the UN General Assembly (UN Charter, article 22), similar to the creation of a UN Human Rights Council in 2006. The same holds for inclusion of special chambers of civil society organizations or a parliamentary assembly in the United Nations. Also, a UN Trusteeship Council for Areas beyond National Jurisdiction, as proposed in chapter 4, could be installed under article 22 by the UN General Assembly without affecting the legal status of the obsolete current trusteeship system as enshrined in the Charter. In addition, article 77.1.c of the UN Charter allows for trusteeship agreements for "territories voluntarily placed under the system by states responsible for their administration." This could apply to Antarctica if members of the Antarctic treaty system agree. This solution would not be ideal, yet it is legally and politically possible. Moreover, a World

Environment Organization or a World Environment Fund can be established through an intergovernmental agreement among those countries willing to join the organization. Other changes can be enacted by decisions under multilateral environmental agreements, including the introduction of qualified majority voting in the conferences of the parties. Inclusion of citizens, civil society, and parliamentarians, as well as many questions of equity and the protection of the most vulnerable people, can also be addressed under multilateral agreements. In sum, many reforms suggested in this book do not rely on a revision of the UN Charter. Support by a majority of countries can allow for transformative change.

The proposal of an "Earth Alliance" would constitute a major reform of global governance, yet it would not be without precedent in national political systems or even global governance. Economic, financial, and trade governance, in particular, have seen tremendous increases in global institutionalization in recent decades, not least through creation of the powerful regulatory systems under the World Trade Organization, the International Monetary Fund, and the World Bank. In international security governance, heads of state who engage in wars of aggression are facing trial at the newly established International Criminal Court. As another example, the United Nations Convention on the Law of the Sea has created an international administration to govern exploitation of mineral resources of the deep sea.

An area that has not seen a similar institutionalization is earth system governance. Yet like economic and financial governance, sustainable development and planetary stewardship require international cooperation and strong institutions to protect the vital planetary systems on which human survival depends. After the creation of the United Nations in 1945 to ensure international peace, and the strengthening of economic governance systems in the 1990s, what is needed now is a new constitutional moment to strengthen the overall institutional framework for effective governance of the interaction of human societies with the planetary system. Achieving this major reform of earth system governance will not be easy, and we cannot expect revolutionary change in the foreseeable future. But the past record of the slow but steady emergence of stronger institutions in global governance gives room for hope.

In sum, I tend to side with the Tailor. Yes, humans can fly, and they can take off to a better future and more effective earth system governance.

Progress is too slow, however, and more effort is needed. The need of the hour is a global and effective architecture for earth system governance that is adaptive to changing circumstances; participatory through involving citizens and civil society at all levels; accountable and legitimate as part of new democratic governance beyond the state; and fair for all participants. This book has tried to sketch some elements of a blueprint for effective earth system governance that could help achieve these major goals.

References

Abbott, Kenneth W. 2012. The Transnational Regime Complex for Climate Change. *Environment and Planning C: Government and Policy* 30 (4): 571–590.

Abbott, Kenneth W., and David Gartner. 2011. The Green Climate Fund and the Future of Environmental Governance. Earth System Governance Working Paper 16. Earth System Governance Project, Lund and Amsterdam.

Abbott, Kenneth W., and Duncan Snidal. 1998. Why States Act through Formal International Organizations. *Journal of Conflict Resolution* 42 (1):3–32.

Abbott, Kenneth W., and Duncan Snidal. 2009. Strengthening International Regulation through Transnational New Governance: Overcoming the Orchestration Deficit. *Vanderbilt Journal of Transnational Law* 42:1–80.

Abbott, Kenneth W., and Duncan Snidal. 2010. International Regulation without International Government: Improving IO Performance through Orchestration. *Review of International Organizations* 5:315–344.

Abrego, Lisandro, Carlo Perroni, John Whalley, and Randall M. Wigle. 2003. Trade and Environment: Bargaining Outcomes from Linked Negotiations. *Review of International Economics* 9 (3):414–428.

Adelle, Camilla, and Andrew Jordan. 2009. The European Union and the "External" Dimension of Sustainable Development. In *International Organizations in Global Environmental Governance*, ed. Frank Biermann, Bernd Siebenhüner, and Anna Schreyögg, 111–130. New York: Routledge.

Adger, W. Neil, Nigel W. Arnell, and Emma L. Tompkins. 2005. Successful Adaptation to Climate Change across Scales. *Global Environmental Change: Human and Policy Dimensions* 15:77–86.

Adger, W. Neil, Katrina Brown, and Mike Hulme. 2005. Redefining Global Environmental Change. *Global Environmental Change: Human and Policy Dimensions* 15:1–4.

Adger, W. Neil, and Andrew J. Jordan, eds. 2009. *Governing Sustainability*. Cambridge, UK: Cambridge University Press.

Adger, W. Neil, Jouni Paavola, Saleemul Huq, and M. J. Mace, eds. 2006. *Fairness in Adaptation to Climate Change*. Cambridge, MA: MIT Press.

Agarwal, Anil, Anju Sharma, and Sunita Narain. 1999. *Global Environmental Negotiations 1: Green Politics.* New Delhi: Center for Science and Environment.

Agreement Governing the Activities of States on the Moon and Other Celestial Bodies. 1979. *International Legal Materials* 18:1434.

Alcántara, Cynthia Hewitt de. 1998. Uses and Abuses of the Concept of Governance. *International Social Science Journal* 155:105–113.

Alcock, Frank. 2008. Conflicts and Coalitions within and across the ENGO Community. *Global Environmental Politics* 8 (4):66–91.

Aldy, Joseph E., Scott Barrett, and Robert N. Stavins. 2003. Thirteen Plus One: A Comparison of Global Climate Policy Architectures. *Climate Policy* 3 (4): 373–397.

Amsterdam Declaration. 2001. Challenges of a Changing Earth. Declaration of the Global Change Open Science Conference Amsterdam, signed by the chairs of the International Geosphere-Biosphere Programme (IGBP), the International Human Dimensions Programme on Global Environmental Change (IHDP), the World Climate Research Programme (WCRP), and the international biodiversity program DIVERSITAS. Amsterdam, The Netherlands, 13 July 2001. Available at http://www.essp.org/index.php?id=41&L= (retrieved 12 January 2014).

Andler, Lydia. 2009. The Secretariat of the Global Environment Facility: From Network to Bureaucracy. In *Managers of Global Change: The Influence of International Environmental Bureaucracies*, ed. Frank Biermann and Bernd Siebenhüner, 203–223. Cambridge, MA: MIT Press.

Andonova, Liliana. B. 2006. Globalization, Agency, and Institutional Innovation: The Rise of Public-Private Partnerships in Global Governance. Working Paper 2006-004. Goldfarb Center, Waterville, ME.

Andonova, Liliana B., Michele M. Betsill, and Harriet Bulkeley. 2009. Transnational Climate Governance. *Global Environmental Politics* 9 (2):52–73.

Andonova, Liliana B., and Marc A. Levy. 2003. Franchising Global Governance: Making Sense of the Johannesburg Type II Partnerships. In *Yearbook of International Cooperation on Environment and Development*, ed. Olav Schram Stokke and Øystein B. Thommessen, 19–32. London: Earthscan.

Andreae, Meinrat O., Liana Talaue-McManus, and P. A. Matson. 2004. Anthropogenic Modification of Land, Coastal, and Atmospheric Systems as Threats to the Functioning of the Earth System. In *Earth System Analysis for Sustainability*, ed. Hans-Joachim Schellnhuber, Paul J. Crutzen, William C. Clark, Martin Claussen, and Hermann Held, 245–264. Cambridge, MA: MIT Press, in cooperation with Dahlem University Press.

Andresen, Steinar. 2001. Global Environmental Governance: UN Fragmentation and Co-ordination. In *Yearbook of International Co-operation on Environment and Development 2001/2002*, ed. Olav Schram Stokke and Øystein B. Thommessen, 19–26. London: Earthscan.

Andresen, Steinar. 2007a. Key Actors in UN Environmental Governance: Influence, Reform and Leadership. *International Environmental Agreements: Politics, Law and Economics* 7 (4):457–468.

Andresen, Steinar. 2007b. The Effectiveness of UN Environmental Institutions. *International Environmental Agreements: Politics, Law and Economics* 7 (4): 317–336.

Andresen, Steinar, and Ellen Hey. 2005. The Effectiveness and Legitimacy of International Environmental Institutions. *International Environmental Agreements: Politics, Law and Economics* 5 (3):211–226.

Andresen, Steinar, and Kirsten Rosendal. 2009. The Role of the United Nations Environment Programme in the Coordination of Multilateral Environmental Agreements. In *International Organizations in Global Environmental Governance*, ed. Frank Biermann, Bernd Siebenhüner, and Anna Schreyögg, 133–150. Abingdon: Routledge.

Andresen, Steinar, and Arild Underdal. 2012. We Do Not Need More Global Sustainability Conferences. Open letter in the internet forum on international environmental governance hosted by the Earth System Governance Project, at www.ieg.earthsystemgovernance.org (retrieved 14 November 2012).

Archibugi, Daniele, and David Held, eds. 1995. *Cosmopolitan Democracy: An Agenda for a New World Order*. Oxford: Polity Press.

Archibugi, Daniele, David Held, and Martin Köhler, eds. 1998. *Re-imagining Political Community: Studies in Cosmopolitan Democracy*. Stanford: Stanford University Press.

Arts, Bas. 1998. *The Political Influence of Global NGOs: Case Studies on the Climate Change and Biodiversity Conventions*. Utrecht: International Books.

Arts, Bas. 2002. Green Alliances of Business and NGOs: New Styles of Self-regulation or Dead-End Roads? *Corporate Social Responsibility and Environmental Management* 9:26–36.

Australian Labor Party. 2006. Labor Calls for International Coalition to Accept Climate Change Refugees. Press release, 9 October.

Ayers, Jessica, Mozaharul Alam, and Saleemul Huq. 2010. Global Adaptation Governance beyond 2012: Developing Country Perspectives. In *Global Climate Governance beyond 2012: Architecture, Agency and Adaptation*, ed. Frank Biermann, Philipp Pattberg, and Fariborz Zelli, 270–285. Cambridge, UK: Cambridge University Press.

Baber, Walter F., and Robert V. Bartlett. 2009. *Global Democracy and Sustainable Jurisprudence: Deliberative Environmental Law*. Cambridge, MA: MIT Press.

Baber, Walter F., and Robert V. Bartlett. 2013. Juristic Democracy: A Deliberative Common Law Strategy for Earth System Governance. Earth System Governance Working Paper 27. Earth System Governance Project, Lund and Amsterdam.

Bäckstrand, Karin. 2006. Multi-stakeholder Partnerships for Sustainable Development: Rethinking Legitimacy, Accountability and Effectiveness. *European Environment* 16 (5):290–306.

Bäckstrand, Karin. 2008. Accountability of Networked Climate Governance: The Rise of Transnational Climate Partnerships. *Global Environmental Politics* 8:74–104.

Bäckstrand, Karin, Sabine Campe, Sander Chan, Ayşem Mert, and Marco Schäfferhof. 2012. Transnational Public-Private Partnerships. In *Global Environmental Governance Reconsidered*, ed. Frank Biermann and Philipp Pattberg, 123–147. Cambridge, MA: MIT Press.

Bäckstrand, Karin, Jamil Khan, Annica Kronsell, and Eva Lövbrand, eds. 2010. *Environmental Politics and Deliberative Democracy: Examining the Promise of New Modes of Governance*. Cheltenham: Edward Elgar.

Bals, Christoph, Koko Warner, and Sonja Butzengeiger. 2006. Insuring the Uninsurable: Design Options for a Climate Change Funding Mechanism. *Climate Policy* 6 (6):637–647.

Barnett, Michael N., and Liv Coleman. 2005. Designing Police: Interpol and the Study of Change in International Organizations. *International Studies Quarterly* 49:593–619.

Barnett, Michael N., and Martha Finnemore. 1999. The Politics, Power, and Pathologies of International Organizations. *International Organization* 53 (4):699–732.

Barnett, Michael N., and Martha Finnemore. 2004. *Rules for the World: International Organizations in Global Politics*. Ithaca: Cornell University Press.

Barrett, Scott. 2007. A Multitrack Climate Treaty System. In *Architectures for Agreement: Addressing Global Climate Change in the Post-Kyoto World*, ed. Joseph E. Aldy and Robert N. Stavins, 237–259. Cambridge, UK: Cambridge University Press.

Barrett, Scott, and Michael Toman. 2010. Contrasting Future Paths for an Evolving Global Climate Regime. World Bank Development Research Group, Environment and Energy Team, Policy Research Working Paper 5164. World Bank, Washington, DC.

Barry, John, and Robyn Eckersley, eds. 2005. *The State and the Global Ecological Crisis*. Cambridge, MA: MIT Press.

Bartlett, Robert V., Priya A. Kurian, and Madhu Malik, eds. 1995. *International Organizations and Environmental Policy*. Westport, CT: Greenwood Press.

Bastos Lima, M. 2012. Personal communication. 14 November.

Bauer, Steffen. 2009a. The Ozone Secretariat: The Good Shepherd of Ozone Politics. In *Managers of Global Change: The Influence of International Environmental Bureaucracies*, ed. Frank Biermann and Bernd Siebenhüner, 225–244. Cambridge, MA: MIT Press.

Bauer, Steffen. 2009b. The Secretariat of the United Nations Environment Programme: Tangled Up in Blue. In *Managers of Global Change: The Influence of International Environmental Bureaucracies*, ed. Frank Biermann and Bernd Siebenhüner, 169–201. Cambridge, MA: MIT Press.

Bauer, Steffen. 2013. Strengthening the United Nations. In *The Handbook of Global Climate and Environment Policy*, ed. Robert Falkner, 320–357. Chichester: John Wiley and Sons.

Bauer, Steffen, Steinar Andresen, and Frank Biermann. 2012. International Bureaucracies. In *Global Environmental Governance Reconsidered*, ed. Frank Biermann and Philipp Pattberg, 27–44. Cambridge, MA: MIT Press.

Bauer, Steffen, and Frank Biermann. 2005. The Debate on a World Environment Organization: An Introduction. In *A World Environment Organization: Solution or Threat for Effective International Environmental Governance?*, ed. Frank Biermann and Steffen Bauer, 1–23. Aldershot, UK: Ashgate.

Beitz, Charles R. 1975. Justice and International Relations. *Philosophy and Public Affairs Journal* 4 (4):360–389.

Beitz, Charles R. 1979. *Political Theory and International Relations*. Princeton: Princeton University Press.

Benecke, Elisabeth. 2011. Networking for Climate Change: Agency in the Context of Renewable Energy Governance in India. *International Environmental Agreements: Politics, Law and Economics* 11 (1):23–42.

Benedick, Richard E. 1998. *Ozone Diplomacy: New Directions in Safeguarding the Planet*. 2nd enl. ed. Cambridge, MA: Harvard University Press.

Benner, Thorsten, Charlotte Streck, and Jan-Martin Witte, eds. 2003. *Progress and Perils: Networks and Partnerships in Global Environmental Governance: The Post-Johannesburg Agenda*. Berlin and Washington, DC: Global Public Policy Institute.

Benvenisti, Eyal, and George W. Downs. 2007. The Empire's New Clothes: Political Economy and the Fragmentation of International Law. *Stanford Law Review* 60:595–632.

Berkes, Fikret, Johan Colding, and Carl Folke, eds. 2003. *Navigating Social-Ecological Systems: Building Resilience for Complexity and Change*. Cambridge, UK: Cambridge University Press.

Berkhout, Frans. 2010. Reconstructing Boundaries and Reason in the Climate Debate. *Global Environmental Change: Human and Policy Dimensions* 20 (4):565–569.

Bernauer, Thomas. 1995. The Effect of International Environmental Institutions: How We Might Learn More. *International Organization* 49 (2):351–377.

Bernstein, Steven. 2005. Legitimacy in Global Environmental Governance. *Journal of International Law and International Relations* 1 (1–2):139–166.

Bernstein, Steven, with Jutta Brunnée. 2011. Consultants' Report on Options for Broader Reform of the Institutional Framework for Sustainable Development (IFSD): Structural, Legal, and Financial Aspects. UN Department of Economic and Social Affairs, New York. Available at http://www.uncsd2012.org/index.php ?page=view&type=400&nr=211&menu=45 (retrieved 12 January 2014).

Bernstein, Steven, and Benjamin Cashore. 2007. Can Non-state Global Governance Be Legitimate? A Theoretical Framework. *Regulation and Governance* 1:1–25.

Bernstein, Steven, and Maria Ivanova. 2007. Institutional Fragmentation and Normative Compromise in Global Environmental Governance: What Prospects for Re-embedding? In *Global Liberalism and Political Order: Towards a New Grand Compromise?*, ed. Steven Bernstein and Louis W. Pauly, 161–185. Albany: State University of New York Press.

Betsill, Michele M., and Harriet Bulkeley. 2004. Transnational Networks and Global Environmental Governance: The Cities for Climate Protection Program. *International Studies Quarterly* 48 (2):471–493.

Betsill, Michele M., and Elisabeth Corell. 2001. NGO Influence in International Environmental Negotiations: A Framework for Analysis. *Global Environmental Politics* 1 (4):65–85.

Biermann, Frank. 1996. Common Concern of Humankind: The Emergence of a New Concept of International Environmental Law. *Archiv des Völkerrechts* 34 (4):426–481.

Biermann, Frank. 1997. Financing Environmental Policies in the South: Experiences from the Multilateral Ozone Fund. *International Environmental Affairs* 9 (3):179–219.

Biermann, Frank. 1998. *Weltumweltpolitik zwischen Nord und Süd. Die neue Verhandlungsmacht der Entwicklungsländer.* Baden-Baden: Nomos.

Biermann, Frank. 2000. The Case for a World Environment Organization. *Environment* 42 (9):22–31.

Biermann, Frank. 2001a. The Emerging Debate on the Need for a World Environment Organization: A Commentary. *Global Environmental Politics* 1 (1):45–55.

Biermann, Frank. 2001b. The Rising Tide of Green Unilateralism in World Trade Law: Options for Reconciling the Emerging North-South Conflict. *Journal of World Trade* 35 (3):421–448.

Biermann, Frank. 2002a. Common Concerns of Humankind and National Sovereignty. In *Globalism: People, Profits and Progress*, 158–212. Proceedings of the 30th Annual Conference of the Canadian Council on International Law, Ottawa, 18–20 October 2001. Dordrecht: Kluwer.

Biermann, Frank. 2002b. Institutions for Scientific Advice: Global Environmental Assessments and Their Influence in Developing Countries. *Global Governance* 8 (2):195–219.

Biermann, Frank. 2002c. Johannesburg Plus 20: From International Environmental Policy to Earth System Governance. *Politics and the Life Sciences* 21 (2):72–77.

Biermann, Frank. 2005a. Earth System Governance: The Challenge for Social Science. Inaugural Lecture delivered on 23 November upon accession to the offices of Professor of Environmental Policy Sciences and Professor of Political

Science at the Vrije Universiteit Amsterdam. Amsterdam: Vrije Universiteit Amsterdam.

Biermann, Frank. 2005b. Between the USA and the South: Strategic Choices for European Climate Policy. *Climate Policy* 5 (3):273–290.

Biermann, Frank. 2006. Whose Experts? The Role of Geographic Representation in Assessment Institutions. In *Global Environmental Assessments: Information and Influence*, ed. Ronald B. Mitchell, William C. Clark, David W. Cash, and Nancy M. Dickson, 87–112. Cambridge, MA: MIT Press.

Biermann, Frank. 2007. "Earth System Governance" as a Crosscutting Theme of Global Change Research. *Global Environmental Change: Human and Policy Dimensions* 17:326–337.

Biermann, Frank. 2008. Earth System Governance: A Research Agenda. In *Institutions and Environmental Change: Principal Findings, Applications and Research Frontiers*, ed. Oran R. Young, Leslie A. King, and Heike Schroeder, 277–301. Cambridge, MA: MIT Press.

Biermann, Frank. 2010. Beyond the Intergovernmental Regime: Recent Trends in Global Carbon Governance. *Current Opinion in Environmental Sustainability* 2 (4):284–288.

Biermann, Frank. 2012a. Greening the United Nations Charter: World Politics in the Anthropocene. *Environment* 54 (3):6–17.

Biermann, Frank. 2012b. Planetary Boundaries and Earth System Governance: Exploring the Links. *Ecological Economics* 81:4–9.

Biermann, Frank. 2013. Curtain Down and Nothing Settled: Global Sustainability Governance after the "Rio+20" Earth Summit. *Environment and Planning C: Government and Policy* 31 (6): 1099–1114.

Biermann, Frank, Kenneth Abbott, Steinar Andresen, Karin Bäckstrand, Steven Bernstein, Michele M. Betsill, Harriet Bulkeley, Benjamin Cashore, Jennifer Clapp, Carl Folke, Aarti Gupta, Joyeeta Gupta, Peter M. Haas, Andrew Jordan, Norichika Kanie, Tatiana Kluvánková-Oravská, Louis Lebel, Diana Liverman, James Meadowcroft, Ronald B. Mitchell, Peter Newell, Sebastian Oberthür, Lennart Olsson, Philipp Pattberg, Roberto Sánchez-Rodríguez, Heike Schroeder, Arild Underdal, Susana Camargo Vieira, Coleen Vogel, Oran R. Young, Andrea Brock, and Ruben Zondervan. 2012. Navigating the Anthropocene: Improving Earth System Governance. *Science* 335 (6074) (16 March): 1306–1307.

Biermann, Frank, and Steffen Bauer, eds. 2005. *A World Environment Organization: Solution or Threat for Effective International Environmental Governance?* Aldershot, UK: Ashgate.

Biermann, Frank, Jesper Berséus, Eleni Dellas, Sofia Frantzi, Peter Janssen, Marcel Kok, Philipp Pattberg, Arthur Petersen, and Martine de Vos. 2011. Modelling International Institutions in Earth System Analysis: The ModelGIGS Approach. Paper presented at the 2011 Colorado Conference on Earth System Governance "Crossing Boundaries and Building Bridges." Fort Collins, CO, 17–20 May 2011. On file with author.

Biermann, Frank, Michele M. Betsill, Joyeeta Gupta, Norichika Kanie, Louis Lebel, Diana Liverman, Heike Schroeder, and Bernd Siebenhüner, with contributions from Ken Conca, Leila da Costa Ferreira, Bharat Desai, Simon Tay, and Ruben Zondervan. 2009. Earth System Governance: People, Places and the Planet. Science and Implementation Plan of the Earth System Governance Project. ESG Report 1. Earth System Governance Project, Bonn.

Biermann, Frank, and Ingrid Boas. 2008. Protecting Climate Refugees: The Case for a Global Protocol. *Environment* 50 (6):8–16.

Biermann, Frank, and Ingrid Boas. 2010a. Global Adaptation Governance: Setting the Stage. In *Global Climate Governance beyond 2012: Architecture, Agency, and Adaptation*, ed. Frank Biermann, Philipp Pattberg, and Fariborz Zelli, 223–234. Cambridge, UK: Cambridge University Press.

Biermann, Frank, and Ingrid Boas. 2010b. Preparing for a Warmer World: Towards a Global Governance System to Protect Climate Refugees. *Global Environmental Politics* 10 (1):60–88.

Biermann, Frank, Man-san Chan, Ayşem Mert, and Philipp Pattberg. 2007. Multi-stakeholder Partnerships for Sustainable Development: Does the Promise Hold? In *Partnerships, Governance and Sustainable Development: Reflections on Theory and Practice*, ed. Pieter Glasbergen, Frank Biermann, and Arthur P. J. Mol, 239–260. Cheltenham: Edward Elgar.

Biermann, Frank, and Klaus Dingwerth. 2004. Global Environmental Change and the Nation State. *Global Environmental Politics* 4 (1):1–22.

Biermann, Frank, and Aarti Gupta. 2011a. Accountability and Legitimacy in Earth System Governance: A Research Framework. *Ecological Economics* 70:1856–1864.

Biermann, Frank, and Aarti Gupta. 2011b. Accountability and Legitimacy: An Analytical Challenge for Earth System Governance. *Ecological Economics* 70:1854–1855.

Biermann, Frank, and Philipp Pattberg, eds. 2012. *Global Environmental Governance Reconsidered*. Cambridge, MA: MIT Press.

Biermann, Frank, Philipp Pattberg, Harro van Asselt, and Fariborz Zelli. 2009. The Fragmentation of Global Governance Architectures: A Framework for Analysis. *Global Environmental Politics* 9 (4):14–40.

Biermann, Frank, Philipp Pattberg, and Fariborz Zelli, eds. 2010. *Global Climate Governance beyond 2012: Architecture, Agency and Adaptation*. Cambridge, UK: Cambridge University Press.

Biermann, Frank, and Bernd Siebenhüner, eds. 2009. *Managers of Global Change: The Influence of International Environmental Bureaucracies*. Cambridge, MA: MIT Press.

Biermann, Frank, Bernd Siebenhüner, and Anna Schreyögg, eds. 2009. *International Organizations and Global Environmental Governance*. London: Routledge.

Boas, Ingrid. 2013. The Securitisation of Climate Migration: Analysing the Inter-action between the UK and Indian Governments and Understanding How Their Actions and Perspectives Are Shaped. Doctoral dissertation, University of Kent, United Kingdom.

Bodansky, Daniel. 1999. Legitimacy of International Governance: A Coming Challenge for International Environmental Law. *American Journal of International Law* 93 (3):596–624.

Bodansky, Daniel. 2002. *U.S. Climate Policy after Kyoto: Elements for Success.* Washington, DC: Carnegie Endowment for International Peace.

Bodansky, Daniel. 2007. Legitimacy. In *The Oxford Handbook of International Environmental Law*, ed. Daniel Bodansky, Jutta Brunnée, and Ellen Hey, 704–723. Oxford: Oxford University Press.

Bodansky, Daniel. 2011. *Multilateral Climate Efforts beyond the UNFCCC.* Arlington, VA: Center for Climate and Energy Solutions.

Bodansky, Daniel, Jutta Brunée, and Ellen Hey, eds. 2007. *The Oxford Handbook of International Environmental Law.* Oxford: Oxford University Press.

Böhringer, Christoph, and Carsten Helm. 2008. On the Fair Division of Greenhouse Gas Abatement Costs. *Resource and Energy Economics* 30 (2):260–276.

Bouteligier, Sofie. 2011. Exploring the Agency of Global Environmental Consultancy Firms in Earth System Governance. *International Environmental Agreements: Politics, Law and Economics* 11 (1):43–61.

Bouwer, Laurens M., and Jeroen C. J. H. Aerts. 2006. Financing Climate Change Adaptation. *Disasters* 30 (1):49–63.

Brouwer, Stijn, and Frank Biermann. 2011. Towards Adaptive Management: Examining the Strategies of Policy Entrepreneurs in Dutch Water Management. *Ecology and Society* [online journal] 16: 4: 5.

Brown Weiss, Edith. 1993. International Environmental Law: Contemporary Issues and the Emergence of a New Order. *Georgetown Law Journal* 81 (3):675–710.

Brown Weiss, Edith, and Harold K. Jacobson, eds. 1998. *Engaging Countries: Strengthening Compliance with International Environmental Accords.* Cambridge, MA: MIT Press.

Bruch, Carl, and John Pendergrass. 2003. Type II Partnerships, International Law, and the Commons. *Georgetown International Environmental Law Review* 15 (4):855–886.

Brunnée, Jutta. 1989. "Common Interest": Echoes from an Empty Shell? Some Thoughts on Common Interest and International Environmental Law. *Zeitschrift für ausländisches öffentliches Recht und Völkerrecht* 49 (3–4): 791–808.

Bulkeley, Harriet, Liliana B. Andonova, Karin Bäckstrand, Michele M. Betsill, Daniel Compagnon, Rosaleen Duffy, Ans Kolk, Matthew Hoffmann, David L. Levy, Peter Newell, Tori Milledge, Matthew Paterson, Philipp Pattberg, and Stacy D. VanDeveer. 2012. Governing Climate Change Transnationally: Assessing the

Evidence from a Database of Sixty Initiatives. *Environment and Planning C: Government and Policy* 30 (4):591–612.

Bulkeley, Harriet, and Michele M. Betsill. 2003. *Cities and Climate Change: Urban Sustainability and Global Environmental Governance.* London: Routledge.

Bulkeley, Harriet, Matthew J. Hoffmann, Stacy D. VanDeveer, and Victoria Milledge. 2012. Transnational Governance Experiments. In *Global Environmental Governance Reconsidered*, ed. Frank Biermann and Philipp Pattberg, 149–171. Cambridge, MA: MIT Press.

Bulkeley, Harriet, and Andrew Jordan. 2012. Transnational Environmental Governance: New Findings and Emerging Research Agendas. *Environment and Planning C: Government and Policy* 30 (4):556–570.

Bulkeley, Harriet, and Heike Schroeder. 2011. Beyond State/Non-state Divides: Global Cities and the Governing of Climate Change. *European Journal of International Relations* 18 (4):743–766.

Bulkeley, Harriet, and Heike Schroeder. 2012. Global Cities and the Politics of Climate Change. In *Handbook of Global Environmental Politics.* 2nd ed., ed. Peter Dauvergne, 249–260. Cheltenham: Edward Elgar.

Bull, Hedley. 1977. *The Anarchical Society: A Study of Order in World Politics.* New York: Columbia University Press.

Bummel, Andreas. 2010. *The Composition of a Parliamentary Assembly at the United Nations.* Berlin: Committee for a Democratic U.N.

Busch, Per-Olof. 2009. The Climate Secretariat: Making a Living in a Straitjacket. In *Managers of Global Change: The Influence of International Environmental Bureaucracies*, ed. Frank Biermann and Bernd Siebenhüner, 245–264. Cambridge, MA: MIT Press.

Busch, Per-Olof, Aarti Gupta, and Robert Falkner. 2012. International-Domestic Linkages and Policy Convergence. In *Global Environmental Governance Reconsidered*, ed. Frank Biermann and Philipp Pattberg, 199–218. Cambridge, MA: MIT Press.

Busch, Per-Olof, and Helge Jörgens. 2005. International Patterns of Environmental Policy Change and Convergence. *European Environment* 15 (2):80–101.

Cairo World Conference on Preparing for Climate Change. 1990. Cairo Compact: Toward a Concerted World-Wide Response to the Climate Crisis (Conference Statement, 1989). Reprinted in *American University Journal of International Law and Policy* 5: 631–634.

Caldwell, Lynton Keith. 1984. *International Environmental Policy: Emergence and Dimensions.* Durham: Duke University Press.

Caney, Simon. 2001. International Distributive Justice: A Review. *Political Studies Journal* 49:974–989.

Caney, Simon. 2006. Cosmopolitan Justice and Institutional Design: An Egalitarian Liberal Conception of Global Governance. *Social Theory and Practice* 32 (4):725–756.

Cartagena Declaration on Refugees. 1984. Cartagena Declaration on Refugees. Adopted by the Colloquium on the International Protection of Refugees in Central America, Mexico and Panama, 22 November. Available at http://www .oas.org/dil/1984_Cartagena_Declaration_on_Refugees.pdf (retrieved 14 January 2014).

Cashore, Benjamin, Graeme Auld, Steven Bernstein, and Constance McDermott. 2007. Can Non-state Governance 'Ratchet Up' Global Environmental Standards? Lessons from the Forest Sector. *Review of European Community and International Environmental Law* 16 (2):158–172.

Center for Participatory Research and Development. 2013. *Loss and Damage Negotiation at the UNFCCC: An Era of Liability and Compensation.* Dhaka: Center for Participatory Research and Development.

Chan, Sander. 2014. Partnerships for Sustainable Development: Emergence, Adaptation, and Impacts in Global and Domestic Governance Contexts. Doctoral dissertation. Amsterdam: VU University Amsterdam.

Chan, Sander, and Philipp Pattberg. 2008. Private Rule-making and the Politics of Accountability: Analyzing Global Forest Governance. *Global Environmental Politics* 8:103–121.

Charnovitz, Steve. 2005. Toward a World Environment Organization: Reflections upon a Vital Debate. In *A World Environment Organization: Solution or Threat for Effective International Environmental Governance?*, ed. Frank Biermann and Steffen Bauer, 87–116. Aldershot, UK: Ashgate.

Charnovitz, Steve. 2007. The WTO's Environmental Progress. *Journal of International Economic Law* 10 (3):685–706.

Chasek, Pamela S. 2000. The UN Commission on Sustainable Development: The First Five Years. In *The Global Environment in the Twenty-first Century: Prospects for International Cooperation*, ed. Pamela S. Chasek, 378–398. New York: UN University.

Chen, Shaohua, and Martin Ravallion. 2008. The Developing World Is Poorer Than We Thought, but No Less Successful in the Fight against Poverty. Policy Research Working Paper 4703. World Bank, Washington DC.

Civil Society Reflection Group. 2012. *No Future without Justice: Report of the Civil Society Reflection Group on Global Development Perspectives.* Development Dialogue 59. Uppsala: Dag Hammarskjöld Foundation.

Clapp, Jennifer. 1997. The Illegal CFC Trade: An Unexpected Wrinkle in the Ozone Protection Regime. *International Environmental Affairs* 9 (4):259–273.

Clapp, Jennifer. 1998. The Privatization of Global Environmental Governance: ISO 14000 and the Developing World. *Global Governance* 4:295–316.

Clapp, Jennifer. 2009. Global Mechanisms for Greening TNCs: Inching Towards Corporate Accountability? In *Handbook on Trade and Environment*, ed. Kevin P. Gallagher, 159–170. Cheltenham: Edward Elgar.

Clapp, Jennifer, and Doris Fuchs, eds. 2009. *Corporate Power in Global Agrifood Governance.* Cambridge, MA: MIT Press.

Clark, William C., Paul J. Crutzen, and Hans-Joachim Schellnhuber. 2005. Science for Global Sustainability: Toward a New Paradigm. Center for International Development, Working Paper 120. Harvard University, Cambridge, MA.

Clò, S. 2009. The Effectiveness of the EU Emissions Trading Scheme. *Climate Policy* 9 (3):227–241.

CNA Corporation. 2007. National Security and the Threat of Climate Change. Available at http://www.cna.org/sites/default/files/National%20Security%20 and%20the%20Threat%20of%20Climate%20Change%20-%20Print.pdf (retrieved 11 January 2014).

Cohen, Maurie J., Halina Szejnwald Brown, and Philip J. Vergragt, eds. 2013. *Innovations in Sustainable Consumption: New Economics, Socio-technical Transitions, and Social Practices.* Cheltenham: Edward Elgar.

Colombia and Guatemala. 2011. Rio + 20: Sustainable Development Goals (SDGs). A Proposal from the Governments of Colombia and Guatemala. Undated (2011). On file with author.

Commission on Global Governance. 1995. *Our Global Neighbourhood: The Report of the Commission on Global Governance.* Oxford: Oxford University Press.

Compagnon, Daniel, Sander Chan, and Ayşem Mert. 2012. The Changing Role of the State. In *Global Environmental Governance Reconsidered,* ed. Frank Biermann and Philipp Pattberg, 217–263. Cambridge, MA: MIT Press.

Conca, Ken. 1995. Greening the United Nations: Environmental Organizations and the UN System. *Third World Quarterly* 16 (3):441–457.

Conca, Ken. 2006. *Governing Water: Contentious Transnational Politics and Global Institution Building.* Cambridge, MA: MIT Press.

Cone, Sydney M., III. 1999. The Appellate Body, the Protection of Sea Turtles and the Technique of "Completing the Analysis." *Journal of World Trade* 33:51–61.

de Coninck, Heleen, Carolyn Fischer, Richard G. Newell, and Takahiro Ueno. 2008. International Technology-Oriented Agreements to Address Climate Change. *Energy Policy* 36 (1):335–356.

Consultative Group of Ministers or High-Level Representatives on International Environmental Governance. 2010. Nairobi-Helsinki Outcome, agreed at the group's second meeting in Espoo, Finland, 21–23 November 2010. On file with author.

Convention Governing the Specific Aspects of Refugee Problems in Africa. 1969. Done at Addis Ababa 10 September 1969, in force 20 June 1974. Available at http://www.afrol.com/archive/documents/refugees_convention.htm (retrieved 14 January 2014).

Convention on Biological Diversity. 1992. Done at Rio de Janeiro 5 June 1992, in force 29 December 1993. *International Legal Materials* 31:818.

Convention on International Trade in Endangered Species of Wild Fauna and Flora (CITES). 1973. Done at Washington 3 March 1973, in force 1 July 1975. *International Legal Materials* 12:1085.

Convention on the Control of Transboundary Movements of Hazardous Wastes and Their Disposal. 1989. Done at Basel 22 March 1989, in force 24 May 1992. *International Legal Materials* 37:22.

Convention on the Law of Treaties. 1969. Done at Vienna 23 May 1969, in force 27 January 1980. *International Legal Materials* 8:679.

Convention on the Protection of the Ozone Layer. 1985. Done at Vienna 22 March 1985, in force 22 September 1988. *International Legal Materials* 26:1529.

Corbera, Esteve, and Heike Schroeder. 2011. Governing and Implementing REDD+. *Environmental Science and Policy* 14:89–99.

Corporate Europe Observatory. 2002. *From Rio to Johannesburg: Girona Declaration*. London.

Crutzen, Paul J. 2002. The Anthropocene: Geology of Mankind. *Nature* 415:23.

Crutzen, Paul J. 2006. Albedo Enhancement by Stratospheric Sulfur Injections: A Contribution to Solve a Policy Dilemma. *Climatic Change* 77:211–219.

Crutzen, Paul J., and Veerabhadran Ramanathan. 2004. Atmospheric Chemistry and Climate in the Anthropocene: Where Are We Heading? In *Earth System Analysis for Sustainability*, ed. Hans-Joachim Schellnhuber, Paul J. Crutzen, William C. Clark, Martin Claussen, and Hermann Held, 266–292. Cambridge, MA: MIT Press, in cooperation with Dahlem University Press.

Crutzen, Paul J., and Eugene F. Stoermer. 2000. The "Anthropocene." *IGBP Newsletter* 41:17–18.

Dauvergne, Peter, ed. 2012. *Handbook of Global Environmental Politics*. 2nd ed. Cheltenham: Edward Elgar.

Dauvergne, Peter, and Jane Lister. 2013. *Eco-Business: A Big-Brand Takeover of Sustainability*. Cambridge, MA: MIT Press.

Davenport, Coral. 2014. A Hotter, More Violent World. *New York Times International*, 15 May, 5.

de Boer, Joop, and Onno Kuik. 2004. The Logic of Sustainability Labels: Their Functions for Stakeholders and Their Role in Markets. In *Sustainability Labelling and Certification*, ed. Mar Campins Eritja, 49–74. Madrid: Marcial Pons.

Dellapenna, Joseph W., and Joyeeta Gupta. 2008. Toward Global Law on Water. *Global Governance* 14 (4):437–453.

Dellapenna, Joseph W., and Joyeeta Gupta. 2009. The Evolution of Global Water Law. In *The Evolution of the Law and Politics of Water*, ed. Joseph W. Dellapenna and Joyeeta Gupta, 3–19. Berlin: Springer Science + Business Media B.V.

Dellas, Eleni. 2011. CSD Water Partnerships: Privatization, Participation, and Legitimacy. *Ecological Economics* 70 (11):1916–1923.

Dellas, Eleni, and Philipp Pattberg. 2014. Assessing the Political Feasibility of Global Options to Reduce Biodiversity Loss. *International Journal of Biodiversity Science, Ecosystem Services and Management* 9 (4): 347–363.

Dellas, Eleni, Philipp Pattberg, Jesper Berséus, Marcel Kok, Sofia Frantzi, Martine de Vos, Peter Janssen, Frank Biermann, and Arthur Petersen. 2011. Modelling Governance and Institutions for Global Sustainability Politics (ModelGIGS). IVM Report W11/005. Institute for Environmental Studies, VU University Amsterdam.

Dellas, Eleni, Philipp Pattberg, and Michele M. Betsill. 2011. Agency in Earth System Governance: Refining a Research Agenda. *International Environmental Agreements: Politics, Law and Economics* 11 (1):85–98.

DeSombre, Elizabeth R., and J. Samuel Barkin. 2002. Turtles and Trade: The WTO's Acceptance of Environmental Trade Restrictions. *Global Environmental Politics* 2 (1):12–18.

Development, Concepts and Doctrine Centre, UK Ministry of Defence. 2010. *Global Strategic Trends: Out to 2014*. London: UK Ministry of Defence.

de Vos, Martine G., Peter H. M. Janssen, Marcel T. J. Kok, Sofia Frantzi, Eleni Dellas, Philipp Pattberg, Arthur C. Petersen, and Frank Biermann. 2013. Formalizing Knowledge on International Environmental Regimes: A First Step towards Integrating Political Science in Integrated Assessments of Global Environmental Change. *Environmental Modelling and Software* 44:101–112.

Diamond, Jared. 2005. *Collapse: How Societies Choose to Fail or Succeed*. New York: Viking Books.

Dimitrov, Radoslav S. 2010. Inside UN Climate Change Negotiations: The Copenhagen Conference. *Review of Policy Research* 27 (6):795–821.

Dingwerth, Klaus. 2005. The Democratic Legitimacy of Public-Private Rule-Making: What Can We Learn from the World Commission on Dams? *Global Governance* 11 (1):65–83.

Dingwerth, Klaus. 2007. *The New Transnationalism: Transnational Governance and Democratic Legitimacy*. Basingstoke: Palgrave Macmillan.

Dingwerth, Klaus. 2008. North-South Parity in Global Governance: The Affirmative Procedures of the Forest Stewardship Council. *Global Governance* 14 (1):53–71.

Dingwerth, Klaus, and Philipp Pattberg. 2009. World Politics and Organizational Fields: The Case of Sustainability Governance. *European Journal of International Relations* 15 (4):707–743.

Dombrowski, Kathrin I. 2013. Bridging the Democratic Gap: Can NGOs Link Local Communities to International Environmental Institutions? Doctoral dissertation, Department of International Relations, London School of Economics and Political Science.

Dryzek, John S. 1999. Transnational Democracy. *Journal of Political Philosophy* 7 (1):30–51.

Dryzek, John S. 2006. *Deliberative Global Politics: Discourse and Democracy in a Divided World*. Cambridge, UK: Polity Press.

Dryzek, John S., André Bächtiger, and Karolina Milewicz. 2011. Toward a Deliberative Global Citizens' Assembly. *Global Policy* 2 (1):33–42.

Dryzek, John, David Downes, Christian Hunhold, David Schlosberg, and Hans-Kristian Hernes. 2003. *Green States and Social Movements: Environmentalism in the United States, United Kingdom and Norway*. Oxford: Oxford University Press.

Dryzek, John S., and Hayley Stevenson. 2011. Global Democracy and Earth System Governance. *Ecological Economics* 70 (11):1865–1874.

Ebbesson, Jonas. 2009. The Rule of Law in Governance of Complex Socio-ecological Changes. *Global Environmental Change: Human and Policy Dimensions* 20:414–422.

Eckersley, Robyn. 2004a. The Big Chill: The WTO and Multilateral Environmental Agreements. *Global Environmental Politics* 4 (2):24–50.

Eckersley, Robyn. 2004b. *The Green State: Rethinking Democracy and Sovereignty*. Cambridge, MA: MIT Press.

Edwards, Julia, Guillermo Kerber, and Sophia Wirsching. 2013. Climate Change-Induced Displacement: What Is at Stake? A Climate Justice Perspective. In *"Climate Refugees": People Displaced by Climate Change and the Role of the Churches*, ed. Sophia Wirsching, Peter Emberson, and Guillermo Kerber, 23–53. Geneva: World Council of Churches.

Eisenack, Klaus, Jürgen P. Kropp, and Heinz Welsch. 2006. A Qualitative Dynamical Modelling Approach to Capital Accumulation in Unregulated Fisheries. *Journal of Economic Dynamics and Control* 30 (12):2613–2636.

El-Hinnawi, Essam. 1985. *Environmental Refugees*. Nairobi: United Nations Environment Programme.

Eliasch, Johan. 2008. *Climate Change: Financing Global Forests: The Eliasch Review*. London: Earthscan.

Elliott, Lorraine. 2005. The United Nations Record on Environmental Governance: An Assessment. In *A World Environment Organization: Solution or Threat for Effective International Environmental Governance?*, ed. Frank Biermann and Steffen Bauer, 27–56. Aldershot, UK: Ashgate.

ENB [Earth Negotiations Bulletin]. 2012. Summary of the 2012 United Nations Conference on Sustainable Development, 13–22 June. Available at http://www .iisd.ca/download/pdf/enb2751e.pdf (retrieved 15 January 2014).

ENB. 2013a. Summary of the Bonn Climate Change Conference, 3–14 June. Available at http://www.iisd.ca/vol12/enb12580e.html (retrieved 14 January 2014).

ENB. 2013b. Summary of the Warsaw Climate Change Conference, 11–23 November. Available at http://www.iisd.ca/climate/cop19/enb (retrieved 3 June 2014).

European Commission. 2013. The 2015 International Climate Change Agreement: Shaping International Climate Policy beyond 2020. Communication from the Commission to the European Parliament, the Council, the European Economic and Social Committee, and the Committee of the Regions. Doc. COM (2013) 167. European Commission, Brussels, 26 March.

European Union. 2011. Submission to the UN Department of Economic and Social Affairs for the UN Conference on Sustainable Development. 1 November.

Falk, Richard, and Andrew Strauss. 2001. Toward Global Parliament. *Foreign Affairs* 80 (1):212–220.

Falkner, Robert. 2003. Private Environmental Governance and International Relations: Exploring the Links. *Global Environmental Politics* 3 (2):72–87.

Falkner, Robert, ed. 2013. *The Handbook of Global Climate and Environment Policy*. Chichester, UK: John Wiley and Sons.

Falkner, Robert, and Aarti Gupta. 2009. Limits of Regulatory Convergence: Globalization and GMO Politics in the South. *International Environmental Agreements: Politics, Law and Economics* 9 (2):113–133.

Falkner, Robert, Hannes Stephan, and John Vogler. 2010. International Climate Policy after Copenhagen: Towards a "Building Blocks" Approach. *Global Policy* 1 (3):252–262.

FAO [Food and Agriculture Organization of the United Nations], IFAD [International Fund for Agricultural Development], and WFP [World Food Programme]. 2013. *State of Food Insecurity in the World*. Rome: Food and Agriculture Organization of the United Nations.

Fauchald, Ole Kristian. 2010. *International Environmental Governance: A Legal Analysis of Selected Options*. FNI Report 16/2010. Lysaker, Norway: Fridtjof Nansen Institute.

Ferguson, Tyrone. 1998. *The Third World and Decision Making in the International Monetary Fund: The Quest for Full and Effective Participation*. London: Pinter Publishers.

Finkelstein, Lawrence S. 1995. What Is Global Governance? *Global Governance* 1:367–372.

Finnemore, Martha. 1993. International Organizations as Teachers of Norms: The United Nations Educational, Scientific, and Cultural Organization and Science Policy. *International Organization* 47 (4):565–598.

Flachsland, Christian, Robert Marschinski, Ottmar Edenhofer, Marian Leimbach, and Lavinia Baumstark. 2010. Developing the International Carbon Market beyond 2012: Options and the Costs of Delay. In *Global Climate Governance beyond 2012: Architecture, Agency and Adaptation*, ed. Frank Biermann, Philipp Pattberg, and Fariborz Zelli, 60–78. Cambridge, UK: Cambridge University Press.

Florini, Ann, ed. 2007. *The Right to Know: Transparency for an Open World*. New York: Columbia University Press.

Folke, Carl. 2006. Resilience: The Emergence of a Perspective for Social-Ecological Systems Analysis. *Global Environmental Change: Human and Policy Dimensions* 16:253–267.

Folke, Carl, Thomas Hahn, Per Olsson, and Jon Norberg. 2005. Adaptive Governance of Social-Ecological Systems. *Annual Review of Environment and Resources* 30:441–473.

Folke, Carl, Lowell Pritchard, Fikret Berkes, Johan Colding, and Uno Svedin. 1998. *The Problem of Fit between Ecosystems and Institutions*. Bonn: International Human Dimensions Programme on Global Environmental Change.

Freeland, Chrystia. 2011. The Super-Rich Pull Even Farther Ahead. *International Herald Tribune*, 26 January, 1 and 13.

Future Earth Transition Team. 2012. Future Earth: Research for Global Sustainability. A Framework Document. Final Version. Unpublished manuscript (February). Available at http://www.icsu.org/future-earth/whats-new/relevant _publications (retrieved 2 January 2013).

Gaffney, Owen, Ninad Bondre, Sybil Seitzinger, Mark Stafford Smith, Frank Biermann, Rik Leemans, John Ingram, et al. 2012. Interconnected Risks and Solutions for a Planet under Pressure: Transition to Sustainability in the Context of a Green Economy and Institutional Frameworks for Sustainable Development. One of nine policy briefs produced by the scientific community to inform the 2012 United Nations Conference on Sustainable Development and commissioned by the international conference "Planet under Pressure: New Knowledge towards Solutions." Available at www.planetunderpressure2012.net (retrieved 21 January 2013).

Galaz, Victor, Per Olsson, Thomas Hahn, Carl Folke, and Uno Svedin. 2008. The Problem of Fit among Biophysical Systems, Environmental and Resource Regimes, and Broader Governance Systems: Insights and Emerging Challenges. In *Institutions and Environmental Change: Principal Findings, Applications, and Research Frontiers*, ed. Oran R. Young, Leslie A. King, and Heike Schroeder, 147–182. Cambridge, MA: MIT Press.

Galaz, Victor, Frank Biermann, Beatrice Crona, Derk Loorbach, Carl Folke, Per Olsson, Måns Nilsson, Jeremy Allouche, Åsa Persson, and Gunilla Reischl. 2012a. Planetary Boundaries: Exploring the Challenges for Global Environmental Governance. *Current Opinion in Environmental Sustainability* 4 (1):80–87.

Galaz, Victor, Frank Biermann, Carl Folke, Per Olsson, and Måns Nilsson, eds. 2012b. Planetary Boundaries: Exploring the Challenges for Global Environmental Governance. *Ecological Economics* 81 (special issue).

Galaz, Victor, Frank Biermann, Carl Folke, Måns Nilsson, and Per Olsson. 2012c. Global Environmental Governance and Planetary Boundaries: An Introduction. *Ecological Economics* 81:1–3.

GEF [Global Environment Facility]. 1994. Instrument for the Establishment of the Restructured Global Environment Facility. *International Legal Materials* 33:1273.

Gehring, Thomas. 2011. The Institutional Complex of Trade and Environment: Toward an Interlocking Governance Structure and a Division of Labor. In *Managing Institutional Complexity: Regime Interplay and Global Environmental Change*, ed. Sebastian Oberthür and Olav Schram Stokke, 227–254. Cambridge, MA: MIT Press.

Gehring, Thomas, and Sebastian Oberthür. 2006. Empirical Analysis and Ideal Types of Institutional Interaction. In *Institutional Interaction in Global Environmental Governance: Synergy and Conflict among International and EU Policies*, ed. Sebastian Oberthür and Thomas Gehring, 307–371. Cambridge, MA: MIT Press.

Gerlak, Andrea K. 2013. Policy Interactions in Human-Landscape Systems. *Environmental Management* 53 (1): 67–75.

German Advisory Council on Global Change. 1997. *World in Transition: The Research Challenge*. Berlin: Springer.

German Advisory Council on Global Change. 2000. *World in Transition: Strategies for Managing Global Environmental Risks*. Berlin: Springer.

German Advisory Council on Global Change. 2007. *World in Transition: Climate Change as a Security Risk*. Berlin: German Advisory Council on Global Change.

Gillis, Justin. 2010. That Wheezing Sound May Be Earth. *International Herald Tribune*, 22 December, 1 and 4.

Gillis, Justin. 2011. A Fence at the Top of the World. *International Herald Tribune*, 25 January, 1 and 4.

Glasbergen, Pieter, Frank Biermann, and Arthur P. J. Mol, eds. 2007. *Partnerships, Governance and Sustainable Development: Reflections on Theory and Practice*. Cheltenham: Edward Elgar.

Gleditsch, Nils Petter, Ragnhild Nordås, and Idean Salehyan. 2007. Climate Change and Conflict: The Migration Link. Coping with Crisis working paper series. International Peace Academy, New York.

Gordenker, Leon, and Thomas G. Weiss. 1996. Pluralizing Global Governance: Analytical Approaches and Dimensions. In *NGOs, the UN, and Global Governance*, ed. Thomas G. Weiss and Leon Gordenker, 17–47. Boulder, CO: Lynne Rienner.

Greiner, Sandra. 2009. CDM: From Policy to Practice. *Climate Policy* 9 (6):681–683.

Gribbin, John. 1988. Any Old Iron. *Nature* 331:570.

Group of 77 and the People's Republic of China. 1989. Draft text proposed. UN Doc. UNEP/OzL.Pro.1/CRP.11 of 4 May.

Gulbrandsen, Lars H. 2004. Overlapping Public and Private Governance: Can Forest Certification Fill the Gaps in the Global Forest Regime? *Global Environmental Politics* 4 (2):75–99.

Gulbrandsen, Lars H. 2010. *Transnational Environmental Governance: The Emergence and Effects of the Certification of Forests and Fisheries*. Cheltenham: Edward Elgar.

Gulbrandsen, Lars H., and Steinar Andresen. 2004. NGO Influence in the Implementation of the Kyoto Protocol: Compliance, Flexibility Mechanisms, and Sinks. *Global Environmental Politics* 4 (4):54–75.

Gupta, Aarti. 2004. When Global Is Local: Negotiating Safe Use of Biotechnology. In *Earthly Politics: Local and Global in Environmental Governance*, ed. Sheila Jasanoff and Marybeth Long Martello, 127–148. Cambridge, MA: MIT Press.

Gupta, Aarti. 2008. Transparency under Scrutiny: Information Disclosure in Global Environmental Governance. *Global Environmental Politics* 8 (2):1–7.

Gupta, Aarti. 2010. Transparency in Global Environmental Governance: A Coming of Age? *Global Environmental Politics* 10 (3):1–9.

Gupta, Aarti, Steinar Andresen, Frank Biermann, and Bernd Siebenhüner. 2012. Science Networks. In *Global Environmental Governance Reconsidered*, ed. Frank Biermann and Philipp Pattberg, 69–93. Cambridge, MA: MIT Press.

Gupta, Aarti, and Robert Falkner. 2006. The Influence of the Cartagena Protocol on Biosafety: Comparing Mexico, China and South Africa. *Global Environmental Politics* 6 (4):23–44.

Gupta, Aarti, Eva Lövbrand, Esther Turnhout, and Marjanneke J. Vijge. 2012. In Pursuit of Carbon Accountability: The Politics of REDD+ Measuring, Reporting and Verification Systems. *Current Opinion in Environmental Sustainability* 4 (6):726–731.

Gupta, Aarti, and Michael Mason, eds. 2014. *Transparency in Global Environmental Governance: Critical Perspectives.* Cambridge, MA: MIT Press.

Gupta, Joyeeta. 2004. Global Sustainable Food Governance and Hunger: Traps and Tragedies. *British Food Journal* 5:406–416.

Gupta, Joyeeta. 2005. Global Environmental Governance: Challenges for the South from a Theoretical Perspective. In *A World Environment Organization: Solution or Threat for Effective International Environmental Governance?*, ed. Frank Biermann and Steffen Bauer, 57–83. Aldershot, UK: Ashgate.

Gupta, Joyeeta, Nicolien van der Grijp, and Onno Kuik, eds. 2013. *Climate Change, Forests, and REDD: Lessons for Institutional Design.* Abingdon, UK: Routledge.

Haas, Peter M. 1990. *Saving the Mediterranean: The Politics of International Environmental Cooperation.* New York: Columbia University Press.

Haas, Peter M. 2004. Addressing the Global Governance Deficit. *Global Environmental Politics* 4 (4):1–15.

Haas, Peter M. 2012. The Road from Rio: Why Environmentalism Needs to Come Down from the Summit. *Foreign Affairs* 16 (August).

Haas, Peter M., Robert O. Keohane, and Marc A. Levy, eds. 1993. *Institutions for the Earth: Sources of Effective International Environmental Protection.* Cambridge, MA: MIT Press.

Haites, Erik, and Michael Mehling. 2009. Linking Existing and Proposed GHG Emissions Trading Schemes in North America. *Climate Policy* 9 (4):373–388.

Hajer, Maarten. 2011. *De energieke samenleving. Op zoek naar een sturingsfilosofie voor een schone economie* [with English summary]. The Hague: Planbureau voor de Leefomgeving.

Hakone Vision on Governance for Sustainability in the 21st Century. 2011. Towards a Charter Moment. Lund: Earth System Governance Project. Available at http://earthsystemgovernance.org/publication/earth-system-governance -project-editor-towards-charter-moment (retrieved 14 January 2014).

Hale, Thomas, and Denise Mauzerall. 2004. Thinking Globally and Acting Locally: Can the Johannesburg Partnerships Coordinate Action on Sustainable Development? *Journal of Environment and Development* 13 (3):220–239.

Hall, Rodney Bruce, and Thomas J. Biersteker, eds. 2002. *The Emergence of Private Authority in Global Governance*. Cambridge, UK: Cambridge University Press.

Halle, Mark. 2012. *Life after Rio: IISD Commentary*. Winnipeg, Canada: International Institute for Sustainable Development.

Hamilton, Clive. 2013. *Earthmasters: The Dawn of the Age of Climate Engineering*. New Haven: Yale University Press.

Hawkins, Darren G., David A. Lake, Daniel L. Nielson, and Michael J. Tierney, eds. 2006a. *Delegation and Agency in International Organizations*. Cambridge, UK: Cambridge University Press.

Hawkins, Darren G., David A. Lake, Daniel L. Nielson, and Michael J. Tierney. 2006b. Delegation under Anarchy: States, International Organizations, and Principal-Agent Theory. In *Delegation and Agency in International Organizations*, ed. Darren G. Hawkins, David A. Lake, Daniel L. Nielson, and Michael J. Tierney, 3–38. Cambridge, UK: Cambridge University Press.

Hedlund-de Witt, Annick. 2013. Worldviews and the Transformation to Sustainable Societies: An Exploration of the Cultural and Psychological Dimensions of Our Global Environmental Challenges. Doctoral dissertation. VU University Amsterdam, The Netherlands.

Heinrich, Dieter. 2010. *The Case for a United Nations Parliamentary Assembly*. Berlin: Committee for a Democratic U.N.

Held, David. 1995. *Democracy and the Global Order: From the Modern State to Cosmopolitan Governance*. Stanford: Stanford University Press.

Held, David. 1997. Democracy and Globalization. *Global Governance* 3 (3):251–267.

Held, David. 1999. The Transformation of Political Community: Rethinking Democracy in the Context of Globalization. In *Democracy's Edges*, ed. Ian Shapiro and Casiano Hacker-Cordon, 84–111. Cambridge, UK: Cambridge University Press.

High Level Dialogue on Institutional Framework for Sustainable Development. 2011. Held 19–21 July in Solo, Indonesia. Chair's summary. On file with author.

High-Level Panel on Global Sustainability. 2012. *Resilient People, Resilient Planet: A Future Worth Choosing. Report of the United Nations Secretary-General's High-Level Panel on Global Sustainability*. New York: United Nations.

Hirschman, Albert O. 1945 [1980]. *National Power and the Structure of Foreign Trade*. Berkeley: University of California Press.

Hof, Andries, Michel den Elzen, and Detlef van Vuuren. 2010. Environmental Effectiveness and Economic Consequences of Fragmented versus Universal Regimes: What Can We Learn from Model Studies? In *Global Climate Governance beyond 2012: Architecture, Agency and Adaptation*, ed. Frank Biermann, Philipp Pattberg, and Fariborz Zelli, 33–59. Cambridge, UK: Cambridge University Press.

Hoffmann, Matthew J. 2011. *Climate Governance at the Crossroads: Experimenting with a Global Response after Kyoto*. Oxford: Oxford University Press.

Hovi, Jon, and Detlef F. Sprinz. 2006. The Limits of the Law of the Least Ambitious Program. *Global Environmental Politics* 6 (3):28–42.

Howse, R. 1998. The Turtles Panel: Another Environmental Disaster in Geneva. *Journal of World Trade* 32:73–100.

Huitema, Dave, Andrew J. Jordan, Eric Massey, Tim Rayner, Harro van Asselt, Constanze Haug, Roger Hildingsson, Suvi Monni, and Johannes Stripple. 2011. The Evaluation of Climate Policy: Theory and Emerging Practice in Europe. *Policy Sciences* 44 (2):179–198.

Huitema, Dave, and Sander Meijerink, eds. 2009. *Water Policy Entrepreneurs: A Research Companion to Water Transitions around the Globe*. Cheltenham: Edward Elgar.

Huitema, Dave, Erik Mostert, Wouter Egas, Sabine Moellenkamp, Claudia Pahl-Wostl, and Resul Yalcin. 2009. Adaptive Water Governance: Assessing Adaptive Management from a Governance Perspective. *Ecology and Society* [online journal] 4 (1):26.

Humphreys, David. 2004. Redefining the Issues: NGO Influence on International Forest Negotiations. *Global Environmental Politics* 4 (2):51–74.

IASC [Inter-Agency Standing Committee Working Group]. 2006. Protecting Persons Affected by Natural Disasters. In *IASC Operational Guidelines on Human Rights and Natural Disasters*. Washington: Brookings-Bern Project on Internal Displacement.

ICJ [International Court of Justice]. 1945. *Statute of the International Court of Justice*. (The Statute forms an integral part of the Charter of the United Nations.) Available at http://www.icj-cij.org/documents/?p1=4&p2=2&p3=0 (retrieved 14 January 2014).

ICJ. 1950. "Asylum Case" (Colombia *v* Peru). ICJ Reports, 266.

ICJ. 1951a. "Anglo-Norwegian Fisheries Case" (United Kingdom *v* Norway). ICJ Reports, 116.

ICJ. 1951b. "Reservations to the Convention on the Prevention and Punishment of the Crime of Genocide Case, Advisory Opinion." ICJ Reports, 15.

ICJ. 1969. "North Sea Continental Shelf Cases" (Federal Republic of Germany *v* Denmark, Federal Republic of Germany *v* The Netherlands). ICJ Reports, 3.

ICJ. 1970. "Barcelona Traction, Light and Power Company Limited Case" (Belgium *v* Spain) (Second Phase). ICJ Reports, 3.

ICJ. 1996. "Legality of the Threat or Use of Nuclear Weapons." Advisory Opinion of 8 July 1996.

ICSU [International Council for Science]. 2010. *Earth System Science for Global Sustainability: The Grand Challenges*. Paris: International Council for Science.

IDGEC [Institutional Dimensions of Global Environmental Change Project]. 1999. Science Plan, by Oran R. Young with contributions from Arun Agrawal, Leslie A. King, Peter H. Sand, Arild Underdal, and Merrilyn Wasson (= IHDP Report No. 9). IHDP, Bonn.

IISD [International Institute for Sustainable Development]. 2002. A Snap-shot of the Summit: General News. WSSD Info. Linkages. IISD.

ILC [International Law Commission]. 2006. *Fragmentation of International Law: Difficulties Arising from the Diversification and Expansion of International Law*. Report of the Study Group of the International Law Commission. UN Doc. A/CN.4/L.682. Geneva: International Law Commission.

IMF [International Monetary Fund]. 2008. IMF Revamps Loans for Countries Facing Price Shocks, Disasters. *IVM Survey Magazine*, 19 September.

India. 1989a. Amendments to the Montreal Protocol on Substances that Deplete the Ozone Layer. Proposals by India. UN Doc. UNEP/OzL.Pro.WG.I(2)/CRP.1 of 28 August 1989 and UN Doc UNEP/OzL.Pro.WG.I(2)/CRP.2 of 29 August 1989.

India. 1989b. Funding Mechanisms for Developing Countries. Communication from the Government of India to the Open-ended Working Group of the Parties to the Montreal Protocol on Substances that Deplete the Ozone Layer to Develop Modalities for Financial and Other Mechanisms to Enable Developing Countries to Meet the Requirements of the Montreal Protocol (Nairobi, 21–25 August 1989). UN Doc UNEP/OzL.Pro.Mech.1/CRP.1 of 21 August 1989.

Informal Working Group of Experts on Financial Mechanisms for the Implementation of the Montreal Protocol on Substances that Deplete the Ozone Layer. 1989. Report of the Meeting in Geneva, 3–7 July 1989. UN Doc. UNEP/OzL. Pro.Mech.1/Inf.1 of 16 August 1989.

Institute for Global Environmental Strategies. 2011. *The IGES Proposal for Rio+20—Version 1. Inputs to the Compilation Document of the Outcome Document of Rio+20*. Kamiyamaguchi, Japan: Institute for Global Environmental Strategies.

IOM [International Organization for Migration]. 2011. Establishment of a Migration Emergency Funding Mechanism. IOM Doc. MC/2335 of 14 November 2011.

IPCC [Intergovernmental Panel on Climate Change]. 2007. *Climate Change 2007: Mitigation of Climate Change. Contribution of Working Group III to the Fourth Assessment Report of the Intergovernmental Panel on Climate Change.* Cambridge, UK: Cambridge University Press.

IPCC. 2012. *Managing the Risks of Extreme Events and Disasters to Advance Climate Change Adaptation. A Special Report of Working Groups I and II of the Intergovernmental Panel on Climate Change.* Cambridge, UK: Cambridge University Press.

IPCC. 2013. Summary for Policymakers. In *Climate Change 2013: The Physical Science Basis. Contribution of Working Group I to the Fifth Assessment Report of the Intergovernmental Panel on Climate Change*, ed. T. F. Stocker, D. Qin, G.-K. Plattner, M. Tignor, S. K. Allen, J. Boschung, A. Nauels, Y. Xia, V. Bex, and P. M. Midgley. Cambridge, UK: Cambridge University Press.

IPCC. 2014a. Contribution of Working Group II to the Fifth Assessment Report of the Intergovernmental Panel on Climate Change. Summary for Policymakers. Advanced approved version pending copyedit.

IPCC. 2014b. Contribution of Working Group III to the Fifth Assessment Report of the Intergovernmental Panel on Climate Change. Summary for Policymakers. Advanced approved version pending copyedit.

ITU [International Telecommunication Union]. 2013. ICT Facts and Figures 2013. Available at http://www.itu.int/en/ITU-D/Statistics/Documents/statistics/2013/ITU_Key_2005-2013_ICT_data.xls (retrieved 3 January 2014).

Ivanova, Maria. 2010. UNEP in Global Environmental Governance: Design, Leadership, Location. *Global Environmental Politics* 10 (1):30–59.

Ivanova, Maria, and Jennifer Roy. 2007. The Architecture of Global Environmental Governance: Pros and Cons of Multiplicity. In *Global Environmental Governance: Perspectives on the Current Debate*, ed. Lydia Swart and Estelle Perry, 48–66. New York: Center for UN Reform.

Jänicke, Martin, and Klaus Jacob. 2006. Lead Markets for Environmental Innovations: A New Role for the Nation State. In *Environmental Governance in Global Perspective: New Approaches to Ecological Modernisation*, ed. Martin Jänicke and Klaus Jacob, 30–50. Berlin: Center for Environmental Policy Analysis.

Jänicke, Martin, and Helge Jörgens. 2000. Strategic Environmental Planning and Uncertainty: A Cross-National Comparison of Green Plans in Industrialized Countries. *Policy Studies Journal* 28 (3):612–632.

Jasanoff, Sheila S. 1987. Contested Boundaries in Policy-Relevant Science. *Social Studies of Science* 17:195–230.

Jasanoff, Sheila S. 1996. Science and Norms in Global Environmental Regimes. In *Earthly Goods: Environmental Change and Social Justice*, ed. Fen Osler Hampson and Judith Reppy, 173–197. Ithaca: Cornell University Press.

Jasanoff, Sheila S., and Marybeth Long Martello, eds. 2004. *Earthly Politics: Local and Global in Environmental Governance.* Cambridge, MA: MIT Press.

Jerneck, Anne, and Lennart Olsson. 2010. Shaping Future Adaptation Governance: Perspectives from the Poorest of the Poor. In *Global Climate Governance beyond 2012: Architecture, Agency and Adaptation*, ed. Frank Biermann, Philipp Pattberg, and Fariborz Zelli, 286–305. Cambridge, UK: Cambridge University Press.

Johnson, Brian. 1972. The United Nations Institutional Response to Stockholm: A Case Study in the International Politics of Institutional Change. *International Organization* 26 (2):255–301.

Joint Inspection Unit. 2008. Management Review of Environmental Governance within the United Nations System, prepared by Tadanori Inomata. UN Doc. JIU/REP/2008/3.

Jordan, Andrew J. 2008. The Governance of Sustainable Development: Taking Stock and Looking Forwards. *Environment and Planning C: Government and Policy* 26:17–33.

Jordan, Andrew, Tim Rayner, Heike Schroeder, Neil Adger, Kevin Anderson, Alice Bows, Corinne Le Quéré, et al. 2013. Going beyond Two Degrees? The Risks and Opportunities of Alternative Options. *Climate Policy* 13 (6):751–769.

Jordan, Andrew J., Harro van Asselt, Frans Berkhout, Dave Huitema, and Tim Rayner. 2012. Understanding the Paradoxes of Multi-level Governing: Climate Change Policy in the European Union. *Global Environmental Politics* 12 (2):41–64.

Jotzo, Frank, and Regina Betz. 2009. Australia's Emissions Trading Scheme: Opportunities and Obstacles for Linking. *Climate Policy* 9 (4):402–414.

Kaasa, Stine Madland. 2007. The UN Commission on Sustainable Development: Which Mechanisms Explain Its Accomplishments? *Global Environmental Politics* 7 (3):107–129.

Kalfagianni, Agni, and Philipp Pattberg. 2013a. Fishing in Muddy Waters: Exploring the Conditions for Effective Governance of Fisheries and Aquaculture. *Marine Policy* 38:124–132.

Kalfagianni, Agni, and Philipp Pattberg. 2013b. Global Fisheries Governance beyond the State: Unraveling the Effectiveness of the Marine Stewardship Council. *Journal of Environmental Studies and Sciences* 3 (2):184–193.

Kalfagianni, Agni, and Philipp Pattberg. 2013c. Participation and Inclusiveness in Private Rule-Setting Organizations: Does It Matter for Effectiveness? *Innovation: The European Journal of Social Science Research* 26 (3): 231–250.

Kanie, Norichika. 2007. Governance with Multilateral Environmental Agreements: A Healthy or Ill-Equipped Fragmentation. In *Global Environmental Governance: Perspectives on the Current Debate*, ed. Lydia Swart and Estelle Perry, 69–86. New York: Center for UN Reform.

Kanie, Norichika, Michele M. Betsill, Ruben Zondervan, Frank Biermann, and Oran R. Young. 2012. A Charter Moment: Restructuring Governance for Sustainability. *Public Administration and Development* 32:292–304.

Kanie, Norichika, Peter M. Haas, Steinar Andresen, Graeme Auld, Benjamin Cashore, Pamela S. Chasek, Jose A. Puppim de Oliveira, et al. 2013. Green Pluralism: Lessons for Improved Environmental Governance in the 21st Century. *Environment: Science and Policy for Sustainable Development* 55 (5):14–30.

Kant, Immanuel. 1795 [1983]. Zum ewigen Frieden. Ein philosophischer Entwurf. In *Werke in 6 Bänden*, ed. Wilhelm Weischedel, vol. 4, *Schriften zur Anthropologie, Geschichtsphilosophie, Politik und Pädagogik*, 191–251. Darmstadt: Wissenschaftliche Buchgesellschaft.

Kara, Jan, and Diana Quarless. 2002. Guiding Principles for Partnerships for Sustainable Development ("Type 2 Outcomes") to Be Elaborated by Interested Parties in the Context of the World Summit on Sustainable Development (WSSD). Presented at the Fourth Summit Preparatory Committee (PREPCOM 4). Bali, Indonesia.

Karlsson-Vinkhuyzen, Sylvia I., and Harro van Asselt. 2009. Introduction: Exploring and Explaining the Asia-Pacific Partnership on Clean Development and Climate. *International Environmental Agreements: Politics, Law and Economics* 3:195–211.

Karlsson-Vinkhuyzen, Sylvia I., and Jeffrey McGee. 2013. Legitimacy in an Era of Fragmentation: The Case of Global Climate Governance. *Global Environmental Politics* 13 (3):56–78.

Kates, Robert W., William C. Clark, Robert Corell, J. Michael Hall, Carlo C. Jaeger, Ian Lowe, James J. McCarthy, et al. 2001. Sustainability Science. *Science* 292:641–642.

Kates, Robert W., Thomas M. Parris, and Anthony A. Leiserowitz. 2005. What Is Sustainable Development? Goals, Indicators, Values, and Practice. *Environment* 47 (3):8–21.

Keane, David. 2004. The Environmental Causes and Consequences of Migration: A Search for the Meaning of "Environmental Refugees." *Georgetown International Environmental Law Review* 16 (2):209–223.

Keck, Margaret E., and Kathryn Sikkink. 1998. *Activists beyond Borders: Advocacy Networks in International Politics*. Ithaca: Cornell University Press.

Kennan, George F. 1970. To Prevent a World Wasteland: A Proposal. *Foreign Affairs* 48 (3):401–413.

Keohane, Robert O. 2003. Global Governance and Democratic Accountability. In *Taming Globalization: Frontiers of Governance*, ed. David Held and Mathias Koenig-Archbugi, 130–159. Cambridge, UK: Polity.

Keohane, Robert O., and Marc A. Levy, eds. 1996. *Institutions for Environmental Aid: Pitfalls and Promise*. Cambridge, MA: Harvard University Press.

Keohane, Robert O., and Joseph S. Nye. 1977. *Power and Interdependence: World Politics in Transition*. Boston: Little Brown.

Keohane, Robert O., and David G. Victor. 2011. The Regime Complex for Climate Change. *Perspectives on Politics* 9 (1):7–23.

Kern, Kristine, Helge Jörgens, and Martin Jänicke. 2001. The Diffusion of Environmental Policy Innovations: A Contribution to the Globalisation of Environmental Policy. Discussion Paper FS II 01–302 of the Social Science Research Center Berlin.

Kingsbury, Benedict. 2007. Global Environmental Governance as Administration: Implications for International Law. In *Oxford Handbook of International Environmental Law*, ed. Daniel Bodansky, Jutta Brunnée, and Ellen Hey, 63–84. New York: Oxford University Press.

Kirchner, Andree, ed. 2003. *International Marine Environmental Law: Institutions, Implementation and Innovations*. The Hague: Kluwer Law International.

Kohler, Daniel F., John Haaga, and Frank Camm. 1987. *Projections of Consumption of Products Using Chlorofluorocarbons in Developing Countries*. Santa Monica, CA: Rand Corporation.

Kotzé, Louis J. 2013. Rethinking Global Environmental Law and Governance in the Anthropocene. Unpublished manuscript. On file with author.

Krasner, Stephen D. 1983. Structural Causes and Regime Consequences: Regimes as Intervening Variables. In *International Regimes*, ed. Stephen D. Krasner, 1–21. Ithaca: Cornell University Press.

Kroll, Luisa, and Allison Fass. 2007. The World's Richest People. Available at http://www.forbes.com/2007/03/06/billionaires-new-richest_07billionaires_cz_lk_af_0308billieintro.html (retrieved 10 January 2014).

Kuin, Frank. 2013. Bike Boom in Manhattan. *NRC Handelsblad* 15–16 (October):10–11.

Kyoto Protocol to the United Nations Framework Convention on Climate Change. 1997. Done at Kyoto 11 December 1997, in force 16 February 2005. 2303 United Nations Treaty Series 148.

Laguna-Celis, Jorge. 2012. Ideas for a Sustainable Development Outlook. Earth System Governance Working Paper 24. Earth System Governance Project, Lund and Amsterdam.

Lebel, Louis, John M. Anderies, Bruce Campbell, Carl Folke, Steve Hatfield-Dodds, Terry P. Hughes, and James Wilson. 2006. Governance and the Capacity to Manage Resilience in Regional Social-Ecological Systems. *Ecology and Society* [online journal] 11 (1):19.

Lederer, Markus. 2011. From CDM to REDD+: What Do We Know for Setting Up Effective and Legitimate Carbon Governance? *Ecological Economics* 70 (11):1900–1907.

Leemans, Rik, Ghassem Asrar, Antonio Busalacchi, Josep Canadell, John Ingram, Anne Larigauderie, Harold Mooney, et al. 2009. Developing a Common Strategy for Integrative Global Environmental Change Research and Outreach: The Earth System Science Partnership (ESSP). *Current Opinion in Environmental Sustainability* 1 (1):4–13.

Leemans, Rik, and William Solecki. 2013. Redefining Environmental Sustainability. *Current Opinion in Environmental Sustainability* 5:272–277.

Lenton, Timothy M., Ken G. Caldeira, and Eörs Szathmáry. 2004. What Does History Teach Us about the Major Transitions and Role of Disturbances in the Evolution of Life and of the Earth System? In *Earth System Analysis for Sustainability*, ed. Hans-Joachim Schellnhuber, Paul J. Crutzen, William C. Clark, Martin Claussen, and Hermann Held, 29–52. Cambridge, MA: MIT Press, in cooperation with Dahlem University Press.

Lenton, Timothy M., Hermann Held, Elmar Kriegler, Jim W. Hall, Wolfgang Lucht, Stefan Rahmstorf, and Hans-Joachim Schellnhuber. 2008. Tipping Elements in the Earth's Climate System. *Proceedings of the National Academy of Sciences of the United States of America* 105 (6):1786–1793.

Levy, David L., and Ans Kolk. 2002. Strategic Responses to Global Climate Change: Conflicting Pressures on Multinationals in the Oil Industry. *Business and Politics* 4:275–300.

Levy, David L., and Peter J. Newell. 2000. Oceans Apart? Business Responses to Global Environmental Issues in Europe and the United States. *Environment* 42:8–20.

Levy, David L., and Peter J. Newell. 2002. Business Strategy and International Environmental Governance. *Global Environmental Politics* 2:84–101.

Linnerooth-Bayer, Joanne, and Reinhard Mechler. 2006. Insurance for Assisting Adaptation to Climate Change in Developing Countries: A Proposed Strategy. *Climate Policy* 6 (6):621–636.

Litfin, Karen T. 1994. *Ozone Discourses: Science and Politics in Global Environmental Cooperation*. New York: Columbia University Press.

Liu, Jianguo, Thomas Dietz, Stephen R. Carpenter, Marina Alberti, Carl Folke, Emilio Moran, Alice N. Pell, et al. 2007. Complexity of Coupled Human and Natural Systems. *Science* 317:1513–1516.

Lodewalk, Magnus, and John Whalley. 2002. Reviewing Proposals for a World Environmental Organisation. *World Economy* 25 (5):601–617.

Lövbrand, Eva, Teresia Rindefjäll, and Joakim Nordqvist. 2009. Closing the Legitimacy Gap in Global Environmental Governance? Lessons from the Emerging CDM Market. *Global Environmental Politics* 9 (2):74–100.

Lynas, Mark. 2007. *Six Degrees: Our Future on a Hotter Planet*. London: Fourth Estate.

Martens, Jens. 2007. *Multistakeholder Partnerships: Future Models of Multilateralism?* Berlin: Friedrich Ebert Foundation.

Mason, Michael. 2008a. The Governance of Transnational Environmental Harm: Addressing New Modes of Accountability/Responsibility. *Global Environmental Politics* 8 (3):8–24.

Mason, Michael. 2008b. Transparency for Whom? Information Disclosure and Power in Global Environmental Governance. *Global Environmental Politics* 8 (2):8–13.

Mattor, Katherine, Michele M. Betsill, Huayhuaca Ch'aska, Heidi Huber-Stearns, Theresa Jedd, Faith Sternlieb, Patrick Bixler, Antony Cheng, and Matthew Luizza.

2013. Transdisciplinary Research on Environmental Governance: A View from the Trenches. Earth System Governance Working Paper 29. Earth System Governance Project, Lund and Amsterdam.

Mavroidis, Petros C. 2000. Trade and Environment after the Shrimps-Turtles Litigation. *Journal of World Trade* 34 (1):73–88.

Mayer, Benoît. 2011a. Fraternity, Responsibility, and Sustainability: The International Legal Protection of Climate (or Environmental) Migrants at the Crossroads. Earth System Governance Working Paper 14. Earth System Governance Project, Amsterdam and Lund.

Mayer, Benoît. 2011b. The International Legal Challenges of Climate-Induced Migration: Proposal for an International Legal Framework. *Colorado Journal of International Environmental Law and Policy* 22 (3):357–416.

McGee, Jeffrey, and Ros Taplin. 2006. The Asia-Pacific Partnership on Clean Development and Climate: A Competitor or Complement to the Kyoto Protocol. *Global Change, Peace and Security* 18 (3):173–192.

Meadowcroft, James. 2004. Participation and Sustainable Development: Modes of Citizen, Community, and Organizational Involvement. In *Governance for Sustainable Development: The Challenge of Adapting Form to Function*, ed. William M. Lafferty, 162–190. Cheltenham: Edward Elgar.

Meadowcroft, James. 2005. From Welfare State to Ecostate. In *The State and the Global Ecological Crisis*, ed. John Barry and Robyn Eckersley, 3–23. Cambridge, MA: MIT Press.

Meadowcroft, James. 2007. Democracy and Accountability: The Challenge for Cross-Sectoral Partnerships. In *Partnerships, Governance and Sustainable Development: Reflections on Theory and Practice*, ed. Pieter Glasbergen, Frank Biermann, and Arthur P. J. Mol, 194–213. Cheltenham: Edward Elgar.

Mert, Ayşem. 2009. Partnerships for Sustainable Development as Discursive Practice: Shifts in Discourses of Environment and Democracy. *Forest Policy and Economics* 11 (5–6):326–339.

Mert, Ayşem. 2014. *Environmental Governance through Transnational Partnerships: A Discourse Theoretical Study*. Cheltenham: Edward Elgar.

Ministry of Transport, Public Works and Water Management, Ministry of Housing, Spatial Planning, and the Environment, and Ministry of Agriculture, Nature Management and Food Quality. 2006. *Spatial Planning Key Decision "Room for the River": Investing in the Safety and Vitality of the Dutch River Basin Region.* The Hague: Ministry of Transport, Public Works and Water Management, Government of the Netherlands.

Mitchell, Ronald B. 2003. International Environmental Agreements: A Survey of Their Features, Formation, and Effects. *Annual Review of Environment and Resources* 28:429–461.

Mitchell, Ronald B. 2007. Compliance Theory: Compliance, Effectiveness, and Behavior Change in International Environmental Law. In *The Oxford Handbook of International Environmental Law*, ed. Daniel Bodansky, Jutta Brunée, and Ellen Hey, 893–921. Oxford: Oxford University Press.

Mitchell, Ronald B. 2008. Evaluating the Performance of Environmental Institutions: What to Evaluate and How to Evaluate It? In *Institutions and Environmental Change: Principal Findings, Applications, and Research Frontiers*, ed. Oran R. Young, Leslie A. King, and Heike Schroeder, 79–114. Cambridge, MA: MIT Press.

Mitchell, Ronald B. 2009. The Influence of International Institutions: Institutional Design, Compliance, Effectiveness, and Endogeneity. In *Power, Interdependence and Non-State Actors in World Politics*, ed. Helen V. Milner and Andrew Moravcsik, 66–83. Princeton: Princeton University Press.

Mitchell, Ronald B. 2011. Transparency for Governance: The Mechanisms and Effectiveness of Disclosure-Based and Education-Based Transparency Policies. *Ecological Economics* 70 (11):1882–1890.

Mitchell, Ronald B. 2013. International Environmental Agreements Database Project (Version 2013.2). Available at http://iea.uoregon.edu/ (retrieved 11 January 2014).

Mitchell, Ronald B., William C. Clark, David W. Cash, and Nancy M. Dickson, eds. 2006. *Global Environmental Assessments: Information and Influence*. Cambridge, MA: MIT Press.

Moltke, Konrad von. 2005. Clustering International Environmental Agreements as an Alternative to a World Environment Organization. In *A World Environment Organization: Solution or Threat for Effective International Environmental Governance?*, ed. Frank Biermann and Steffen Bauer, 175–204. Aldershot, UK: Ashgate.

Montreal Protocol. 1987. Protocol (to the 1985 Vienna Convention) on Substances that Deplete the Ozone Layer. Done at Montreal 16 September 1987, in force 1 January 1989. *International Legal Materials* 26:1550.

Montreal Protocol. 1990. Protocol (to the 1985 Vienna Convention) on Substances that Deplete the Ozone Layer as amended in London, 26–29 June 1990. Amendment in force 10 August 1992.

Mukhtarov, Farhad, and Andrea K. Gerlak. 2013. River Basin Organizations in the Global Water Discourse: An Exploration of Agency and Strategy. *Global Governance* 19:307–326.

Müller, Benito. 2002. *Equity in Climate Change: The Great Divide*. Oxford: Oxford Institute for Energy Studies.

Müller, Benito, and Cameron Hepburn. 2006. *IATAL: An Outline Proposal for an International Air Travel Adaptation Levy*. Oxford: Oxford Institute for Energy Studies.

Myers, Norman. 2002. Environmental Refugees: A Growing Phenomenon of the 21st Century. *Philosophical Transactions of the Royal Society of London. Series B, Biological Sciences* 357 (1420):609–613.

Myers, Norman, and Jennifer Kent. 1995. *Environmental Exodus: An Emergent Crisis in the Global Arena*. Washington, DC: Climate Institute.

Najam, Adil. 2005. Neither Necessary, nor Sufficient: Why Organizational Tinkering Will Not Improve Environmental Governance. In *A World Environment Organization: Solution or Threat for Effective International Environmental Governance?*, ed. Frank Biermann and Steffen Bauer, 235–256. Aldershot, UK: Ashgate.

Nansen Initiative. 2012. The Nansen Initiative: A Protection Agenda for Disaster-Induced Cross-Border Displacement. Concept Note. No place. On file with author.

Nelson, Donald R., W. Neil Adger, and Katrina Brown. 2007. Adaptation to Environmental Change: Contributions of a Resilience Framework. *Annual Review of Environment and Resources* 32:395–419.

Newell, Peter J. 2005. Race, Class, and the Global Politics of Environmental Inequality. *Global Environmental Politics* 5 (3):70–94.

Newell, Peter J. 2008. Civil Society, Corporate Accountability and the Politics of Climate Change. *Global Environmental Politics* 8 (3):122–153.

Newell, Peter, Philipp Pattberg, and Heike Schroeder. 2012. Multiactor Governance and the Environment. *Annual Review of Environment and Resources* 37:365–387.

Nozick, Robert. 1974. *Anarchy, State, and Utopia*. New York: Basic Books.

Oberthür, Sebastian. 1996. Die Reflexivität internationaler Regime: Erkenntnisse aus der Untersuchung von drei umweltpolitischen Problemfeldern. *Zeitschrift für Internationale Beziehungen* 3 (1):7–44.

Oberthür, Sebastian. 2002. Clustering of Multilateral Environmental Agreements: Potentials and Limitations. *International Environmental Agreements: Politics, Law and Economics* 2:317–340.

Oberthür, Sebastian, and Thomas Gehring. 2005. Reforming International Environmental Governance: An Institutional Perspective on Proposals for a World Environment Organization. In *A World Environment Organization: Solution or Threat for Effective International Environmental Governance?*, ed. Frank Biermann and Steffen Bauer, 205–234. Aldershot, UK: Ashgate.

Oberthür, Sebastian, and Thomas Gehring, eds. 2006a. *Institutional Interaction in Global Environmental Governance: Synergy and Conflict among International and EU Policies*. Cambridge, MA: MIT Press.

Oberthür, Sebastian, and Thomas Gehring. 2006b. Institutional Interaction in Global Environmental Governance: The Case of the Cartagena Protocol and the World Trade Organization. *Global Environmental Politics* 6 (2): 1–31.

Oberthür, Sebastian, and Olav Schram Stokke. 2011a. Conclusions: Decentralized Interplay Management in an Evolving Interinstitutional Order. In *Managing Institutional Complexity: Regime Interplay and Global Environmental Change*, ed. Sebastian Oberthür and Olav Schram Stokke, 313–341. Cambridge, MA: MIT Press.

Oberthür, Sebastian, and Olav Schram Stokke, eds. 2011b. *Managing Institutional Complexity: Regime Interplay and Global Environmental Change.* Cambridge, MA: MIT Press.

OECD [Organization for Economic Cooperation and Development]. 2006. *Evaluating the Effectiveness and Efficiency of Partnerships.* Paris: OECD.

Office of the High Commissioner for Human Rights. 1998. Guiding Principles on Internal Displacement. Document E/CN.4/1998/53/Add.2. Geneva, 11 February 1998.

Okereke, Chukwumerije, Harriet Bulkeley, and Heike Schroeder. 2009. Conceptualizing Climate Governance beyond the International Regime. *Global Environmental Politics* 9 (1):58–78.

Okereke, Chukwumerije, and Philip Mann with contributions by Henny Osbahr, Benito Müller, and Johannes Ebeling. 2007. Assessment of Key Negotiating Issues at Nairobi Climate COP/MOP and What It Means for the Future of the Climate Regime. Tyndall Centre Working Paper 106. Tyndall Centre for Climate Change Research, Norwich, UK.

Oliver-Smith, Anthony. 2009. Climate Change and Populations Displacement: Disasters and Diasporas in the Twenty-First Century. In *Anthropology and Climate Change: From Encounters to Actions,* ed. Susan Crate and Mark Nuttall, 116–136. Walnut Creek, CA: Left Coast Press.

Olsson, Per, Lance H. Gunderson, Steve R. Carpenter, Paul Ryan, Louis Lebel, Carl Folke, and C. S. Holling. 2006. Shooting the Rapids: Navigating Transitions to Adaptive Governance of Social-Ecological Systems. *Ecology and Society* [online journal] 11 (1):18.

Olsson, Lennart, Jean-Charles Hourcade, and Jonathan Köhler. 2014. Sustainable Development in a Globalized World. *Journal of Environment and Development* 23 (1): 3–14.

Ottaway, Marina. 2001. Corporatism Goes Global: International Organizations, Nongovernmental Organization Networks, and Transnational Business. *Global Governance* 7 (3):265–292.

Overbeek, Henk, Klaus Dingwerth, Philipp Pattberg, and Daniel Compagnon. 2010. Forum: Global Governance: Decline or Maturation of an Academic Concept? *International Studies Review* 12:696–719.

Paavola, Jouni, and W. Neil Adger. 2002. Justice and Adaptation to Climate Change. Tyndall Centre Working Paper 23. Tyndall Centre for Climate Change Research, Norwich, UK.

Pahl-Wostl, Claudia, Marc Craps, Art Dewulf, Erik Mostert, David Tàbara, and Tharsi Taillieu. 2007. Social Learning and Water Resources Management. *Ecology and Society* 12(2): art. 5.

Pahl-Wostl, Claudia, Joyeeta Gupta, and Daniel Petry. 2008. Governance and the Global Water System: A Theoretical Exploration. *Global Governance* 14 (4):419–435.

Parliament of the Commonwealth of Australia. 2007. Migration (Climate Refugees) Amendment Bill (Senator Nettle). Available at http://parlinfo.aph.gov.au/parlInfo/download/legislation/bills/s585_first/toc_pdf/0714120.pdf;fileType=application%2Fpdf#search=%22legislation/bills/s585_first/0000%22 (retrieved 14 January 2014).

Parson, Edward A. 2003. *Protecting the Ozone Layer: Science and Strategy.* Oxford: Oxford University Press.

Partzsch, Lena, and Rafael Ziegler. 2011. Social Entrepreneurs as Change Agents: A Case Study on Power and Authority in the Water Sector. *International Environmental Agreements: Politics, Law and Economics* 11 (1):63–83.

Pattberg, Philipp. 2005a. The Forest Stewardship Council: Risk and Potential of Private Forest Governance. *Journal of Environment and Development* 14 (3):356–374.

Pattberg, Philipp. 2005b. The Institutionalization of Private Governance: How Business and Non-profits Agree on Transnational Rules. *Governance: An International Journal of Policy, Administration and Institutions* 18 (4):589–610.

Pattberg, Philipp. 2006. Private Governance and the South: Lessons from Global Forest Politics. *Third World Quarterly* 27 (4):579–593.

Pattberg, Philipp. 2007. *Private Institutions and Global Governance: The New Politics of Environmental Sustainability.* Cheltenham: Edward Elgar.

Pattberg, Philipp. 2012. Transnational Environmental Regimes. In *Global Environmental Governance Reconsidered*, ed. Frank Biermann and Philipp Pattberg, 97–121. Cambridge, MA: MIT Press.

Pattberg, Philipp, Frank Biermann, Sander Chan, and Ayşem Mert, eds. 2012. *Public-Private Partnerships for Sustainable Development: Emergence, Influence, and Legitimacy.* Cheltenham, UK: Edward Elgar.

Pattberg, Philipp, and Ayşem Mert. 2013. The Future We Get Might Not Be the Future We Want: Analyzing the Rio+20 Outcomes. *Global Policy* 4 (3):305–310.

Pattberg, Philipp, and Johannes Stripple. 2008. Beyond the Public and Private Divide: Remapping Transnational Climate Governance in the 21st Century. *International Environmental Agreements: Politics, Law and Economics* 8 (4):367–388.

PCIJ [Permanent Court of International Justice]. 1928. "Factory at Charzow (Claim for Indemnity) Case (Germany *v* Poland)" (Merits). PCIJ Ser. A, No. 17.

Peters, Glen P., Gregg Marland, Corinne Le Quéré, Thomas Boden, Josep G. Canadell, and Michael R. Raupach. 2012. Rapid Growth in CO_2 Emissions after the 2008–2009 Global Financial Crisis. *Nature Climate Change* 2:2–4.

Petit, J. R., J. Jouzel, D. Raynaud, N. I. Barkov, J.-M. Barnola, I. Basile, M. Bender, J. Chappellaz, M. Davisk, G. Delaygue, M. Delmotte, V. M. Kotlyakov, M. Legrand, V. Y. Lipenkov, C. Lorius, L. Pepin, C. Ritz, E. Saltzmank, and M. Stievenard. 1999. Climate and Atmospheric History of the Past 420,000 Years from the Vostok Ice Core, Antarctica. *Nature* 399 (3 June): 429–436.

Pfanner, Eric. 2013. The World Is Watching. *International New York Times*, 15 October, S6.

Planet under Pressure Conference. 2012. U.N. Overhaul Required to Govern Planet's Life Support System. Press release by the consortium organizing the Planet under Pressure conference held 26–29 March 2012 in London, released 23 November 2011 (on file with author).

Powers, Diana S. 2013. Commitment to Solar Shows Progress. *International New York Times*, 11 November, 10–11.

Princen, Thomas. 2003. Principles for Sustainability: From Cooperation and Efficiency to Sufficiency. *Global Environmental Politics* 3 (1):33–50.

Princen, Thomas. 2005. *The Logic of Sufficiency*. Cambridge, MA: MIT Press.

Princen, Thomas, Matthias Finger, and Jack Manno. 1995. Nongovernmental Organizations in World Environmental Politics. *International Environmental Affairs* 7 (1):42–58.

Rahmstorf, Stefan, and Frank Sirocko. 2004. Modes of Oceanic and Atmospheric Circulation during the Quaternary. In *Earth System Analysis for Sustainability*, ed. Hans-Joachim Schellnhuber, Paul J. Crutzen, William C. Clark, Martin Claussen, and Hermann Held, 157–170. Cambridge, MA: MIT Press, in cooperation with Dahlem University Press.

Rajan, Mukund Govind. 1997. *Global Environmental Politics: India and the North-South Politics of Global Environmental Issues*. Delhi: Oxford University Press.

Raustiala, Kal, and David Victor. 2004. The Regime Complex for Plant Genetic Resources. *International Organization* 58 (2):277–309.

Raustiala, Kal. 1997. States, NGOs, and International Environmental Institutions. *International Studies Quarterly* 42 (4):719–740.

Rawls, John. 1971. *A Theory of Justice*. Cambridge, MA: Harvard University Press.

Rawls, John. 1999. *The Law of Peoples with "The Idea of Public Reason Revisited."* Cambridge, MA: Harvard University Press.

Reinicke, Wolfgang H. 1998. *Global Public Policy: Governing without Government?* Washington, DC: Brookings Institution.

Reinicke, Wolfgang H., Francis M. Deng, Jan Martin Witte, Thorsten Benner, Beth Witaker, and John Gershman. 2000. *Critical Choices: The United Nations Networks, and the Future of Global Governance*. Ottawa: International Development Research Centre.

Renaud, Fabrice, Janos J. Bogardi, Olivia Dun, and Koko Warner. 2007. Control, Adapt, or Flee: How to Face Environmental Migration? Interdisciplinary Security Connections 5/ 2007. United Nations University Institute for Environment and Human Security, Bonn.

Rietig, Katharina. 2013. The Influence of Academics on the Political Dynamics of International Negotiations. Paper presented at the 2013 Tokyo Conference on

Earth System Governance. Tokyo, 29–30 January. Available at http://tokyo2013 .earthsystemgovernance.org/ (retrieved 30 January 2013).

Rietig, Katharina. 2014. "Neutral" Experts? How Input of Scientific Expertise Matters in International Environmental Negotiations. *Policy Sciences* 47 (2): 141–160.

Rindefjäll, Teresia, Emma Lund, and Johannes Stripple. 2011. Wine, Fruit, and Emission Reductions: The CDM as Development Strategy in Chile. *International Environmental Agreements: Politics, Law and Economics* 11 (1):7–22.

Rio Declaration. 1992. Rio Declaration on Environment and Development. Annex I to the Report of the United Nations Conference on Environment and Development, held in Rio de Janeiro, 3–14 June 1992. UN Doc. A/CONF.151/26 (Vol. I) of 12 August 1992.

Robinson, Alexander, Reinhard Calov, and Andrey Ganopolski. 2012. Multistability and Critical Thresholds of the Greenland Ice Sheet. *Nature Climate Change* 2:429–432.

Robinson, John. 2004. Squaring the Circle? Some Thoughts on the Idea of Sustainable Development. *Ecological Economics* 48:369–384.

Rockström, Johan, Will Steffen, Kevin Noone, Åsa Persson, F. Stuart Chapin, Eric F. Lambin, Timothy M. Lenton, Marten Scheffer, Carl Folke, Hans-Joachim Schellnhuber, Björn Nykvist, Cynthia A. de Wit, Terry Hughes, Sander van der Leeuw, Henning Rodhe, Sverker Sörlin, Peter K. Snyder, Robert Costanza, Uno Svedin, Malin Falkenmark, Louise Karlberg, Robert W. Corell, Victoria J. Fabry, James Hansen, Brian Walker, Diana Liverman, Katherine Richardson, Paul Crutzen, and Jonathan A. Foley. 2009. A Safe Operating Space for Humanity. *Nature* 461 (24 September):472–475.

Rosenau, James N. 1995. Governance in the Twenty-First Century. *Global Governance* 1 (1):13–43.

Rosenau, James N. 2002. Globalization and Governance: Sustainability between Fragmentation and Integration. Paper presented at the Conference on Governance and Sustainability: New Challenges for the State, Business, and Civil Society, Berlin, 30 September.

Rosendal, G. Kristin. 2006. The Convention on Biological Diversity: Tensions with the WTO TRIPS Agreement over Access to Genetic Resources and the Sharing of Benefits. In *Institutional Interaction in Global Environmental Governance: Synergy and Conflict among International and EU Policies*, ed. Sebastian Oberthür and Thomas Gehring, 79–102. Cambridge, MA: MIT Press.

Rosendal, G. Kristin, and Steinar Andresen. 2011. Institutional Design for Improved Forest Governance through REDD. Lessons from the Global Environment Facility. *Ecological Economics* 70 (11):1908–1915.

Rosenthal, Elisabeth. 2010. Heating a City with Nothing but Detritus. *International Herald Tribune*, 13 December, 1 and 3.

Roth, Dik, and Jeroen Warner. 2007. Flood Risk, Uncertainty and Changing River Protection Policy in the Netherlands: The Case of "Calamity Polders." *Journal of Economic and Social Geography* 98 (4):519–525.

Ruggie, John Gerard. 2002. The Theory and Practice of Learning Networks: Corporate Social Responsibility and the Global Compact. *Journal of Corporate Citizenship* 5:27–36.

Schalatek, Liane. 2013. Upping the Ante: The 5th Green Climate Fund Board Meeting Speeds up the Progress on the Fund's Business Model and Sets a Time-line for Its Resource Mobilization. Heinrich Böll Foundation, Washington, DC.

Scharf, Michael P. 2013. *Customary International Law in Times of Fundamental Change: Recognizing Grotian Moments.* Cambridge, UK: Cambridge University Press.

Scharpf, Fritz W. 1997. Economic Integration, Democracy and the Welfare State. *Journal of European Public Policy* 4:18–36.

Scheffer, Marten, Jordi Bascompte, William A. Brock, Victor Brovkin, Stephen R. Carpenter, Vasilis Dakos, Hermann Held, Egbert H. van Nes, Max Rietkerk, and George Sugihara. 2009. Early-Warning Signals for Critical Transitions. *Nature* 461 (3 September): 53–59.

Schellnhuber, Hans-Joachim. 1998. Earth System Analysis: The Scope of the Challenge. In *Earth System Analysis: Integrating Science for Sustainability*, ed. Hans-Joachim Schellnhuber and Volker Wenzel, 3–195. Berlin: Springer.

Schellnhuber, Hans-Joachim. 1999. "Earth System" Analysis and the Second Copernican Revolution. *Nature* 402 (Supp.):C19–C23.

Schellnhuber, Hans-Joachim, Paul J. Crutzen, William C. Clark, Martin Claussen, and Hermann Held, eds. 2004. *Earth System Analysis for Sustainability.* Cambridge, MA: MIT Press, in cooperation with Dahlem University Press.

Schellnhuber, Hans-Joachim, and Dork Sahagian. 2002. The Twenty-three GAIM Questions. *Global Change Newsletter* (International Geosphere-Biosphere Programme) 49: 20–21.

Schellnhuber, Hans-Joachim, and Ferenc L. Tóth. 1999. Earth System Analysis and Management. *Environmental Modeling and Assessment* 4:201–207.

Schellnhuber, Hans-Joachim, and Volker Wenzel. 1998. Preface. In *Earth System Analysis: Integrating Science for Sustainability*, ed. Hans-Joachim Schellnhuber and Volker Wenzel, vii–xvi. Berlin: Springer.

Scholte, Jan Aart. 2002. Civil Society and Democracy in Global Governance. *Global Governance* 8 (3):281–304.

Scholte, Jan Aart. 2004. Civil Society and Democratically Accountable Global Governance. *Government and Opposition* 39:211–233.

Schouten, Greetje. 2013. Tabling Sustainable Commodities through Private Governance: Processes of Legitimization in the Roundtables on Sustainable Palm Oil and Responsible Soy. Doctoral dissertation, University of Utrecht.

Schouten, Greetje, and Pieter Glasbergen. 2011. Creating Legitimacy in Global Private Governance: The Case of the Roundtable on Sustainable Palm Oil. *Ecological Economics* 70:1891–1899.

Schroeder, Heike. 2010. Agency in International Climate Negotiations: The Case of Indigenous Peoples and Avoided Deforestation. *International Environmental Agreements: Politics, Law and Economics* 10 (4): 317–332.

Schroeder, Heike, Maxwell T. Boykoff, and Laura Spiers. 2012. Equity and State Representations in Climate Negotiations. *Nature Climate Change* 2:834–836.

Schroeder, Heike, and Heather Lovell. 2012. The Role of Non-Nation-State Actors and Side Events in the International Climate Negotiations. *Climate Policy* 12 (1):23–37.

Schwartzberg, Joseph E. 2004. *Revitalizing the United Nations: Reform through Weighted Voting*. New York and The Hague: World Federalist Movement and Institute for Global Policy.

Schwartzberg, Joseph E. 2009. Universal Weighted Regional Representation as a Basis for Security Council Reform. Presentation at the opening panel on "Reform of the Security Council" at the International Law Weekend Conference of the American Branch of the International Law Association. New York, 22 October.

Schwartzberg, Joseph E. 2012. *Creating a World Parliamentary Assembly: An Evolutionary Journey*. Berlin: Committee for a Democratic U.N.

SCOSTEP [Scientific Committee on Solar-Terrestrial Physics]. 1997. *International STEP Newsletter* 3 (1) (March). Available at http://www.scostep.ucar.edu/archives/newsletters/Mar97news.html (retrieved 27 January 2011).

SDIN [Sustainable Development Issues Network]. 2002. Taking Issue: Questioning Partnerships. SDIN Paper No.1. Sustainable Development Issues Network.

Seyfang, Gill, and Andrew Jordan. 2002. The Johannesburg Summit and Sustainable Development: How Effective Are Environmental Mega-Conferences? In *Yearbook of International Co-operation on Environment and Development 2002/2003*, ed. Olav Schram Stokke and Øystein B. Thommessen, 19–26. London: Earthscan Publications.

Shindell, D., J. C. I. Kuylenstierna, E. Vignati, R. van Dingenen, M. Amann, Z. Klimont, S. C. Anenberg, et al. 2012. Simultaneously Mitigating Near-Term Climate Change and Improving Human Health and Food Security. *Science* 335:183–189.

Siebenhüner, Bernd. 2002a. How Do Scientific Assessments Learn? Part 1. Conceptual Framework and Case Study of the IPCC. *Environmental Science and Policy* 5:411–420.

Siebenhüner, Bernd. 2002b. How Do Scientific Assessments Learn? Part 2. Case Study of the LRTAP Assessment and Comparative Conclusions. *Environmental Science and Policy* 5:421–427.

Skjærseth, Jon Birger, and Jørgen Wettestad. 2008. Implementing EU Emissions Trading: Success or Failure. *International Environmental Agreements: Politics, Law and Economics* 8 (3):275–290.

Skjærseth, Jon Birger, and Jørgen Wettestad. 2009. The Origin, Evolution and Consequences of the EU Emissions Trading System. *Global Environmental Politics* 9 (2):101–122.

Skodvin, Tora, and Steinar Andresen. 2003. Nonstate Influence in the International Whaling Commission, 1970–1990. *Global Environmental Politics* 3 (4):61–86.

Smismans, Stijn. 2000. The European Economic and Social Committee: Towards Deliberative Democracy via a Functional Assembly. European Integration Online Papers 4 (12). Available at http://eiop.or.at/eiop/texte/2000-012a.htm (retrieved 14 January 2014).

Smith, Kirk R., J. Swisher, and D. R. Ahuja. 1993. Who Pays (to Solve the Problem and How Much)? In *The Global Greenhouse Regime: Who Pays? Science, Economics and North-South Politics in the Climate Change Convention*, ed. Peter Hayes and Kirk Smith, 70–98. London: Earthscan Publications/United Nations University Press.

Smouts, Marie-Claude. 1998. The Proper Use of Governance in International Relations. *International Social Science Journal* 155:81–89.

South Centre. 1996. *For a Strong and Democratic United Nations: A South Perspective on UN Reform*. Geneva: South Centre.

Spagnuolo, Francesca. 2011. Diversity and Pluralism in Earth System Governance: Contemplating the Role for Global Administrative Law. *Ecological Economics* 70 (11):1875–1881.

Speth, James Gustave. 2004. Perspective on the Johannesburg Summit. In *Green Planet Blues: Environmental Politics from Stockholm to Johannesburg*, ed. Ken Conca and Geoffrey D. Dabelko, 156–163. Boulder, CO: Westview Press.

Stadelmann, Martin, Åsa Persson, Izabela Ratajczak-Juszko, and Axel Michaelowa. 2014. Equity and Cost-Effectiveness of Multilateral Adaptation Finance: Are They Friends or Foes? *International Environmental Agreements: Politics, Law and Economics* 14 (2): 101–120.

State of the Planet Declaration. 2012. By the Co-chairs of the Planet under Pressure conference (London, 26–29 March 2012) supported by the conference Scientific Organizing Committee. On file with author.

Steffen, Will, Meinrat O. Andreae, Bert Bolin, Peter M. Cox, Paul J. Crutzen, Ulrich Cubasch, Hermann Held, Nebojsa Nakicenovic, Liana Talaue-McManus, and Billie L. Turner, II. 2004. Earth System Dynamics in the Anthropocene. In *Earth System Analysis for Sustainability*, ed. Hans-Joachim Schellnhuber, Paul J. Crutzen, William C. Clark, Martin Claussen, and Hermann Held, 313–340. Cambridge, MA: MIT Press, in cooperation with Dahlem University Press.

Steffen, Will, Jacques Grinevald, Paul Crutzen, and John McNeill. 2011. The Anthropocene: Conceptual and Historical Perspectives. *Philosophical Transactions of the Royal Society A* 369:842–867.

Steffen, Will, Angelina Sanderson, Peter D. Tyson, Jill Jäger, Pamela A. Matson, Berrien Moore III, Frank Oldfield, Katherine Richardson, Hans-Joachim Schellnhuber, B. L. Turner II, and Robert J. Wasson. 2004. *Global Change and the Earth System: A Planet under Pressure*. New York: Springer.

Sterk, Wolfgang, and Joseph Kruger. 2009. Establishing a Transatlantic Carbon Market. *Climate Policy* 9 (4):389–401.

Stern, Nicholas. 2007. *The Stern Review on the Economics of Climate Change*. Cambridge, UK: Cambridge University Press.

Stewart, Richard B., and Jonathan B. Wiener. 2003. *Reconstructing Climate Policy: Beyond Kyoto*. Washington, DC: AEI Press.

Stiglitz, Joseph E. 2013. Inequality Is a Choice. *International New York Times*, 15 October, S17.

Stockholm Convention on Persistent Organic Pollutants. 2001. Done at Stockholm 22 May 2001, in force 17 May 2004.

Stockholm Declaration. 1972. Stockholm Declaration of the United Nations Conference on the Human Environment (16 June 1972). *International Legal Materials* 11: 1416.

Stokke, Olav Schram. 2012. *Disaggregating International Regimes: A New Approach to Evaluation and Comparison*. Cambridge, MA: MIT Press.

Streck, Charlotte. 2004. New Partnerships in Global Environmental Policy: The Clean Development Mechanism. *Journal of Environment and Development* 13 (3):295–322.

Stripple, Johannes. 2010. Weberian Climate Policy: Administrative Rationality Organized as a Market. In *Environmental Politics and Deliberative Democracy: Examining the Promise of New Modes of Governance*, ed. Karin Bäckstrand, Jamil Khan Karin, Annica Kronsell, and Eva Lövbrand, 67–84. Cheltenham: Edward Elgar.

Stripple, Johannes, and Eva Lövbrand. 2010. Carbon Market Governance beyond the Public-Private Divide. In *Global Climate Governance beyond 2012: Architecture, Agency, and Adaptation*, ed. Frank Biermann, Philipp Pattberg, and Fariborz Zelli, 167–182. Cambridge, UK: Cambridge University Press.

Sugiyama, Taishi, and Jonathan Sinton. 2005. Orchestra of Treaties: A Future Climate Regime Scenario with Multiple Treaties among Like-Minded Countries. *International Environmental Agreements: Politics, Law and Economics* 5 (1):65–88.

Szulecki, Kacper, Philipp Pattberg, and Frank Biermann. 2011. Explaining Variation in the Effectiveness of Transnational Energy Partnerships. *Governance: An International Journal of Policy, Administration and Institutions* 24 (4):713–736.

Takken, Hille. 2013. Bedrijfsleiders gaan tien dagen op autodieet. *NRC Handelsblad* 9–10 (October):20.

Tamiotti, Ludivine. 2001. Environmental Organizations: Changing Roles and Functions in Global Politics. *Global Environmental Politics* 1 (1):56–76.

The Future We Want. 2012. The Future We Want. Outcome document of the United Nations Conference on Sustainable Development, held 20–22 June 2012 in Rio de Janeiro. UN Doc. A/RES/66/288.

Third Nobel Laureate Symposium on Global Sustainability. 2011. Stockholm Memorandum, agreed upon at the Third Nobel Laureate Symposium on Global Sustainability "Transforming the World in an Era of Global Change," held in May 2011 in Stockholm. Available at http://globalsymposium2011.org/wp -content/uploads/2011/05/The-Stockholm-Memorandum.pdf (retrieved 22 December 2011).

Tienhaara, Kyla, Amandine Orsini, and Robert Falkner. 2012. Global Corporations. In *Global Environmental Governance Reconsidered*, ed. Frank Biermann and Philipp Pattberg, 45–67. Cambridge, MA: MIT Press.

Tokyo Conference on the Global Environment and Human Response toward Sustainable Development. 1989. Chairman's Statement, Tokyo, 13 September 1989, section II C. Reprinted in *American University Journal of International Law and Policy* 5 (1990): 577–588.

Töpfer, Klaus. 2003. Presentation at the Global Governance Speakers Series. Potsdam Institute for Climate Impact Research, Potsdam, Germany, 28 February.

Trail Smelter Arbitration. 1938/1941. USA *v* Canada, 1938/1941. UNRIAA III, 1911.

Tuerk, Andreas, Michael Mehling, Christian Flachsland, and Wolfgang Sterk. 2009. Linking Carbon Markets: Concepts, Case Studies and Pathways. *Climate Policy* 9 (4):341–357.

Uhlmann, Eva M. Kornicker. 1998. State Community Interests, *Jus Cogens* and Protection of the Global Environment: Developing Criteria for Peremptory Norms. *Georgetown International Environmental Law Review* 11: 120–135.

Uhrqvist, Ola, and Eva Lövbrand. 2013. Rendering Global Change Problematic: The Constitutive Effects of Earth System Research in the IGBP and the IHDP. *Environmental Politics* 23 (3):339–356.

UN [United Nations]. 1945. *Charter of the United Nations*. Done 26 June 1945, in force 24 October 1945. 1 United Nations Treaty Series XVI.

UN. 1992. *Agenda 21: The United Nations Programme of Action from Rio*. New York: United Nations.

UNDP [United Nations Development Programme]. 1998. *Human Development Report 1998*. Oxford: Oxford University Press.

UNDP. 2006. *Human Development Report 2006. Beyond Scarcity: Power, Poverty and the Global Water Crisis*. New York: United Nations Development Programme.

UNDP. 2007. *Human Development Report 2007/2008. Fighting Climate Change: Human Solidarity in a Divided World*. New York: United Nations Development Programme.

UNEP [United Nations Environment Programme]. 2012a. *21 Issues for the 21st Century: Result of the UNEP Foresight Process on Emerging Environmental Issues*. Nairobi: United Nations Environment Programme.

UNEP. 2012b. *Global Environmental Outlook 5 (GEO5). Environment for the Future We Want*. Nairobi: United Nations Environment Programme.

UNESCO [United Nations Educational, Scientific, and Cultural Organization]. 2002. Harnessing Science to Society. Analytical Report to Governments and International Partners on the Follow-up to the World Conference on Science, "Science for the Twenty-First Century: A New Commitment" (Budapest, 26 June–1 July 1999). UNESCO, Paris.

UNFCCC [United Nations Framework Convention on Climate Change]. 1992. Done at New York 9 May 1992, in force 21 March 1994. *International Legal Materials* 31:849.

UNFCCC. 1996. Draft Rules of Procedure of the Conference of the Parties and Its Subsidiary Bodies. Conference of the Parties to the United Nations Framework Convention on Climate Change, 2nd Session. UN Doc. FCCC/CP/1996/2 of 22 May.

UNFCCC. 2007. Bali Action Plan. Decision 1/CP.13 of the 13th meeting of the Conference of the Parties. UN Doc. FCCC/CP/2007/6/Add.1* of 14 March 2008.

UNFCCC. 2010. The Cancun Agreements: Outcome of the Work of the Ad Hoc Working Group on Long-term Cooperative Action under the Convention. Conference of the Parties to the United Nations Framework Convention on Climate Change, Decision 1/CP.16 adopted at its 16th session, held in Cancun, 29 November to 10 December 2010. UN Doc. FCCC/CP/2010/7/Add.1 of 15 March 2011.

UNFCCC. 2011a. Launching the Green Climate Fund. Conference of the Parties to the United Nations Framework Convention on Climate Change, Decision 3/CP.17 of 11 December 2011. UN Doc. FCCC/CP/2011/9/Add.1 of 15 March 2012.

UNFCCC. 2011b. Revised Proposal from Papua New Guinea and Mexico to Amend Articles 7 and 18 of the Convention. Conference of the Parties to the United Nations Framework Convention on Climate Change, 17th Session. UN Doc. FCCC/CP/2011/4/Rev.1 of 9 December.

UNFCCC. 2012. Approaches to Address Loss and Damage Associated with Climate Change Impacts in Developing Countries that Are Particularly Vulnerable to the Adverse Effects of Climate Change to Enhance Adaptive Capacity. Decision 3/CP.18 of the 18th Conference of the Parties. UN Doc. FCCC/CP/2012/8/Add.1 of 28 February 2013.

UNGA [United Nations General Assembly]. 1989. Protection of Global Climate for Present and Future Generations of Mankind. Resolution 43/53 of 6 December 1988. UN Doc. A/RES/43/53 (27 January 1989). *International Legal Materials* 28:1326.

UNGA. 2000. United Nations Millennium Declaration. Resolution 55/2 of 8 September 2000. Available at http://www.un.org/millennium/declaration/ares552e.htm (retrieved 11 January 2013).

UNHCR [United Nations High Commissioner for Refugees]. 2007. Internally Displaced People: Questions and Answers. UNHCR, Geneva. Available at http://www.unhcr.org/basics/BASICS/405ef8c64.pdf (accessed 14 January 2014).

UNHCR. 2013. Populations of Concern to UNHCR. UNHCR, Geneva.

UNICEF [United Nations Children's Fund]. 2004. *Childhood under Threat. The State of the World's Children 2005*. New York: UNICEF.

UNSC [United Nations Security Council]. 2007. Security Council Holds First-Ever Debate on Impact of Climate Change on Peace, Security, Hearing over 50 Speakers. 5663rd Meeting, 17 April, 2007. United Nations, New York. Available at: http://www.un.org/News/Press/docs/2007/sc9000.doc.htm (retrieved 14 January 2014).

UN Secretary-General. 1997. Renewing the United Nations: A Programme for Reform. Report of the Secretary General. UN Doc A/51/950 of 14 July 1997.

UN Secretary-General. 2005. In Larger Freedom: Towards Development, Security and Human Rights for All. Report of the Secretary-General. UN Doc. A/59/2005 of 21 March 2005.

UN Secretary-General. 2012. Report of the Special Rapporteur on the Human Rights of Migrants. Submitted to the Sixty-seventh Session of the United Nations General Assembly. UN Doc. A/67/299 of 13 August 2012.

Urpelainen, Johannes. 2013. A Model of Dynamic Climate Governance: Dream Big, Win Small. *International Environmental Agreements: Politics, Law and Economics* 13:107–125.

Usui, Mikoto. 2003. Sustainable Development Diplomacy in the Private Business Sector: An Integrative Perspective on Game Change Strategies at Multiple Levels. *International Negotiation* 8:267–310.

Vajpayee, Atal Bihari. 2002. Speech of Prime Minister Shri Atal Bihari Vajpayee at the Eighth Session of Conference of the Parties to the UN Framework Convention on Climate Change, 30 October 2002. Available at http://pib.nic.in/archieve/lreleng/lyr2002/roct2002/30102002/r301020023.html (retrieved 12 January 2014).

van Asselt, Harro. 2014. *The Fragmentation of Global Climate Governance: Consequences and Management of Regime Interactions*. Cheltenham: Edward Elgar.

van Asselt, Harro, and Frank Biermann. 2007. European Emissions Trading and the International Competiveness of Energy-Intensive Industries: A Legal and Political Evaluation of Possible Supporting Measures. *Energy Policy* 35 (1):297–306.

van Asselt, Harro, and Fariborz Zelli. 2014. Connect the Dots: Managing the Fragmentation of Global Climate Change. *Environmental Economics and Policy Studies* 16:137–155.

van de Graaf, Thijs. 2013a. Fragmentation in Global Energy Governance: Explaining the Creation of IRENA. *Global Environmental Politics* 13 (3):14–33.

van de Graaf, Thijs. 2013b. *The Politics and Institutions of Global Energy Governance.* Houndmills, Basingstoke: Palgrave Macmillan.

van der Woerd, K. Frans, David L. Levy, and Katie Begg, eds. 2005. *Corporate Responses to Climate Change.* Sheffield: Greenleaf Publishing.

van Kersbergen, Kees, and Frans van Waarden. 2004. "Governance" as a Bridge between Disciplines: Cross-disciplinary Inspiration Regarding Shifts in Governance and Problems of Governability, Accountability and Legitimacy. *European Journal of Political Research* 43:143–171.

van Vuuren, Detlef, Marcel Kok, Stefan van der Esch, Michel Jeuken, Paul Lucas, Anne Gerdien Prins, Rob Alkemade, et al. 2012. *Roads from Rio+20: Pathways to Achieve Global Sustainability Goals by 2050.* The Hague: PBL Netherlands Environmental Assessment Agency.

Verdross, Alfred. 1966. Jus Dispositivum and Jus Cogens in International Law. *American Journal of International Law* 60:55–63.

Vestergaard, Jakob. 2011. *The G20 and Beyond: Towards Effective Global Economic Governance.* DIIS Report 2011:04. Copenhagen: Danish Institute for International Studies.

Victor, David G. 2007. Fragmented Carbon Markets and Reluctant Nations: Implications for the Design of Effective Architectures. In *Architectures for Agreement: Addressing Global Climate Change in the Post-Kyoto World,* ed. Joseph E. Aldy and Robert N. Stavins, 133–160. Cambridge, UK: Cambridge University Press.

Vieira, Susana C. 2012. From Sustainable Development to Earth System Governance: A View from the South. *Anuário Brasileiro de Direito Internacional/ Brazilian Yearbook of International Law/Annuaire Brésilien de Droit International* 2 (11): 167–176.

Vienna Convention on the Law of Treaties. 1969. Done 22 May 1969, in force 27 January 1980. 1155 United Nations Treaty Series 331.

Vihma, Antto, and Kati Kulovesi. 2012. Strengthening Global Climate Change Negotiations: Improving the Efficiency of the UNFCCC Process. Nordic Working Papers. Nordic Council of Ministers, Copenhagen.

Vijge, Marjanneke J. 2010. Towards a World Environment Organization: Identifying the Barriers to International Environmental Governance Reform. Global Governance Working Paper 40. Global Governance Project, Amsterdam. Available at http://www.glogov.org/images/doc/WP40.pdf (retrieved 11 January 2014).

Vijge, Marjanneke J. 2013. The Promise of New Institutionalism: Explaining the Absence of a World or United Nations Environment Organization. *International Environmental Agreements: Politics, Law and Economics* 13 (2):153–176.

Visseren-Hamakers, Ingrid J., and Philipp Pattberg. 2013. We Can't See the Forest for the Trees: The Environmental Impact of Global Forest Certification Is

Unknown. *GAIA: Ecological Perspectives for Science and Society* 22 (1):25–28.

Vitousek, Peter M., Harold A. Mooney, Jane Jubchenco, and Jerry M. Melillo. 1997. Human Domination of Earth's Ecosystems. *Science* 277:494–499.

Vormedal, Irja. 2008. The Influence of Business and Industry NGOs in the Negotiation of the Kyoto Mechanisms: The Case of Carbon Capture and Storage in the CDM. *Global Environmental Politics* 8 (4):36–65.

Waddell, Steve. 2011. *Global Action Networks: Creating Our Future Together.* Milan: Bocconi University Press.

Wapner, Paul K. 1996. *Environmental Activism and World Civic Politics.* Albany: State University of New York Press.

Wapner, Paul K. 2002. Horizontal Politics: Transnational Environmental Activism and Global Cultural Change. *Global Environmental Politics* 2 (2): 37–62.

Wapner, Paul K. 2003. World Summit on Sustainable Development: Toward a Post-Jo'Burg Environmentalism. *Global Environmental Politics* 3 (1):1–10.

Warner, Koko, Nicoloa Ranger, Swenja Surminski, Margaret Arnold, Joanne Linnnerooth-Bayer, Erwann Michel-Kerjan, Paul Kovacs, and Celine Herweijer, with contributions from Christoph Bals, Laurens Bouwer, Ian Burton, Susan Cutter, Balgis Osman Elasha, Peter Hoeppe, Thomas Loster, Olivier Mahul, Robin Mearns, Youba Sokona, and Bob Ward. 2009. *Adaptation to Climate Change: Linking Disaster Risk Reduction and Insurance.* Geneva: United Nations International Strategy for Disaster Reduction Secretariat.

Warren, Rachel, Nigel Arnell, Robert Nicholls, Peter Levy, and Jeff Price. 2006. Understanding the Regional Impacts of Climate Change. Research report prepared for the Stern review on the economics of climate change. Tyndall Centre Working Paper 90. Tyndall Centre for Climate Change Research, Norwich, UK.

Watson, Robert. 2008. Climate Change: Prepare for Global Temperature rise of 4C, Warns Top Scientist [interview with *The Guardian*]. Press report (7 August 2008). Available at: http://www.guardian.co.uk/environment/2008/aug/06/climatechange.scienceofclimatechange (retrieved 14 January 2014).

Whalley, John, and Ben Zissimos. 2001. What Could a World Environment Organization Do? *Global Environmental Politics* 1 (1):29–34.

Widerberg, Oscar, and Frank van Laerhoven. 2014. Measuring the Autonomous Influence of an International Bureaucracy: The Division for Sustainable Development. *International Environmental Agreements: Politics, Law and Economics* (in press).

Winkler, Harald, Ogunlade Davidson, and Stanford Mwakasonda. 2005. Developing Institutions for the Clean Development Mechanism (CDM): African Perspectives. *Climate Policy* 5:207–218.

Witte, J. Martin, Charlotte Streck, and Thorsten Brenner. 2003. The Road from Johannesburg: What Future for Partnerships in Global Environmental

Governance? In *Progress or Peril? Networks and Partnerships in Global Environmental Governance. The Post-Johannesburg Agenda*, ed. Thorsten Benner, Charlotte Streck, and J. Martin Witte, 59–84. Berlin: Global Public Policy Institute.

Wolfrum, Rüdiger. 1990. Purposes and Principles of International Environmental Law. *Jahrbuch für Internationales Recht. German Yearbook of International Law* 33:308–330.

World Bank. 2008. *World Development Indicators 2008*. Washington, DC: International Bank for Reconstruction and Development/The World Bank.

World Bank. 2010. World Bank Group Voice Reform: Enhancing Voice and Participation in Developing and Transition Countries in 2010 and Beyond. Doc. DC 2010–0006/1 of 25 April. World Bank, Washington, DC. Available at http://siteresources.worldbank.org/NEWS/Resources/IBRD2010VotingPower RealignmentFINAL.pdf (retrieved 15 October 2013).

World Bank. 2012. *Turn Down the Heat: Why a 4°C Warmer World Must Be Avoided*. Washington, DC: World Bank.

World Commission on Environment and Development. 1987. *Our Common Future: Report of the World Commission on Environment and Development*. Oxford: Oxford University Press.

WTO [World Trade Organization] Appellate Body. 1998. United States—Import Prohibition of Certain Shrimp and Shrimp Products. Report of the Appellate Body, AB-1998–4. WTO Doc. WT/DS58/AB/R of 12 Oct. 1998. *International Legal Materials* 38:118.

Yale Center for Environmental Law and Policy. 2012. *Climate Change and the International Court of Justice*. New Haven: Yale University.

Young, Oran R. 1980. International Regimes: Problems of Concept Formation. *World Politics* 32 (4):331–356.

Young, Oran R. 1986. International Regimes: Toward a New Theory of Institutions. *World Politics* 39:104.

Young, Oran R. 1989a. *International Cooperation: Building Regimes for Natural Resources and the Environment*. Ithaca: Cornell University Press.

Young, Oran R. 1989b. The Politics of International Regime Formation: Managing Natural Resources and the Environment. *International Organization* 43:349–376.

Young, Oran R. 1994. *International Governance: Protecting the Environment in a Stateless Society*. Ithaca: Cornell University Press.

Young, Oran R. 1996. Institutional Linkages in International Society: Polar Perspectives. *Global Governance* 2 (1):1–24.

Young, Oran R., ed. 1997. *Global Governance: Drawing Insights from the Environmental Experience*. Cambridge, MA: MIT Press.

Young, Oran R. 1999. *Governance in World Affairs*. Ithaca: Cornell University Press.

Young, Oran R. 2001. Inferences and Indices: Evaluating the Effectiveness of International Environmental Regimes. *Global Environmental Politics* 1 (1):99–121.

Young, Oran R. 2002. *The Institutional Dimension of Environmental Change: Fit, Interplay and Scale.* Cambridge, MA: MIT Press.

Young, Oran R. 2008. The Architecture of Global Environmental Governance: Bringing Science to Bear on Policy. *Global Environmental Politics* 8 (1):14–32.

Young, Oran R., Leslie A. King, and Heike Schroeder, eds. 2008. *Institutions and Environmental Change: Principal Findings, Applications and Research Frontiers.* Cambridge, MA: MIT Press.

Young, Oran R., Eric F. Lambin, Frank Alcock, Helmut Haberl, Sylvia I. Karlsson, William J. McConnell, Tun Myint, Claudia Pahl-Wostl, Colin Polsky, P. S. Ramakrishnan, Heike Schroeder, Marie Scouvart, and Peter H. Verburg. 2006. A Portfolio Approach to Analyzing Complex Human-Environment Interactions: Institutions and Land Change. *Ecology and Society* [online journal] 11 (2): 31. http://www.ecologyandsociety.org/vol11/iss2/art31/.

Young, Oran R., Marc A. Levy, and Gail Osherenko, eds. 1999. *Effectiveness of International Environmental Regimes: Causal Connections and Behavioral Mechanisms.* Cambridge, MA: MIT Press.

Zalasiewicz, Jan, Mark Williams, Alan Haywood, and Michael Ellis. 2011. The Anthropocene: A New Epoch of Geological Time? *Philosophical Transactions of the Royal Society A* 369:835–841.

Zalasiewicz, Jan, Mark Williams, Alan Smith, Tiffany L. Barry, Angela L. Coe, Paul R. Brown, Patrick Brenchley, et al. 2008. Are We Now Living in the Anthropocene? *GSA Today* 18 (2):4–8.

Zelli, Fariborz. 2007. The World Trade Organization: Free Trade and Its Environmental Impacts. In *Handbook of Globalization and the Environment*, ed. Khi V. Thai, Dianne Rahm, and Jerrell D. Coggburn, 177–216. London: Taylor and Francis.

Zelli, Fariborz. 2010. The Regime Environment of Environmental Regimes: Conceptualizing, Theorizing, and Examining Conflicts among International Regimes on Environmental Issues. Doctoral dissertation, University of Tübingen, Germany.

Zelli, Fariborz. 2011a. The Fragmentation of the Climate Governance Architecture. *Wiley Interdisciplinary Reviews: Climate Change* 2 (2): 255–270.

Zelli, Fariborz. 2011b. Regime Conflict and Interplay Management in Global Environmental Governance. In *Managing Institutional Complexity: Regime Interplay and Global Environmental Change*, ed. Sebastian Oberthür and Olav Schram Stokke, 199–226. Cambridge, MA: MIT Press.

Zelli, Fariborz, and Harro van Asselt. 2010. The Overlap between the UN Climate Regime and the World Trade Organization: Lessons for Climate Governance beyond 2012. In *Global Climate Governance beyond 2012: Architecture, Agency and Adaptation*, ed. Frank Biermann, Philipp Pattberg, and Fariborz Zelli, 79–96. Cambridge, UK: Cambridge University Press.

Zelli, Fariborz, and Harro van Asselt. 2013. The Institutional Fragmentation of Global Environmental Governance: Causes, Consequences, and Responses. *Global Environmental Politics* 13 (3):1–13.

Zelli, Fariborz, Aarti Gupta, and Harro van Asselt. 2012. Horizontal Institutional Interlinkages. In *Global Environmental Governance Reconsidered*, ed. Frank Biermann and Philipp Pattberg, 175–198. Cambridge, MA: MIT Press.

Zelli, Fariborz, Philipp Pattberg, Hannes Stephan, and Harro van Asselt. 2013. Global Climate Governance and Energy Choices. In *The Handbook of Global Energy Policy*, ed. Andreas Goldthau, 340–357. Hoboken, NJ: Wiley-Blackwell.

Zetter, Roger. 2011. Protecting Environmentally Displaced People: Developing the Capacity of Legal and Normative Frameworks. Refugee Studies Centre, Oxford Department of International Development, University of Oxford.

Zhao, Jimin. 2005. Implementing International Environmental Treaties in Developing Countries: China's Compliance with the Montreal Protocol. *Global Environmental Politics* 5 (1):58–81.

Zürn, Michael, and Benjamin Faude. 2013. On Fragmentation, Differentiation, and Coordination. *Global Environmental Politics* 13 (3):119–130.

Index

Accountability, 10, 11, 13, 27, 36–38, 45, 47, 55, 59–61, 77, 81, 106, 121–133, 137–146, 180–184, 189, 209
  challenges, 74, 78
  mechanisms, 138
  relationships, 122, 123, 127, 129, 142
Adaptability, 41, 81, 131, 179–181, 200
Adaptation, 13, 41, 42, 45, 49, 50, 53, 79, 146, 152, 154, 176, 182, 184, 190–201
  funding, 87, 153, 189, 191
  governance, 13, 41, 176, 184–185, 189, 190, 192, 196, 200, 201
Adaptation Fund, 152, 190, 197
Africa, 55, 95, 97, 109, 127, 145, 153, 155, 168, 177, 199
African Union, 55, 69, 74
Agency, 9, 11, 47, 48, 53, 67–70, 74, 75, 77, 88, 146, 156, 172, 179, 188, 197
"Agenda 21," 22, 55, 95, 136, 186
Agreement on Trade-Related Aspects of Intellectual Property Rights (TRIPS), 86
Alliance of Small Island States, 190
Allocation, 13, 27, 36–43, 47, 78, 145–173, 183
Annan, Kofi, 104
Antarctica, 6, 104, 105, 115, 208
Antarctic Treaty system, 105, 211

Anthropocene, 4, 10, 12, 15, 16, 26, 27, 35, 44, 52, 113, 148, 207
Aquaculture Stewardship Council, 54
Argentina, 112, 140
Asia, 40, 95, 97, 109, 127, 142, 168, 177, 199
Australia, 96, 154, 186

Bali action plan, 191
Bangladesh, 25, 112
Belarus, 106
Benedick, Richard E., 169
Biodiversity, 23, 31, 32, 38, 39, 49, 60, 61, 70, 92, 115
  conventions, 115, 151, 170
  governance, 42, 82
  protection, 61, 128
Brazil, 25, 68, 69, 96, 106, 110, 119, 138, 140
Bretton Woods institutions, 95, 102, 210. See also International Monetary Fund; World Bank
Brown, Noel J., 22
Bureaucracies. See International bureaucracies

Canada, 96, 117
Carbon, 2, 32, 35, 44, 127, 155, 158, 175, 200, 203, 205
  cycle, 28
  markets, 87
Carbon Disclosure Project, 85
Caribbean island states, 190

Cartagena Declaration on Refugees, 187

Cartagena Protocol on Biosafety, 167. *See also* Convention on Biological Diversity

Central America, 188

Certification, 71, 165. *See also* Labeling schemes

Chile, 106

China, 43, 86, 90, 96, 106, 107, 108, 110, 111, 140, 141, 155, 157, 169, 170, 179

Chlorofluorocarbons, 3, 109, 113, 117, 169, 170

Civil society, 31, 42, 59, 103, 118, 131–140, 142, 183, 204, 205, 211
   networks, 138
   organizations, 11, 54, 127, 132–139, 189, 209, 211
   representatives, 73, 134, 135–137, 162, 183

Clean Development Mechanism (CDM), 85, 125, 155

Climate change, 2, 6–8, 23, 31, 32, 37, 38, 42, 43, 49, 50, 56, 91, 93, 106, 115, 118, 128, 129, 141, 148, 159, 168, 169, 176, 177, 179, 188–190, 196, 198, 199, 200
   adaptation, 190, 192, 199
   impacts, 86, 152, 184, 185, 190–194, 197, 199, 200
   mitigation, 117, 158, 184, 199
   refugees, 186, 188 (*see also* Climate migration)

Climate convention. *See* United Nations Framework Convention on Climate Change

Climate governance, 38, 39, 85–87, 98–99, 106, 126, 128, 156, 158, 168, 191
   architecture, 82

Climate migration, 185, 189, 192, 194, 196, 197

Colombia, 103

Commission on Global Governance. *See* United Nations Commission on Global Governance

Commission on Sustainable Development. *See* United Nations Commission on Sustainable Development

Committee on the Peaceful Uses of Outer Space, 105

Convention on Biological Diversity, 68, 86

Convention on the Prevention of Marine Pollution by Dumping of Wastes and Other Matter, 92

Cosmopolitanism, 134, 149

Crutzen, Paul, 4, 6, 8

Cyprus, 168

Decision-making procedures, 24, 81, 83–84, 85, 108–109, 194, 196
   reform, 119, 189

Deforestation and forest degradation, 93, 128, 155, 156

Deliberative democracy, 123, 124, 134, 135, 141

Developed countries. *See* Industrialized countries

Developing countries, 35, 40–43, 50, 58, 59, 64, 69, 76, 77, 87, 91, 97, 99–100, 101, 103, 106–109, 123–127, 130, 135, 150–159, 162–172, 179, 184, 185, 190–192, 195–200
   least developed countries, 58, 91, 190, 198

Dingwerth, Klaus, 49, 124

Diversitas, 17, 61

Earth system analysis, 17, 23, 29

Earth system boundaries, 16, 31–36, 44, 47, 74, 91–93, 175

Earth System Governance Project, 11, 29

Earth system governance research, 11, 22, 25, 26, 28, 30

Earth system management, 15, 22–24

Earth system science, 17, 18, 20, 64

Earth System Science Partnership, 17, 18

East African Legislative Assembly, 140

Eastern Europe, 95
Ecocolonialism, 77
Economic development, 31, 33, 35,
    52, 69, 100–101, 110, 159, 164
Ecosystem, 3, 4, 8, 9, 39, 40, 51,
    185
  degradation, 34
  services, 146
Egalitarian perspectives, 154, 164,
    165, 171
Environmental protection, 8, 28, 34,
    100–101, 149, 162, 210
Equity, 13, 28, 41, 43, 45, 78, 90, 110,
    147, 173, 180–184, 191, 194, 195,
    209, 211
  intergenerational, 38
European Union (EU), 56, 68, 69, 74,
    96, 97, 106, 112, 135
  Commission, 89
  Economic and Social Committee,
    136
  Parliament, 139, 140

Fiji, 191
Food governance, 178, 179, 184
Forest Stewardship Council, 54, 122,
    136, 137
France, 68, 96, 111, 179
Future Earth: Research for Global
    Sustainability, 18, 62

Galaz, Victor, 86
General Agreement on Tariffs and
    Trade (GATT), 118, 160, 161
Geoengineering, 23, 105
Germany, 19, 23, 68, 96, 104, 108,
    111, 155, 205
  Advisory Council on Global Change,
    32
Global Aquaculture Alliance, 54
Global Carbon Project, 18, 62
Global environmental change, 17, 18,
    173. *See also* Climate change
Global Environmental Change and
    Food Systems Project, 18, 62
Global Environmental Change and
    Human Health Project, 18, 62

Global Environment Facility (GEF),
    94, 109, 125, 151, 152, 154, 156,
    162, 167, 170–172, 199
Global Ministerial Environment
    Forum, 70
Global warming, 3, 34, 91, 105, 115,
    127, 156, 159, 175, 176, 185, 199.
    See also Climate change
Governance
  architecture, 42, 81–89, 90, 94, 166,
    180, 184
  dilemmas, 131, 180, 200
  fragmentation, 39, 45, 76, 82–86,
    87–91, 94, 97, 113, 119, 171, 172
  functions, 40
  gaps, 56
  mechanisms, 30, 54, 71, 91, 98, 123,
    131, 137, 176, 177, 200, 201
  performance, 86, 87, 91
  structures, 173, 185
  studies, 9, 12, 22, 24, 25
Green Climate Fund, 153, 162, 164,
    167, 190, 197
Greenland, 6, 7, 175
Group of 77, 90, 157
Group of 20, 94–97, 111–112, 207
Guatemala, 103

Hajer, Maarten, 204
Halle, Mark, 205
Hayek, Friedrich, 148
Health governance, 15, 44, 137,
    179

India, 6, 76, 96, 107, 108, 110, 111,
    134, 136, 140, 141, 145, 155, 161,
    163, 168, 169
Indigenous people, 59, 128, 136,
    189
Indonesia, 69, 96, 106, 110, 136,
    140
Industrialized countries, 7, 36, 42, 43,
    55, 59, 95, 96–97, 107–111, 126,
    127, 135, 138, 141, 151–158, 162,
    163, 169–171, 191, 194, 197, 198
Institutionalization, 56, 62, 71, 75, 78,
    82, 83, 121, 123, 178–180, 212

Institutions, 9, 11, 20, 21, 24–29, 31, 47, 54, 65, 66, 72, 81–99, 101, 105–106, 110, 124, 127, 131, 138, 140–143, 173, 176–180, 187, 189, 191, 193, 203, 208–212
architecture of, 10, 93, 208
financial, 65, 108, 179
global, 11, 20, 62, 138, 140, 204, 207, 209
intergovernmental/international, 51, 52, 73, 83, 106, 113, 115, 133–137, 176, 181, 183, 189, 200, 203, 209
local, 44
multilateral, 11, 12, 27, 79, 93–94, 108, 127, 134, 137, 207–208
nonstate, 12, 49, 124
regional, 179
research, 17, 37, 45, 69
scientific assessment, 48, 72, 210
transnational, 41, 85
Interdependence, 38, 39, 42, 50, 129
ecological, 39, 50
functional, 38, 39, 77, 129, 180
interstate, 49
spatial, 39–41, 51, 129, 130
temporal, 38, 51, 77, 127
Intergovernmental bureaucracies. *See* International bureaucracies
Intergovernmental Panel on Climate Change (IPCC), 37, 63–65, 72, 73, 126, 135, 136, 178, 185, 210
International bureaucracies, 9, 12, 65–67, 77, 79
International Civil Aviation Organization (ICAO), 75, 106
International Council for Science (ICSU), 21, 22, 203
International Court of Justice (ICJ), 73, 117, 118
International Criminal Court, 113, 212
International Human Dimensions Programme on Global Environmental Change, 23, 61
International Labor Organization (ILO), 94, 134

International Maritime Organization (IMO), 110, 112, 182
International Monetary Fund (IMF), 94, 108, 212
International norms, 54, 83, 93, 166
International Organization for Migration (IOM), 199
International Tribunal on the Law of the Sea, 113
Italy, 96, 108, 142

Japan, 69, 96, 111, 191
Juma, Calestous, 68

Kant, Immanuel, 50, 168
Kenya, 67
Keohane, Robert O., 50, 123
Kiribati, 191
Korea, Republic of, 96
Kuwait, 106, 109, 168
Kyoto Protocol, 85, 88, 89, 92, 117, 152, 155, 190

Labeling schemes, 75, 123, 130, 160, 165
Latin America, 78, 86, 95, 97, 127, 168
Latin American Parliament, 140
Least Developed Countries Fund, 152, 153, 190
Lebanon, 168
Legitimacy, 11, 25, 29, 48, 51, 59, 63, 90, 97, 105, 108, 110, 112, 124, 126, 131, 143, 160, 163, 164, 166, 179, 182, 183, 187, 189, 200, 207, 209
and accountability, 10, 13, 27, 36, 45, 47, 54, 55, 74, 77, 121–123, 126–129, 131, 133, 142, 146, 180, 185, 192
civil society organizations, 138, 139
earth system governance, 3, 4, 13, 122, 125–127, 131–133
input and output, 125
internal and external, 125
private actors, 138
state action, 51, 52

Liberal institutionalism, 134, 139
Libertarian perspective, 148, 149, 153,
  154, 157–159, 163–165, 169, 171
Liechtenstein, 107, 119
Local level, 19, 20, 205
Locke, John, 148
Luxembourg, 57

Malaysia, 161
Maldives, Republic of the, 193
Marine Stewardship Council, 54, 122,
  137
Market-based mechanisms, 154,
  157
Mercosur, 140
Mexico, 72, 96, 106, 107, 169, 188
Migration Emergency Funding
  Mechanism, 199
Millennium Development Goals, 58,
  61, 103
Monaco, 107, 119, 134
Montreal Protocol on Substances that
  Deplete the Ozone Layer, 42, 76,
  84, 108–109, 113, 118, 151, 164,
  167, 169, 170, 181
Municipalities, 121, 146, 205

Nairobi, 67, 69
National Adaptation Programs of
  Actions, 152, 190, 199
Nauru, 191
Netherlands, 138, 184
Nigeria, 110, 112, 169
Nongovernmental organizations
  (NGOs), 48, 49, 55, 60, 62, 77,
  134, 136–138, 140, 162, 163, 191,
  206, 209
Nonstate actors, 24, 25, 42, 48, 49,
  53, 54, 56, 59, 60, 63, 89, 121,
  122, 124, 135, 139
Normative theory, 10, 27, 36, 37,
  148
North Atlantic Treaty Organization
  (NATO), 179
North-South, 152, 155, 156, 167
  cooperation, 43
  divide, 108, 133

quotas, 135, 136
  relationship, 130, 172
Nozick, Robert, 148, 165

Oceania, 199
Organisation for Economic
  Cooperation and Development
  (OECD), 58, 64, 110, 141
Ozone layer, 169
  depleting substances, 67, 108, 118,
  151, 167, 169
  depletion, 3, 6, 31, 35, 37, 42, 49,
  66, 84, 93, 113, 126, 129, 170
  regime, 66, 153, 154, 158, 168

Pacific Islands Energy for Sustainable
  Development partnership, 57
Pakistan, 110, 112, 161
Palau, 104, 118
Pan-African Parliament, 140
Panama, 188
Papua New Guinea, 106, 107, 191
Participation deficit, 59, 60
Planetary boundaries. *See* Earth
  system boundaries
Planetary Boundaries Initiative, 91
Potsdam Institute for Climate Impact
  Research, 23, 32
Poverty, 35, 69, 130, 145, 146, 159, 179
Private actors, 24, 25, 48, 54, 63, 90,
  134, 138, 153, 183, 207
Private funding mechanisms, 172
Private governance, 71, 72, 121, 123,
  137
Protocol Relating to the Status of
  Refugees, 187
Public-private partnerships, 61, 85

Rawls, John, 148, 149, 165
Redistribution of wealth, 148, 149,
  158
Reduced emissions from deforestation
  and forest degradation (REDD),
  128, 129, 155, 156
Renewable Energy and Energy
  Efficiency Partnership, 57
Resilience theory, 17, 19–21, 44

Rio Declaration on Environment and
    Development, 42, 166
Rockström, Johan, 31, 32, 34–36, 91,
    175
Roundtable on Sustainable Palm Oil,
    123, 125, 136
Russia, 69, 96, 106, 179

Saudi Arabia, 96, 106
Schellnhuber, Hans-Joachim, 17, 23, 29
Scholte, Jan Aart, 132, 137, 138
Science networks, 47, 49, 62, 77, 78
Singapore, 68, 109
Slovenia, 168
South Africa, 68, 96, 170
Sovereignty, 52, 113–116, 196
Special Climate Change Fund, 152,
    153, 190
State actors, 9, 59, 122
Sustainability science, 18–21, 28, 30,
    44
Sustainable development, 18, 30, 31,
    42, 60, 65, 70, 94–97, 101–103,
    112, 119, 135, 136, 155, 157
Sustainable Development Goals, 103

Thailand, 161
Tipping points, 6, 31, 32, 175, 206
Töpfer, Klaus, 100
Trade restrictions, 118, 160, 161,
    164–166
Transnational partnerships, 54, 71,
    131, 207
Transnational public policy networks,
    12, 55–57, 59, 60, 71, 77, 78, 124
Transparency, 112, 123, 132, 171, 183
Turkey, 96
Tuvalu, 187, 191

Ukraine, 106
United Kingdom, 8, 96, 175, 179
United Nations
    Charter, 102, 180, 211–212
    Commission on Global Governance,
        26, 27, 104, 135
    Commission on Sustainable
        Development (CSD), 95–96, 131
    Convention on the Law of the Sea,
        212
    Development Programme (UNDP),
        100–101, 171, 172, 178, 190, 197
    Economic and Social Council
        (ECOSOC), 67, 70, 94–95, 110,
        117
    Educational, Scientific and Cultural
        Organization (UNESCO), 22, 178
    Environment Organization, 69,
        74. See also World Environment
        Organization
    Environment Programme (UNEP), 8,
        63, 68–78, 94, 97–101, 117, 151,
        171, 178, 186
    Framework Convention on Climate
        Change (UNFCCC), 85, 195
    General Assembly, 8, 67, 68, 70, 73,
        96, 102, 105, 107, 110, 115, 117,
        118, 127, 135, 143, 188, 195, 210,
        211
    Global Environmental Assessment
        Commission, 72–74, 78, 208, 210
    Joint Inspection Unit, 93, 94
    reform, 97, 102, 105, 211–212
    Security Council, 102, 104, 110,
        117, 179, 211
    Sustainable Development Council,
        102–103, 112, 119, 135–136,
        139–140, 208, 210, 211
    Trusteeship Council for Areas
        beyond National Jurisdiction, 104,
        105, 119, 135, 140, 208, 210, 211
    trusteeship system, 104–105, 211
United States of America, 56, 69, 70,
    86, 96, 103, 110, 111, 127, 134,
    136, 140, 142, 145, 146, 161, 179,
    199
Urpelainen, Johannes, 98

Venezuela, 169
Voting systems, 105–110, 152
    majority voting, 77, 105–107,
        108–110, 113, 133, 167, 170, 184,
        189, 208–209
    one-country-one-vote, 107, 110, 112,
        133, 136, 140

Water governance, 178, 179, 184
Watson, Robert, 175
Weber, Max, 48
Western Europe, 95
World Bank, 2, 35, 54, 94, 96, 97,
    100, 101, 108, 109, 145, 151, 152,
    162, 171, 172, 175, 178, 179, 185,
    190, 191, 197, 199, 212
World Climate Research Programme,
    17, 61
World Commission on Dams, 124,
    164
World Commission on Environment
    and Development, 18, 31, 186
World Environment Assembly, 75, 99
World Environment Fund, 171–173,
    209–212
World Environment Organization,
    69, 74–78, 99–101, 139, 140, 143,
    172, 208, 210, 212
World Health Assembly, 75
World Health Organization (WHO),
    75, 118, 179, 197, 208
World Heritage Convention, 150
World Intellectual Property
    Organization, 69, 86, 98
World Meteorological Organization
    (WMO), 63, 69, 117
World parliamentary assembly, 139,
    140
World Trade Organization (WTO), 94,
    98, 99–100, 160
  Appellate Body, 161
  dispute settlement system, 100, 113
World Water Council, 178
World Wildlife Fund, 138